MULK RAJ ANAND

HIS ART AND CONCERNS

C.J. George

ATLANTIC

PUBLISHERS & DISTRIBUTORS (P) LTD

Published by

ATLANTIC

PUBLISHERS & DISTRIBUTORS (P) LTD

B-2, Vishal Enclave, Opp. Rajouri Garden,
New Delhi-110027
Phones : +91-11-25413460, 25429987, 25466842

Sales Office
7/22, Ansari Road, Darya Ganj,
New Delhi-110002
Phones : +91-11-23273880, 23275880, 23280451
Fax : +91-11-23285873
Web : www.atlanticbooks.com
E-mail : info@atlanticbooks.com

Branch Office
5, Nallathambi Street, Wallajah Road,
Chennai-600002
Phones : +91-44-64611085, 32413319
E-mail : chennai@atlanticbooks.com

ISBN 978-81-7156-445-3

Printed in India
at Nice Printing Press, Delhi

DEDICATED

TO

MY PARENTS

Foreword

Mulk Raj Anand has deservedly come to be regarded as a pioneer of the Indian novel in English. He has endeared himself to millions of readers, throughout the English-speaking world, because of his flair for story-telling and his impassioned humanism. His novels are saturated with deep feeling about the people and places he knows from first hand experience. He is a realist. He has an imaginative and sensuous apprehension of the Indian society in all its ramifications. And he has an uncanny capacity for empathising with the lowliest of the lowly. He sees people struggling to free themselves from all forms of serfdom. He celebrates the unadorned dignity of the ordinary individual. He is a crusader. There is a sense of battle in his prose. His use of vernacular words and phrases or turns of speech has been criticised in some quarters. Some have wrongly attributed it to his imperfect command of the English idiom. But this is no more incongruous or vulgar than Dickens's use of the cockney or Hardy's use of the dialect. It ensures a kind of authenticity otherwise unattainable. It is a strength, not a weakness. Anand's English narrative can artistically accommodate his sprinkling of the pungent native idiom. It adds local colour to his tales without deflecting attention from the commanding drift of the story.

Dr George has made a sensitive analysis of all the major novels of Mulk Raj Anand in this book. He has been able to demonstrate successfully how Anand's radical social and moral concerns inform his moving fictions about real people seen toiling through vividly depicted sociological vignettes. Dr George's discovery of the sociological question as the mainspring of Anand's fictional imagination deserves appreciation.

NOORUL HASAN

Preface

Ever since the first Indo-Anglian novel, *Rajmohan's Wife* by Bankim Chandra Chatterjee was published in 1864, some seven years after the Sepoy Mutiny, many other men of vision and imagination could follow his footprints on the sands of time and succeed remarkably by their creative writing in English, thereby discrediting the skeptical view that Indians cannot write English creatively. Indians, in fact, are blessed with the gift of the tongue and George Orwell in his review on Mulk Raj Anand's *The Sword and the Sickle*, acknowledged it by saying, "On average, Indians write and even pronounce English far better than any European race."

The Indo-Anglian writers not only interpreted India to the West but also made known to the British Masters the natives' displeasure with the colonial rule which in gist, in myriad of voices, echoed the lines:

> You taught me language, and my profit on't
> Is, I know how to curse; the red plague rid you
> For learning me your language.

Among the Indo-Anglian novelists, certainly, Mulk Raj Anand occupies an enviable position. He modernized the Indian novel. His love for novelty and originality enabled him to carry the tradition of Tagore and Premchand, Bankim and Sarat Chandra to new heights. With his first novel, *Untouchable*, he, in fact, inaugurated the literature of the underdog. He not only interpreted the soul of India, the real India of the villages to the West, but also convincingly made known to the Colonial rulers the debilitating aspects of their presence in India. After the departure of the British, he shifted his concerns towards the social predicaments and upheavals faced by the emerging republic.

In all his novels Anand stresses the need for a humanistic approach to life. He is an artist with a mission and a poet of the aspiring spirit. Like most Indo-Anglian novelists, he is inevitably concerned with man in society, "man in his circumambient universe". He is an artist saturated with a moral understanding of Indian masses. He understands their mute anguish and always succeeds in bringing out their insulted humanity. His novels expose the silent passions that burst in the hearts of the people who are forbidden to rise up and express themselves. His aim is to evoke generosity and compassion in the minds of the privileged sections of society, to which the bulk of his readers belong.

In this book, I make appraisals of Anand's all major novels, novels which are truly representative of his artistic genius. However, I have not allotted chapters to his *Seven Summers* (1951), *Morning Face* (1968), *Confessions of a Lover* (1976), *The Bubble* (1984) and his latest novel, *Little Plays of Mahatma Gandhi* (1991) which is actually the first part of his forthcoming epic novel in seven parts, *And So He Plays His Part*. I only make a brief reference to them at the introductory Chapter. In the opinion of Saros Cowasjee, they "though often referred to as novels, are dramatised autobiographies with fictional overtones". Disagreeing with Cowasjee, in a letter to the Critic, Anand says: "They are not autobiographies. They are autobiographical novels. I protest, as did Tolstoy, about *Childhood, Boyhood and Youth*, when the reviewers called the book autobiography; the distinction is really important." Whether they are autobiographies or autobiographical novels, I have not dealt with them here in detail on two counts: (1) They can be grouped together and studied under a separate project work. (2) Anand's concerns expressed in these novels with autobiographical references are mere repetitions of the same themes he had given with force and necessary detachment in other novels. Hence studying these works under this project will produce no fresh and significant insight into his social concerns.

Some readers of this book may rightly feel that I have dealt with the plot and story of the novels too elaborately. Well, I have done this to offer the readers a detailed understanding of each of the novels, even if they have no time to go through the original texts. This will also enable the readers to have an emotional understanding of the dramatic or fictional situations which necessitated the major critical pronouncements of various characters.

The twelve novels I study in this book in detail are twelve beacon lights on the shores of life. Anyone who goes to them is sure to get inspiration and illumination. Their monumental magnificance, inspiring power and radiating energy differ from one another. To be precise, *Untouchable*, a Penguin World Classic translated into more than 38 world languages cannot be equated with a less well-known novel like *The Road*. But all his novels are, undoubtedly, the creations of a great artist who has discovered the effectiveness of novel form and efficiently employed it to express his passionate love for the suffering people, who after long struggle managed to get political freedom but not yet, in spite of the continuous struggle, have succeeded in getting freedom from caste and class feeling, freedom from the belief in *karma* and superstition, freedom from religious hypocrisy, parochialism and fanaticism, freedom from poverty and exploitation, freedom from sexual discrimination and so many other freedoms. In fact, Anand's social concerns are the driving force behind all his writings. They act as a catalyst to his creative output.

This book is, by and large, a reproduction of my doctoral thesis, "The Artist as Social Critic: A Study of Mulk Raj Anand's Major Novels", which was prepared under the able and loving guidance of Prof. Noorul Hasan, Dean, School of Languages, North-Eastern Hill University, Shillong. I am also grateful to him for giving a scholarly and thought-provoking "Foreword" to this book.

My thanks are also due to M/s Atlantic Publishers and Distributors for undertaking the publication of this work.

C.J. GEORGE

Contents

I

INTRODUCTION
Mulk Raj Anand : The Emergence of the Novelist

In his "Foreword" to G.S. Balarama Gupta's *Mulk Raj Anand*, K.R. Srinivasa Iyengar remarks:

> There are novelists about whom one critical study could be written, but one would be enough. There are novelists who would be effectively suffocated even by one research performance. And there are the novelists who are large — who invoke multitudes — who can survive several attempts to probe and sound and contain them. Mulk Raj Anand is surely one of the last category. Each new study adds a little to our understanding of Anand and his work, yet leaves the subject unexhausted.[1]

Anand is a celebrated Indo-Anglian[2] novelist with global recognition. He has to his credit a score of novels, hundreds of short stories, a number of books on varying themes and a host of essays and articles on different subjects. Though many approaches to his life and works are possible, his social criticism through imaginative literature

---

1. Iyengar, K.R. Srinivasa: "Foreword" to : G.S. Balarama Gupta's *Mulk Raj Anand* (*A Study of his Fiction in Humanist Perspective*), Bareilly: Prakash Book Depot, 1974, p. (v).
2. The terms (a) "Indo-Anglian", (b) "Anglo-Indian" and (c) "Indo-English" with reference to literature could be distinguished in this way:
   (a) Indo-Anglian Literature is the original literary creation in the English language by Indians.
   Example: R.K. Narayan's *The Guide*.
   (b) Anglo-Indian Literature is writing of Englishmen in English about India and Indian life.
   Example: E.M. Forster's *A Passage to India*.
   (c) Indo-English Literature is the translations into English from literature in Indian languages.
   Example: Rabindranath Tagore's *Gitanjali*.

and his candid endeavour to demonstrate social evils has appealed to me much and so I attempt to focus in this book (making appraisals of his non-autobiographical novels) his artist's concern with the ills of Indian society.

Every novelist is an artist and the greatness of a novelist is directly proportional to the artistic quality of his output. The artistic quality of Anand's literary works has been widely acclaimed:

> It happens now and then in a person's life to pick up a book and suddenly realize, after ten minutes reading that one has made contact with a writer of genius. Sartre, Faulkner, Maurice and Sholokove have given countless readers that shock of discovery and joy. So too has Mulk Raj Anand! When, rather by chance his great little novel *Coolie* came into my hands I knew almost at once that its author was another of those miraculous creators who can make one feel the beauty and horror that lies beneath life's outer surface.
>
> — Ira Morris[3]

> Even if the four volumes so far published of *The Seven Ages of Man* were Anand's only fiction, they place him in the front ranks of the writers like Joyce and D.H. Lawrence and Thomas Wolfe, who deal importantly with the traditional themes of the *Bildungsroman*.
>
> — Marlene Fisher[4]

> Anand's achievement in the first two volumes of the *Trilogy* has not yet been surpassed by an Indo-Anglian novelist.
>
> — Meenakshi Mukherjee[5]

> It (*Untouchable*) is an excellent work and I am delighted it is being re-printed. I hope it will be again favourably received.
>
> — E.M. Forster[6]

3. Ira Morris, "Messages and Souvenirs", *Contemporary Indian Literature*, November-December, 1965, p. 9.
4. Fisher, Marlene: *The Widsom of the Heart* (*A Study of the Works of Mulk Raj Anand*), New Delhi: Sterling Publishers Private Limited, 1985, p. 151.
5. Mukherjee, Meenakshi: "Beyond The Village: An aspect of Mulk Raj Anand", In: *Critical Essays on Indian Writing in English*, ed: M.K. Naik, S.K. Desai and G.S. Amur, Madras: The Macmillan Co. of India Ltd., 1977, p. 239.
6. See: Blurb, In: Anand, Mulk Raj: *Untouchable*, Arnold-Heinemann Publishers Pvt. Ltd., 1984.

The whole 'story' is touching and tender.

— Eric Gill on *Untouchable*[7]

How much of the special atmosphere of English language Indian literature is due to its subject-matter is uncertain, but in reading Mr. Anand's work, it is difficult not to feel that by this time another dialect, comparable perhaps to Irish-English, has grown up....... *The Sword and the Sickle* is obviously the work of a man who is not only at ease with the English language but thinks in it and would probably write in it by preference.

— George Orwell[8]

He (Anand) is one of the most stimulating men I have ever met. Mulk possesses that special kind of talent which helps to fertilize the living mind and gives it the sense of a base on which to build. Such men are rare, in any country. Standing in his own permanence, professional, dedicated, he has sought to interpret in terms of art the MORES of his own people. Above all, he has insisted on the need for VALUES – the civilizing values which help nourish an enlightened and humane society. This has been an essential part of Mulk's character; and the aspirations to which he has given expression are now part of India's cultural and intellectual history. His work stands as a nobly proportioned edifice.

– C.B. Christesen, Editor and Publisher of *Meanjin Quarterly*[9]

As a disciple of Tagore and Nehru, Dr. Anand has made painstaking efforts to understand the soul of this land which has been expressing itself through Indian thoughts and Indian culture.

— S. Lakshman Shastry, the editor of *Contemporary Indian Literature*[10]

---

7. Eric Gill, in his letter dated 10th August, 1935 (an unpublished letter in Anand's file) and quoted by G.S. Balarama Gupta, In: *Mulk Raj Anand (A Study of his Fiction in Humanist Perspective)*, Bareilly: Prakash Book Depot, 1974, p. 135.

8. Orwell, George: "Review: *The Sword and the Sickle* by Mulk Raj Anand", In: *The Collected Essays, Journalism and Letters of George Orwell, Vol. II*, Harmondsworth: Penguin Books, 1970, p. 252.

9. C.B. Christesen, "Messages and Souvenirs", *Contemporary Indian Literature*, November-December 1965, p. 50.

10. S. Lakshman Shastry, "A Few Words About This Issue" (Editorial), *Contemporary Indian Literature*, November-December, 1965, p. 10.

> Apart from the artistic realisation of Indian themes, Anand has done commendable experimentation with the so called alien language in order to give it an Indian flavour.
>
> — Premila Paul[11]

> English people who will not trouble to write their own language well enough ought to be shamed by reading the English of such Indian writers as Mulk Raj Anand.
>
> — Marjourie Boulton[12]

> As a writer of fiction, Anand's notable marks are vitality and a keen sense of actuality. He is a veritable Dickens for describing the inequities and idiosyncrasies in the current human situation with candour as well as accuracy.
>
> — K.R. Srinivasa Iyengar[13]

> *Untouchable* and *Coolie*, the earlier books of Mulk Raj Anand, are not only the best Indian novels of the last twenty years, but they have a place in English Literature.
>
> — V.S. Pritchett[14]

> The Foremost of Indian novelists.
>
> — *Daily Telegraph* commenting on Anand's *The Village*[15]

> The best Indian War Novel.
>
> — *Indian Literary Review on Across the Black Waters*[16]

Such comments from critics and reviewers give a secure place to Anand among the leading Indian novelists of the times. He was not

11. Paul, Premila: *The Novels of Mulk Raj Anand: A Thematic Study*, Delhi: Sterling Publishers Pvt. Ltd., 1983, p. 158.
12. Boulton, Marjorie: *The Anatomy of Prose*, London: 1954, p. 91 and quoted by Krishna Nandan Sinha, In: *Mulk Raj Anand*, New York: Twayne Publishers, 1972, p. 130.
13. Iyengar, K.R. Srinivasa: *Indian Writing in English*, Bombay: Asia Publishing House, 1973, p. 130.
14. Quoted by P.P. Mehta, In: *Indo-Anglian Fiction: An Assessment*, Bareilly: Prakash Book Depot, 1979, p. 123.
15. See: Blurb, In: Anand, Mulk Raj: *The Village*, Delhi: Arnold-Heinemann Publishers (India) Pvt. Ltd., 1984.
16. See: Blurb, In: Anand, Mulk Raj: *Across the Black Waters*, Delhi: Orient Paperbacks, 1980.

only appreciated by most of the leading novelists and thinkers of the time but also was befriended by them. As Saros Cowasjee's carefully documented account indicates, his circle of friends and acquaintances included the following writers: E.M. Forster, Herbert Read, Bonamy Dobree, T.S. Eliot, Laurence Binyon, Aldous Huxley, Middleton Murry, Sir Francis Young Husband, Stephen Spender, V.S. Pritchett, Victor Gollancz, Louis Mac Neice, John Strachey, Virginia Woolf, George Orwell, Cyril Conolly, Edward Thompson, Maurice Brown, Walter Allen, John Cornford, C. Day Lewis, Ralph Fox, Dylan Thomas, Naomi Mitchison, Lowes Dickinson, Lawrence Durell, Edgell Rickword, Andre Malraux, Ernest Toller, Henry Miller, Dorothy Richardson, Jack Lindsay and H.G. Wells.[17] It will be difficult for a critic to find a more detailed or distinguished list and there is enough evidence to support the fact that Anand was a friend well-appreciated and respected by many of them. Cowasjee quotes Henry Miller, for instance saying in a personal letter to him, "I remember Mulk Raj Anand vividly. He was an exciting person to know and great stimulation to every one"[18], or take Julian Symons, writing in *The Sunday Times*: "Mulk Raj Anand was a figure valued not only as a novelist, but for the generosity and enthusiasm of a person untouched by the period's political in-fighting".[19]

As Anand became eminent in the circle of other novelists, critics started to evaluate his works. There is now a large body of writing on Anand, who has been the subject both of some book-length critical works and of several articles. Most of his major critics have acclaimed him as a powerful novelist. The simple fact that his novels *Untouchable* and *Coolie* are available in 38 languages of the world substantiates the point we have tried to focus so far that Mulk Raj Anand is an artist of universal recognition and greatness.

An important aspect of Anand's fiction is its concern with the reality of organised evil. In all his novels he appears as a social critic. The society he has seen and observed is the field of his work. His writings probe deeply into the social process. For him "literature is an expression of society" and the large majority of the questions raised by him are social questions: questions of tradition and

---

17. Cowasjee, Saros: So Many Freedoms: *A Study of the Major Fiction of Mulk Raj Anand*, Delhi: OUP, 1977, p. 27.
18. *Ibid*., p. 27.
19. *Ibid*., p. 28.

convention, norms and genres, symbols and myth. Before his *Untouchable* in 1935, Indo-Anglian novels were mainly based on history or romance and they were primarily written for mere enjoyment or escapist light reading. Anand's temperament and social concern have not been suited to such ventures. His missionary zeal for the welfare of the masses had added purpose and brought a new direction to the Indo-Anglian novels. His purpose in writing fiction has been to focus attention on the suffering, misery and wretchedness of the poor and the underdogs of society caused by the exploitations of capitalists or the feudal lords or by the impact of industry on the traditional and agricultural way of life. Through his art he has been trying to awaken our sympathy for the underdog of society which in turn can urge us to take part in the drama of revolt leading to social reform. Both *Untouchable* and *Coolie* are excellent examples in this respect. They depict the wretched condition and ordeals of the oppressed people and their struggle for a better life. Almost all his novels that followed are variation on the same theme and are intended to bring home to the reader the abject condition of the overburdened peasant who is powerless to fight superstition and social convention and is hindered at every step in his search for a better life. In other words, Anand is a humanist, a proletarian who does not believe in the "Art for Art's sake", but writes to awaken the social conscience. He is audacious enough to admit that he is using literature as a means to some other end, and that this end is the alleviation of the suffering of fellow human beings. He has made his position clear in his *Apology for Heroism*: "Any writer who said that he was not interested in 'la condition humaine' was either posing or yielding to a fanatical love of isolationism".[20] Again in the same book he asserts, "just as I desire a total and truly humane view of experience, a view of the whole man, in order that a completely new kind of revolutionary human may arise, so I have been inclined to stress the need for a truly humanist art commensurate with the needs of our time".[21] Anand has all along written novels and short stories with a view of teaching men to recognize the fundamental principles of human living and exercise vigilance in regard to the real enemies of freedom and socialism. It has been a life time apostolate for him (which he still continues) to

20. Anand, Mulk Raj: *Apology for Heroism*, Delhi: Arnold-Heinemann Pvt. Ltd., 1975, p. 123.

21. *Ibid.*, p. 129.

help raise the untouchables, the peasants, the serfs, the coolies and the other suppressed members of society to fight for human dignity deliberately denied to them by the privileged sections of society.

Of all the great Indian novelists in English, Anand is perhaps the one whose life is most closely and most obviously connected with his work. For him, his life is his art and art, his life. For convenience, his life may be studied under three periods: the early years in India until his departure for England, 1905-1925; the years abroad, 1925-1945; and the later years in India, from 1945 to the present day.

The first period (1905-1925) is a period of formation. It starts on 11th December 1905 when he was born in Peshawar in a family of *Kshatriyas* to Lalchand, a silversmith, and Ishwar Kaur. His father was ambitious enough to rise above the status of silversmith. Hence he worked hard and passed matriculation and it helped him to become Head Clerk in the 38 Dogra Regiment of the British Indian Army. His mother was from a traditional peasant family who believed in every legend, mythology and social conventions. She "would place brass idols of the gods and goddesses of the Hindu pantheon side by side with a crucifix which she had picked up somewhere, a picture of the Aga Khan, and of Guru Nanak, the first saint of the Sikhs, on a raised platform for worship on various festivals".[22] That always seemed to be incongruous to Anand, the child. Her excessive religious enthusiasm had negative effect on Anand from his early childhood. In fact, it developed in him a dislike for religion. His mother's lessons to him in the reading of *Bhagavad Gita* was for him a source of amusement. When his father had some visitors, sometimes to make them happy, he used to mimic the way his mother used to read the *Gita* and the prodigious feat of his mimicking often earned him silver coins from his father or his friends.

His father's attitude in such matters was a compromise between traditional beliefs and the secular life he led in the British-Indian army. Often his father reconciled God with Mammon in the inimitable way of his English masters, of whom he was a loyal subject. He shrewdly paid lip service to the tenets of Hinduism, while in his heart of hearts he sought to amass a fortune through efficient service, as well as through various sidelines in money lending, buying and selling homes, accepting mortgages of property and bribes.[23]

22. *Ibid.*, p. 29.
23. *Ibid.*, p. 33.

Anand's early education was in cantonment schools. The education imparted in these schools was imitative, giving very little idea of Indian tradition, but mainly 'bastardized' version of English curricula, in English, with particular emphasis on English history, ideas, forms and institutions, deliberately calculated to show everything relating to Indian history and tradition as inferior. This had disastrous effect on Anand. He "acquired a bias against all indigeneous customs and grew up hating everything Indian".[24]

There are a few incidents in his childhood days that made lasting impressions on him. The first, the death of his cousin Kaushalya, aged nine, when he himself was only eleven:

> My first real essay was a letter to God Almighty, asking Him why He has caused the death of my little cousin Kaushalya, at the age of nine, by inflicting on her the dread disease of lungs, when she had not done anything bad. I put the letter in the hands of the priests of the temple: But God did not answer my protest. So I have tended to regard Him, since then, as the enemy of mankind. In fact, from that time my belief in the man with the big beard sitting on top of the sky, determining the fate of every one has been shaken more or less completely.[25]

Equally significant was the dreadful end of his aunt Devaki, driven to suicide as a result of her excommunication by an Orthodox Hindu Society, for among other things, calling on a Muslim woman. Anand quotes this tragic happening as the initial fire of his protest that enkindled his whole life, a protest against a hide-bound society bigoted by caste and class and a religion which supported its perversity. But perhaps most important for the nationalist Anand was to become, was his arrest and caning for unintentionally violating the curfew after the ruthless massacre at Jallianwala Bagh in 1919.

After completing his school, Anand joined the Khalsa College at Amritsar and he was there from 1921 to 1924. At Khalsa, he revealed his literary taste by writing poems in Urdu. He frequently met poet Mohammad Iqbal and had many literary discussions with him. But for that, his college days were generally not a happy one. In those days, he was active in the non-violent campaign and once he

---

24. *Ibid*., p. 34.
25. Anand, Mulk Raj: "Why I Write?", In: *Indo-English Literature*, Ed. Dr. K.K. Sharma, Ghaziabad: Vimal Prakashan, 1978, p. 13.

suffered a brief imprisonment. The most terrible thing that happened to him at Khalsa was his abortive amorous affair with a Muslim married woman named Yasmin. Just before the final examination, unable to forget Yasmin, he made up his mind to elope with her to Kashmir getting the assistance of his friend, Noor. Knowing Yasmin's plan, her husband killed her on the day she was to flee. It became a big social issue. Her death led Anand to despair. Anand's *Confessions of a Lover* (1976) is a moving and honest story of his love for Yasmin and its consequences.

The second period of Anand's life can be presented as from 1924. After his graduation from Khalsa College, though his father did not like the idea, he managed to leave for England for higher studies and research in philosophy. On his arrival in London, he registered at the University College to do research for a Doctor's degree in Philosophy, under Professor G. Dawes Hicks, the famous Kantian scholar and co-editor of the *Hibbert Journal.*[26] Professor Hicks set Anand to work on the theory of knowledge and in particular, on the treatment of such relations as cause and effect, identity, etc., by Hume and his predecessors.

Soon Anand found a place to reside at Dolgelly village, with a friendly parson and started his study seriously. In the village he took pleasure in climbing the mountain. One day when he was coming down the mountain, he saw a boy and a girl. As he believed that suppressed behaviour towards girls is treated as dishonesty in the Western world, he took courage and told the girl that he liked her. The girl, Irene, smiled at him and invited him to come to her house. Her father was a professor of Biology at the University of Wales. Irene found Anand to be an excellent conversationalist. She also discovered his story telling faculty from the way he narrated the story of his mother, aunt and cousins. Hence she requested him to write down his life story. To please her, he began a *Confession* modelled on Rousseau's *Confessions*. On week-ends he read out to her all that he wrote. Week-ends followed week-ends. The writing continued and within a few months it reached more than 2000 pages. Irene typed it out. She made up her mind to be married to him if it could be published. But the size of the work caused difficulty in finding a publisher. In the days that followed, the relationship between Irene

---

26. Anand, Mulk Raj: *Apology for Heroism*, Delhi: Arnold Heinemann Pvt. Ltd., 1975, p. 46.

and Anand also slowly cooled down. However, the work was not a waste. It served as a reservoir, a source book for Anand's future novels like *Seven Summers* and *Morning Face*.

In 1926 there was a coal miner's strike under the leadership of Arther Cook. This strike, as well as his involvement with Irene, disturbed his academic pursuit. During the strike, Anand, together with some other students, was assaulted for supporting the workers. The General Strike which followed almost immediately was ruthlessly broken by the Government. What became obvious through these events, Anand tells us, was the connection between British rule in India and the situation in Britain itself. "Britain was organized and run", he writes, "in the interests of a small minority which could suppress the majority as violently at home as it did in the Empire."[27]

Despite the many extra-academic involvements Anand had, he could pursue his studies and in 1929 he was awarded the Ph.D. degree for his thesis on the philosophy of Berkeley, Hume and Russel. With this degree in hand, he did not think of gloriously returning to India. Instead, during the next few years, at the invitation of T.S. Eliot, he wrote a number of articles for *Criterion*. Soon other journals also invited him to contribute articles. He also made several memorable acquaintances. They included D.H. Lawrence, F.R. Leavis, Middleton Murry, Herbert Read, Aldous Huxley, Eric Gill and Anand Coomaraswamy.

His contact with Anand Coomaraswamy inspired him to recognize the latent glory of Indian art. He began to work on Indian art studies under the guidance of Coomaraswamy. The output of this study resulted in his books, *Hindu View of Art*, *Persian Painting* and *Golden Breath* published in 1932.

His appreciation of Indian art and architecture grew and he felt an irresistable urge to return to India to study the ancient monuments. There was also another reason for his return to India in 1932. Anand gives the immediate reason for it in his essay, "Why I Write?"

> One day, I read an article in 'Young India' by Gandhiji, describing how he met Uka, a sweeper boy, and, finding him with torn clothes and hungry, took him to his *ashram*. This narrative was simple, austere and seemed to me more truthful than my artificially concoted novel *Untouchable*. I

27. *Ibid.*, p. 64.

> told Irene this. And, in a sudden fit of revulsion against my experience, in elitist Bloomsbury, I decided to go and see the old man.
>
> I wrote to the Mahatma asking for an appointment. He efficiently wrote back and said he would give me an interview if I came to India. I raised the fare and went to Ahmedabad in the Spring of 1932.[28]

Anand stayed in the Sabarmati *Ashram* with the Mahatma for three months. During that period he revised the manuscript of the novel, *Untouchable*, he had brought from England. What Anand has to say about its revision in the Sabarmati *Ashram* and the mental agony he suffered before the publication of it in England is worth quoting:

> I read the new novel to the old man, who more or less approved, though he gave me Tolstoy's *Childhood, Boyhood and Youth* as a model of sincere writing. He said one must not write anything which was not based on one's experience.
>
> I worked hard to achieve sincerity. I cut and cut, trying to combine the Tolstoyan emphasis on the truth of life in the raw and the Flaubertian objectivity. I had already been made to discard my corduroy suit and necktie and had got into *Kurta-Pyjamas*, thus being converted to the Indian I once was, and I have tried since then to take off the mask of the "Brown Sahib" I had become in England.
>
> I brought the novel back to London (in 1933) glowing with pride about the austerities I had practised.
>
> My novel was turned down by nineteen publishers.
>
> After I had despaired and contemplated suicide, the twentieth accepted it, because E.M. Forster, to whom a poet friend of mine had taken the book offered to write a Preface for it.[29]

Thus, *Untouchable* was published on 1 May 1935. Richard Maine in one of his broadcasts on the B.B.C. praised it as a "classic" and of all Anand's major works, it still receives the greatest critical acclaim.

---

28. Anand, Mulk Raj: "Why I Write?", In: *Indo-English Literature*, Ed. Dr. K.K. Sharma, Ghaziabad: Vimal Prakashan, 1978, p. 18.
29. *Ibid.*, p. 19.

The public response to *Untouchable* encouraged Anand to devote more time to imaginary writing. The following fiction were soon available for the public reading: *Coolie* (1935), *Two Leaves and a Bud* (1937), The Lal Singh *Trilogy* (1942), *The Barber's Trade Union and Other Stories* (1944) and *The Big Heart* (1945).

Thus the period between 1935 and 1945 was the most productive period in Anand's career as a novelist. Though he was busy in this period writing novels after novels, he found sufficient time to involve in other activities too: In 1935 he represented India in the International Writers Conference against Fascism (This gave him the opportunity to come into close contact with Kathleen Van Gelder, a stage actress. Their admiration for each other eventually led to their marriage). In 1936, he joined the International Brigade in Spain during the Spanish Civil War. Between 1937 and 1945 he associated himself with the British Labour Party and the Indian National Congress. He became a zealous activist of India League organized by Krishna Menon in England for the cause of Indian Independence. A study of India League clearly illustrates that along with Krishna Menon, Anand did yeoman service to his country by tilting the British public opinion in England in favour of India's aspiration and struggle for freedom.

The third phase of Anand's life began in 1945 when he returned to India for good. After one year of stay in Lahore, he came to Bombay and started the art magazine MARG at the advice of a smart and gifted woman called Anil de Silva. In the same year (1946) his *Apology for Heroism* was published. The next year (1947) a collection of his short stories under the title *The Tractor and the Corn Goddess and Other Stories* was available.

Anand's love for Anil grew rapidly and soon he was infatuated by her. It in turn eclipsed his love for Kathleen and in 1948 he went to London and secured a divorce from her with the purpose of marrying Anil. However, the divorce instead of settling his problems increased his mental agony and he suffered nervous breakdown as Anil breaking her promise to Anand, married a Frenchman. To save himself from the mental illness, Melpo, a Greek dancer who nursed him in Bombay suggested to him to write it out. The result was the famous novel *Private Life of an Indian Prince* published in 1953.

After his return to Bombay apart from editing the art magazine, MARG, Anand was busy in attending or oganizing many conferences. In 1950, he attended the World Peace Council Session in Berlin. In 1956 he helped to organize the First Asian Writers Conference in

New Delhi. In 1958 he visited U.S.S.R. as joint leader of Indian delegation to Afro-Asian Writers' Conference. In 1960 he visited Japan for a special meeting of Afro Asian Writers Bureau. In 1961, he visited Australia on a lecture tour and attended Australian Peace Conference, in Melbourne. He also organized there an exhibition of Contemporary Indian Painting. The next year, he visited Cairo as a leader of Indian delegation to Afro-Asian Writers' Conference; he also sponsored formation of the Bureau of Afro-Asian Writers in Colombo and the Indian Committee of Writers for Afro-Asian Solidarity, in New Delhi. In 1965 he visited Weimer as a delegate to the World Writers' Meeting; he also visited Helsinki for World Peace Congress. In 1968 he attended Commonwealth Writers' Conference in Australia. The next year he visited Cairo for a meeting of Afro-Asian Writers. In 1970, when the Fourth Conference of Afro-Asian Writers was held in New Delhi he was its Organiser Secretary-General. The next year he visited Middle East on Research tour. Now, though he is old, he continues to attend or organise many national and international conferences. He is also a visiting Professor at many Universities in India and abroad.

Anand's frequent foreign trips to attend or organize conferences, lecture tours and so on have not prevented him from writing fiction. His great works after his return to India include: *The Tractor and the Corn Goddess and Other Stories* (1947), *Private Life of an Indian Prince* (1953), *Reflections of the Golden Bed and Other Stories* (1953), *The Power of Darkness and Other Stories* (1959), *Gauri* (1960), *The Road* (1963), *Death of a Hero* (1964) and *Lajwanti and Other Stories* (1966).

Anand's most ambitious project is not yet completed: It is an autobiographical novel in seven volumes, under the title *Seven Ages of Man*. Anand appears in these novels under the name Krishan Chander. He took inspiration for *Seven Ages of Man* from Shakespeare's *As You Like It* (II:vii) where man's life is analysed into seven ages:

> All the world's a stage,
> And all the men and women merely players:
> They have their exits and their entrances;
> And one man in his time plays many parts,
> His acts being *Seven ages*. At first the infant,
> Mewling and puking in the nurse's arms.
> And then the whining school-boy, with his satchel,
> And shining *morning face*, creeping like snail
> Unwilling to school. And then the *lover*

Sighing like furnace, with a woeful ballad
Made to his mistress' eyebrow. Then a soldier,
Full of strange oaths, and bearded like a pard,
Jealous in honour, sudden and quick in quarrel
Seeking *the bubble* reputation
Even in the cannon's mouth. And then the justice,
In fair round belly with good capon lin'd,
With eyes severe, and beard of formal cut,
Full of wise saws and modern instances;
And so he plays his part. The sixth age shifts
Into the lean and slipper'd pantaloon,
With spectacles on nose and pouch on side,
His youthful hose well sav'd, *a world too wide*
For his shrunk shank; and his big manly voice,
Turning again toward childish treble, pipes
And whistles in his sound. *Last scene* of all,
That ends this strange eventful history,
Is second childishness and mere oblivion
Sans teeth, sans eyes, sans taste, sans everything.[30]

The words *italicised* in the lines quoted above are significant. The author has found them appropriate names for his seven volumed fiction — *Seven Ages of Man*.

So far Anand has completed only 4 volumes of *Seven Ages of Man*. The first volume titled *Seven Summers* was completed as early as in 1951. It covers the first seven years of the hero-narrator's life. It is Anand's recapitulation of his own childhood. The locale is Punjab and the period is the opening decades of the present century. The novel ends with the breaking out of the war in 1914.

The second volume *Morning Face* (1968) appeared only 17 years after the publication of the first volume. It suggests that Anand's initial enthusiasm for the autobiographical fiction in Seven Volumes was not sustained for long. Probably the failure of *The Old Woman and the Cow* or *Gauri*, *The Road* and *Death of a Hero* left him with no alternative but to go back to his autobiographical project. *Morning Face* deals with only six years in Krishan's life: from the beginning of World War I to the Jallianwala Bagh Massacre in 1919. As Krishan grew from a child to a boy, his features also grew to be attractive. He attained a "shining morning face". From Amritsar to Ludhiana, from Ludhiana to the Jhelum cantonment, the story moves in the picaresque tradition. The tyranny of the *Angrezi* Sarkar, General Dyer's blood hunting and the ever increasing fear of the people at the horrible happenings of the time come out in these pages

30. Shakespeare, William: *As You Like It*, II: (vii): 139-166.

vividly enough. The novel is a great artistic achievement and in the year 1972 it won the Central *Sahitya* Academy Award.

The third volume, *Confessions of a Lover* was published in 1976. It deals with Krishan Chander's life at Khalsa College from 1921 to 1924. The book focuses on Anand's multifarious loves: his love of political and social freedoms, his love of the Mahatma, his love of verse, and above all his love for Yasmin. Of these, the author's presentation of Krishan's love for Yasmin and the objective analysis of his psyche and motives is a remarkable accomplishment. The novel can be compared to D.H. Lawrence's *Sons and Lovers*. Krishan's mental suffering borne out of sexual awakening as presented in *Confessions of a Lover* is similar to Paul Morel's agonizing sexual experience in *Sons and Lovers*.

The fourth volume, *The Bubble* was published in 1984. It is divided into ten parts encompassing letters, diaries, journals and third person narration. It covers Krishan's years abroad from 1925 to 1929. Though we come across a number of alive characters both fictional and historical in its pages, its cynosure is Krishan's emotional encounter with Irene: walking on Mount Snowdon one day, Krishan meets an art student named Irene Rhys and immediately he becomes a victim of Cupid's golden arrow. She is fairy-like in her radiant beauty. His close contact and intimacy with her makes him realise her elf-like insistence upon her freedom of self. This is something unacceptable to Krishan. The kind of love he wants from her cannot give way to her quest for self. Hence, rejecting him with great sadness, Irene goes off to Ireland, her native land, to participate in the country's struggle for Independence. Gradually, Krishan realises his selfishness and parochialism. Irene's commitment to Ireland becomes a source of inspiration to him to work for his own country's freedom. His last letter to Irene before his departure to India is redemptive: "... And now each of us is a fuller being than when we met, and we are free to grow into each other and into ourselves".[31]

The novel's dominant imagery is fire. Krishan seeks "the bubble reputaton/Even in the cannon's mouth".[32] He is indeed a kind of "soldier", engaged in a vigorous, time-consuming battle with his weapon of inexperience. The bubbles of Krishan's early com-

31. Anand, Mulk Raj: *The Bubble*, New Delhi: Arnold-Heinemann, 1984, p. 599.
32. Shakespeare, William: *As You Like It*, II: (vii): 152-153.

placency are constantly burst. However his "various bubbling selves"[33] and his spontaneous risking of those selves even in the cannon's mouth explain his will to live, to love and to grow.

For the past few years, Anand has been steadily working on the fifth volume of his epic novel, *Seven Ages of Man*, to be entitled as, *And So He Plays His Part*. This novel with seven parts, or rather with seven novels within it, is nearing its completion. In it, the self-searching-Narcissist-psuedo-poet, Krishan Chander Azad, presents his conversion from exile in the West to his "home coming" to achieve sincerity in his creativity and to take off the mask of the "Brown Sahib" he had become in England. It expresses new and different sensibilities of Krishan and other characters from his remembrances of things past and its varied technique is based in large measure upon Anand's own distinction between the recital of the Indian epics and the narrative of the modern fiction. In this novel, the innovative author gives up the conventional novel form and by a deliberate departure from the popular novel, it includes dramatic dialogue, diary, journal and exchange of ideas as part of his new fiction-faction. In this endeavour, the author is inspired and illumined by the successful revolutionary technique of fiction writing adopted by Marcel Proust in *Remembrances of Things Past*, James Joyce in *Ulysses* and Andre Guide in *The Counterfeiters*.

As mentioned earlier, *And So He Plays His Part* is seven novels in one. The author has decided to issue it in parts and its first part, *Little Plays of Mahatma Gandhi* (1991) is already published and is now available in many libraries around the world. This novel (*Little Plays of Mahatma Gandhi*) is written in dramatic dialogue and its locale is the Sabarmati Ashram, where Krishan Chander Azad comes down to earth from the elitist snobbery of Bloomsbury to learn practical lessons on humility and sincerity from the Mahatma and with the newly acquired experience to modify his maiden creative undertaking. The novel presents the Mahatma – an interesting combination of a saint and politician – as an intimate down to earth human being, having an eye on the gates of heaven. The author does not fail to expose the contradictory and peculiar aspects of the Mahatma's personality such as his advice to peasants, to whom he has preached non-violence, to answer back the police violently if the latter molest the former's women, or his confession that he has slept

33. Anand, Mulk Raj: *The Bubble*, New Delhi: Arnold- Heinemann, 1984, p. 225.

with two girls for teaching himself how to resist the concupiscence of the flesh.

Although Anand is now an octogenarian, with four score and seven years of earthly experience, yet he is like Tennyson's *Ulysses*, "strong in will to strive, to seek, to find and not to yield".[34] He has been living for the past many years in Khandala (a small hill station 80 miles from Bombay) where he has a well-furnished house. Besides editing *Marg* and contributing to a host of Magazines and Journals, he is also sturdily engaged with life in India. His Ulysses-like attitude to life gives us hope that all the seven novels within the novel, *And So He Plays His Part* will be soon published and that we need not wait for long for the pleasure of reading the sixth and the seventh volumes of his *Seven Ages of Man* which he intends to entitle as *A World Too Wide* and *Last Scene*.

At the beginning of this chapter we focused on two points: that Anand is a great artist and that he is primarily a social critic. What are his chief concerns as a social critic? A projection of the spectrum of social criticism found in his novels will reveal his social concerns.

Anand appears in his fiction as a crusader against injustice of every type. He steadfastly opposes the exploitation of the poor by any class. This includes the Imperial masters, the village money-lenders, the unscrupulous traders, the native rulers, priests and tea-planters. So deep is his concern for the poor and the underdog that in his novels we find him cry with anguish against the injustice so prevalent in those days. In fact what has urged him to write novels is the breakdown of decencies in society:

> There is no avoiding the disgust one feels at the breakdown of decencies in present day India. Perhaps I ought to write more novels because, certainly, nowhere is the drama of meanness, hypocrisy, and double dealing in the interest of power and money and privilege being more actively played, every hour than it is in our country to-day.[35]

The passage quoted above is part of a letter Anand wrote to Saros Cowasjee. It reveals what impelled Anand to write novels. It

---

34. Lord Alfred Tennyson: *Ulysses* (1842), Lines: 70-71.

35. Anand, Mulk Raj: *Author to Critic: The Letters of Mulk Raj Anand to Saros Cowasjee*, Ed. Saros Cowasjee, Calcutta: Writers Workshop, 1973, p. 78 (letter dated: 2 Nov. 1969).

also shows his faith in the power of fiction to awaken "the slumbering conscience of man".

The social evil Anand first attacked is casteism. He finds it to be the greatest evil of Indian society. He knows that India, the emerging republic from colonial rule could become a powerful nation only if caste system is done away with.

Just as the caste system has been in India since times immemorial, attempts to abolish it have also been there from that time onwards. Swami Vivekananda wrote, "The caste system is opposed to the religion of the *Vedanta*. Caste is a social custom and all our great preachers have tried to break it down. From Buddhism downwards, every sect has preached against caste and every time it has only riveted the chains."[36] Thus, right from the days of *Upanishades* thinkers have spoken against the caste system. Buddha preached against it 2500 years ago. In the nineteenth century, there were four major movements with the main aim, among other things, to abolish caste system. They are: *Brahmo Samaj, Arya Samaj*, Rama Krishna Movement and the Theosophical Movement. These Movements tried hard to educate the people about the evils of caste system.

Around the 1930s when the freedom movement picked up momentum and united the whole nation into a great force, the Gandhian protest against caste system became an equally powerful force. The famous fast undertaken by Gandhi in 1932 to prevent the establishment of a separate electorates for the untouchables was the climax of protest against caste system in India. In many universities, the students took a vow not to observe the hierarchy of castes in their social dealings with others.

The angry young man in Mulk Raj Anand found the time perfectly ripe to present his long preserved feeling of protest against caste system. His method of protest was quite different from that of others. Instead of writing a tract against untouchability as suggested to him by Mahatma Gandhi, he wrote a novel, as "novel was more human and could reproduce contrary emotions and shades of feeling".[37] According to Mulk Raj Anand :

---

36. Swami Vivekananda: *Caste, Culture and Socialism* (Published by Swami Ananyananda), Calcutta: Ashutosh Lithographic Co., 1983, p. 31.
37. Anand, Mulk Raj: "The Story of My Experiment with a White Lie", In: *Critical Essays on Indian Writing in English*, ed: Naik, M.K., *et al*, Madras: The Macmillan Co. of India Ltd., 1977, p. 11.

> *Untouchable* was in its sources a ballad born of the freedom I had tried to win for truth against the age-old lies of the Hindus by which they upheld discrimination. The profound thoughts of the upper orders in ancient India about caste were often noble. Someone in the great *Mahabharata* had cried, "Caste, caste– There is no caste!" And I wanted to repeat this truth to the "dead souls" from the compassion of my self explanation in the various Hindu hells, in the hope that I would, myself come clean after I had been through sewer, as it were.[38]

To Mulk Raj Anand, casteism is an age-old lie made by the powerful and wicked in society to uphold discrimination. His prime concern as a social critic is to remove caste system as it damages social cohesion by giving certain sections of society an unfair advantage over others permanently. Casteism is a hydra-headed evil contagious like small pox. It is a heinous crime. It poisons and destroys the dignity of man. Hence it must be rejected. Anand is right in beginning his career as a novelist by presenting the evils of caste system. Besides *Untouchable* (1935), *The Road* (1961) and *The Big Heart* (1945) also project caste system in different perspectives as the greatest malady of Indian society.

When the British first landed in India, many might have thought them to be mere traders. This may have been a true view only in the initial stages of the Company's contact with India. But the situation soon changed by the arrival of the British army in support of the traders. By the beginning of nineteenth century the traders backed by their forces, entrenched themselves as colonisers. In their Satanic shrewdness, they found a moral sanction in the colonization of India. They said that they had come at great personal cost to lighten our darkness. They had a mission to fulfil; a moral responsibility in our dark, under-humanized, anti-democratic land. Very soon, many men of consequence were converted to such a view and they were less concerned about the reality of colonial exploitation and the sole debate whether it was amongst the British reformers or their Indian counterparts in the Bengali "Bhadra-lok", focused on the question of reform of Indian religion, Indian character and Indian customs — all of which were labelled as equally vicious or obsolete. Thus the ideology of colonialism had fulfilled its function: the British presence

38. *Ibid*., p. 16.

in India and its harmful effects were ignored. Indian intellectuals were kept busy reforming the Indians themselves.

But, by the arrival of Gandhiji to India and the movement that followed, Britishers found it hard to hide their real intentions. Pamphlets and publications awakened nationalism in the Indian mind. Creative writers like Mulk Raj Anand and Raja Rao began to expose in artistic form the reality of British presence in India and its intentions. The effect was tremendous.

By going through novels like *Coolie* (1935) and *Two Leaves and a Bud* (1942), we will be able to perceive Anand's opposition to Capitalism and Imperialism. The British imperialists found India an ideal place for practising Capitalism in its most cruel form. They exploited the poverty and misery of India to make maximum profit. Munoo in *Coolie* and Gangu in *Two Leaves and a Bud* are victims in the tragic drama of exploitation, illustrating how capital lives by sucking living labour. The capitalism that we see in Anand's novels is part of the British Imperialism. It makes us think on the ironic comments of G.B. Shaw on English men:

> There is nothing so bad or so good that you will not find English men doing it; but you will never find an Englishman in the wrong. He does everything on principle. He fights you on patriotic principles; he robs you on business principles; he enslaves you on imperial principles.[39]

The Senecan view, "Vivere militare est", to live means to struggle, is more true in the case of Indian peasants and tenants than of any other section of Indian society. The struggle of the peasants and tenants for "daybreak and daily bread" is a major theme in Anand's novels. In his novels, landlords, money-lenders and lawyers are satanic triplets in search of the blood of peasants. Poor peasants are subjected to boundless tyranny by these social leeches. Most of the produce of the peasants is usurped, either in the name of rent or debt, and they are compelled to live for ever in the fear of losing their lands, lives and even the chastity of their wives and daughters. These feudal lords are like demi-gods, leading self-indulgent, idle and de luxe lives, at the expense of the toiling and sweating tenants who are despicably treated, despite the legal as well as illegal taxes and 'nazaranas' extorted from them. The humanist in Mulk Raj Anand

39. From: *Best Quotations for all Occasions*, arranged and edited by Lewis C. Henry, London: Premier Publishers Pvt. Ltd., 1968, p. 68.

could not be a passive spectator to such a social situation. He protests vehemently against the evils of feudalism. This can be noticed in many of his novels but particularly it is pronounced in *The Village* (1942), *The Sword and the Sickle* (1942) and *Private Life of an Indian Prince* (1953).

It was Anand's desire to return to his native land for good from England during the year 1939 itself. But this could not be as World War II broke out. Till the dust of the war settled in 1945, the situation compelled him to stay on in England. The ongoing war made him ponder on the brutality and the terrible nature of it. As he himself shared the misery of war by participating in the trench warfare in Spain he was in a position to place himself in the shoes of the poor Indian soldiers who were exploited for the glory of British Crown in the war at Flanders during World War I. Anand being a humanist could not discover any glory in war. Honour in war appears to him like bubble. His character Kirpu (in *Across the Black Waters*) is like Shakespeare's Falstaff at Shrewsbury. To him the honour of war is something unreal and unsubstantial. For Kirpu, as in the case of Falstaff, "honour is a mere scutcheon" and "discretion is the better part of valour". The philosophy of humanism, which Anand tries to live, is antithetical to war. Hence he considers war as a deadly evil, the greatest plague that afflicts humanity. He wants mankind to avoid it for its own survival.

Just like war, its aftermath also makes Anand unhappy. His point of view is similar to the lines by Francis Moore in *Almanac*:

> When after many battles past,
> Both tir'd with blows, make peace at last,
> What is it, after all, the people get?
> Why! taxes, widows, wooden legs and debt.[40]

In his novels, Anand draws our tears by his descriptions of the consequences of war on the poor villagers and the soldiers. The Empire's ingratitude to the soldiers who fight for it, the untold misery they suffer on their return to their native land, the wretchedness of the villagers who are forced to pay war taxes up to the hilt are vividly presented in his novel *The Sword and the Sickle*. This social criticism of Anand is an appeal to the British Crown not to make the poor Indian soldiers a prey in their petty quarrels with somebody else and if it does not heed to his appeal, at least to show compassion to them and their family during and after the war.

40. *Ibid.*, p. 224.

A few years before India became Independent, there was much discussion in intellectual circles as to how the future Republic should be. Some were for all out industrialization even without any considerations of the infrastructure required for it. They wanted to make India a modern industrial power in no time. Some others were at the other end of the pole, strongly supporting the view that India should focus all its attention upon agricutlure and make its economy agriculture oriented. There were some others who had a middle view. They recognized the importance of the machine for nation building. They could not agree with "Gandhi's natural rejection of machine". However, they were moderate in their acceptance of the machine for the emerging republic. They were aware that the sudden all-out industrialization can expose Indian society to the plague of utilitarianism and *laissez faire* as was experienced by the industrialization of England. Mulk Raj Anand belongs to this last group of thinkers. He believes in the machine as a powerful tool of prosperity for mankind. His *The Big Heart* artistically presents the need for controlled industrialization. He presents in this novel a situation in which uncontrolled industrialization causes tremendous problems to the accepted social values. The novel is a protest against the indiscreet introduction of the machine.

The social life in India is traditionally controlled by man and the customary laws that we have been following for ages is framed by man to suit his selfish end. As such woman gets only an inferior status. She is often subjected to endless torture by the pleasure seeking selfish husband, the merciless mother-in-law and the nagging sister-in-law. In this land of male chauvinists, woman leading a happy life is a rare phenomenon. Burning woman to death or offering her for prostitution by the 'faithful' husband or torturing her till she runs away are day to day news items in the newspapers of this 'spiritual' land. We often preach of noble things like non-violence and tolerance. But every night in each lane of our villages or towns we are sure to hear at least one woman crying aloud after becoming a victim of violence. Anand, the champion of the down-trodden, outcastes, waifs and the abandoned does not fail to portray in his novels the predicament of woman who is a pitiable victim of the rigid social system. Of all his novels, *The Old Woman and the Cow* or *Gauri* (1960) considers the cause of woman most extensively. In fact, *Gauri* is Anand's only novel with a woman as the protagonist. The woman's point of view presented in this novel can have a purging effect on the reader. A nation which gives inferior status to woman is not a free nation. Hence, the compassionate heart of Anand eloquently protests in his novels and especially in *Gauri* against the ill-treatment of woman.

At the beginning of this chapter when we spoke of Anand's childhood days, we referred to the type of education he received at schools. The 'bastard type' of early education at schools and the 'false and stupid' type of education that he had at college provoked him to think of the system of education our country needs. Anand has been a visiting professor in a number of Indian and foreign universities. From 1939 to 1942 he was lecturer in philosophy and literature with the London County Council Adult Education School. He is associated with the establishment of a number of schools. His experience in the field of education and the disappointing nature of the system of education our country provides aroused his concern. He wrote a number of articles on the futility of our system of education. His most comprehensive view on the system of education needed for our country can be seen in his book, *On Education*. Being an artist, Anand could not be satisfied with writing only essays and books on education. He wanted to appeal emotionally to his countrymen on the need of reforming the educational system. His autobiographical novels *The Seven Summers, Morning Face* and *Confessions of a Lover* and his *Lament on the death of a Master of Arts* contain references to the futility of our present system of education. The last novel is a solid protest of an artist and social critic on the lamentable condition of our educational system.

India is a birth place of many religions: Buddhism, Sikhism and Jainism are contributions of our land. India is also a host to Jewism, Christianity and Islam. These religions have transformed our history and will continue to last till the end of our history. Majority of our countrymen are too serious about our religions. We are prepared to noisily argue for it; write for it; fight for it; die for it; anything but -- live it. This has caused immense problems to the unity and solidarity of our country. The frequent quarrels in the name of one religion or the other that abruptly floods our streets with blood, is a mockery of true religion. Very often these quarrels are the machinations of certain machiavellians who have no interest in any religion. Anand's exposition of this fact is dexterous in *Coolie*. His humanism considers any quarrel in the name of religion as nonsensical. He wants to lead the Indian society from the darkness of religious fanaticism and nationalism based on it, to the light of secularism. It is with this view that he came out with the novel *Death of a Hero*.

Most of Anand's protagonists are non-conformists who hurl defiance at religion. Like Maxim Gorky, Anand too considers God a fabrication and gets amused by the Ethiop gods having Ethiop lips. Gorky affirms that man sublimated the best in him in the image of God in accordance with the laws of abstraction and concretization. Anand is rather convinced that religion is the opium of the people and considers it as one of Capitalism's protective institutions.

Anand's religion is his humanism. To be good and to do good is the gist of his religion. He does not approve institutionalised religion as that is a barrier to social cohesion. Anand's position on religion is clearly stated in answer to a questionnaire submitted to him by G.S. Balarama Gupta:

> I do not believe in institutionalised religion. And like Tolstoy, I would like to leave the beliefs of people to their private conscience, collaborating with them for certain secular ends, without objecting to their pet religion.[41]

Anand is angered by the Hindu society's acceptance of Casteism and *Karma* as the fundamental truth of its religion. He protests against the Christian theories of revelation, pre-destination, original sin and human depravity as they are impediments to human progress. He ridicules the inept practices of Islam. He attacks impartially the awkwardness that has intruded into every religion. He wants people to practise the true religion which is nothing but humanism. He disapproves the way religion is reduced to mere rituals and dead customs.

Though Anand's criticism of religion and hypocrisy is a major theme in *Death of a Hero*, this theme is artistically 'sprayed' in all his fiction. Its exposure in every novel is intended to show that the institutionalised religions have become a constant threat to every sphere of our social life. Anand wants us to resist this threat by acquiring a more rational outlook.

In the last few pages of this chapter we have considered the chief concerns of Anand as a social critic. The spectrum of the social criticism seen in his novels makes us convinced that he is not an artist

41. Quoted by G.S. Balarama Gupta, In: *Mulk Raj Anand (A Study of his Fiction in Humanist Perspective)*, Bareilly: Prakash Book Depot, 1974, p. 21.

for arts own sake. He himself in one of his letters to Saros Cowasjee confirms this:

> Writing novels for the sake of writing novels was, as you know, never my intention. I felt compelled to answer challenges and tried to get out of my own confusion.[42]

Anand is an artist with a vision. He penetrates deep into our social system and identifies the causes of the social evils: "Our inability to evolve a wide, generous and fine civilized order is to a large extent due to past repressions of our emotional life, the hangover of the petty restraints imposed by the old system of life".[43] Hence what is needed for the creation of a healthy society is social change. Since 'the kingdom of God is within you', for any social change, a pre-requisite condition is change of heart. As Anand says, "What is needed is the big heartedness, the understanding, the generous, the wise heart, informed by passion and schooled by a knowledge born of love."[44]

Anand's social pre-occupations and the presentation of social criticism are found by some critics as a cancer eating away the artistic quality of his works. Some accuse him of being a propagandist and some others of being a Marxist humanist, and Anand denies both these charges. Those who blame him of being a Marxist assert that his writing is weakened by his obvious and, many would imply, dogmatic commitment to the Marxist creed. They say that his novels are designed to fit a thesis and his work, they feel, fails because it is too programatic.[45] Against this we have to set the fact that in 1949, exactly when he had just finished writing what we might consider the most committed of his novels, the Marxist Progressive Writers' Association declared him a decadent because he portrayed workers and peasants as both good and bad. Anand's own stand on this, is more carefully, if evasively, defined. In a later edition of *Apology for Heroism*, he insists that he is, if anything, a humanist and is not a

42. Anand, Mulk Raj: *Author to Critic: The Letters of Mulk Raj Anand to Saros Cowasjee*, ed: Saros Cowasjee, Calcutta: Writers Workshop, 1973, p. 100 (letter dated: 22 Sept. 1970).

43. Anand, Mulk Raj: *Apology for Heroism*, Delhi: Arnold-Heinemann Pvt. Ltd., 1975, p. 156.

44. *Ibid*.

45. H.H. Anaiah Gowda is the main exponent of this view. See: "Mulk Raj Anand", In: *The Literary Half Yearly VI*, January, 1965.

member of the Communist Party. For, he could never show adherence to "the almost religious discipline demanded by a group of people who evolved changing tactics around a minimum manifesto with maximum sanctions".[46] In the same book he also refers to his disappointment with communism as it "denies to the people the very liberties and human rights for which the revolutions were fought".[47]

Although Anand has often denied that he is a member of the Communist Party, and there are evidences that he has not been a hard-boiled leftist, yet the way he makes his characters — like Gama in *Lament on the Death of a Master of Arts* (1939), Lal Singh in *The Sword and the Sickle* (1942) and Ananta in *The Big Heart* (1951) — adore the workers' raj in Russia and the frequent trips he had made to the erstwhile communist countries prevent him from denying that he has been an ardent admirer of Communism or at the least a man leaned towards Marxism. For instance, Gama in *Lament on the Death of a Master of Arts* with vehement desire tells his dying friend Nur, "We want a workers' raj just as it is prevailing in Russia, because the condition here will be as it is in Russia. There was a time when Czar ruled Russia as the *Budshah* of *Vilayat* rules us. But one day he was shot down. And the peasants and labourers are ruling there...."[48] It was when Stalin with a frightening and repressive dictatorship turned the Soviet Union into a centralised one party state supervised by the Satanic hand of the Secret Police that Anand wrote the most Marxist oriented novel, *The Sword and the Sickle* (1942), clearly revealing his political orientation. In this novel, dominated by revolutionaries and comrades, the hero, Comrade Lal Singh wound up one of his speeches addressed to the peasants by saying, "......today, the gates of a new life will begin to open to you. For, in far land called *Roos*, too, the peasants once suffered as you do, and then they set up their own Raj.... And now the peasants and workers are ruling there and all men there live like brothers...."[49] Certainly, the reality has been quite different. The CPSU which was born in 1917 did dig its own grave in August 1991 and in to-day's Commonwealth of Independent

46. Anand, Mulk Raj : *Apology for Heroism*, Delhi: Arnold-Heinemann Pvt. Ltd., 1975, p. 185.
47. *Ibid.*, p. 202.
48. Anand, Mulk Raj : *Lament on the Death of a Master of Arts*, Delhi: Hind Pocket Books, 1963, p. 41.
49. Anand, Mulk Raj : *The Sword and the Sickle*, Delhi: Arnold-Heinemann, 1984, p. 133.

States, the iron rule of Stalin is replaced by the golden rule of *perestroika* and *glasnost* which enables the world to know how oppressive was Stalinism. The break-up of the Soviet Union and the dismantling of the Communist Party, after the unsuccessful *coup d'etat* in the Kremlin, mark the end of one Soviet dream and the beginning of another. The recent dramatic events in that country and in the Eastern bloc, both now no more exist, must have badly shaken the novelist's own ideological moorings. Now Anand's wishful thinkers and the author's own limited vision of the Soviet myth and the workers' raj make some of his novels obsolete.

Those who accuse Anand of being a propagandist say that his humanitarian zeal often carries him off his feet and his art degenerates into propaganda and that he plays the part of a social reformer at the expense of a novelist. They are of the opinion that he often seems to use the novel for the distillation of his social and political ideas, and his characters mostly work out to be little more than elucidators and amplifiers.[50] Anand's defence against the charge of propaganda is this:

> In so far I have dealt with challenges like those of colour and caste, even without giving responses, I have been accused of indulging in political and social propaganda. But, fundamentally, my exposition of character and situation is to reveal life in as total a manner as possible. My adverse critics have seldom seen the symbolism, the attitudes and the rugged poetry beneath the prose .... Therefore, if the attempt to discover the meaning of life in any given human environment is propaganda, then I am a propagandist, otherwise, it is expressionism, which I define as an enactment of the body-soul drama of human beings through the imagination.[51]

Anand's spirited defence against the charge of propaganda is not sufficient to dispel an honest researcher's fear whether he has committed an act of transgression in his novels. One thing is certain:

---

50. Paul C. Varghese and R.K. Kaushik are the main exponents of this view. See: (i) Varghese, Paul C.: *Problems of the Indian Creative Writer in English*, Bombay: Somaiya Publications Pvt. Ltd., 1968, Chapter 9. (ii) R.K. Kaushik, "Red, Brown and Grey — Ideological Commitment in Mulk Raj Anand's Novels", In: *Indo-English Literature*, ed: Dr. K.K. Sharma, Ghaziabad: Vimal Prakashan, 1978.

51. Quoted by Raghukul Tilak, In: *Untouchable – A Critical Study*, Delhi: Rama Brothers, 1983, p. 57.

a supersaturated level of social criticism and contrivance of situation to project the author's views and opinions can turn a novel into a mere tract. As this book is to deal with the author's art and concerns as presented in his non-autobiographical novels, apart from presenting his social criticism, one consideration throughout this study will be, how far the novelist succeeds in reconciling the artist to the social critic in him and whether his social criticism is a help or hindrance to his art.

II

UNTOUCHABLE AND *THE ROAD*

Mulk Raj Anand's childhood friends were mainly children from the cantonment. They included a dhobi boy called Ramcharan, a Muslim child named Ali, son of a cobler called Chota and a sweeper boy named Bakha. He mixed with them freely without giving any importance to the caste feeling his elders were trying to infuse in him. One day while playing with them, a stone thrown by Ramcharan hit him and he was flattened to the ground. Immediately, with great anxiety, they rushed towards their hero. Though he was in need of their help, they were afraid even to touch him for fear of committing the sin of 'pollution'. However, Bakha, the sweeper boy, took courage and carried him to his home to be only scolded by Anand's mother.[1] Her getting angry with Bakha in return of his act of kindness and generosity was something shocking for young Anand. At that very instant, all the sensitiveness in him got polarised and it turned out to be a vow to fight for the cause of innumerable Bakhas in India. While Bankim Chander Chatterji, Ratannath Sarshar and Rabindranath Tagore had not accepted in their novels a place of heroship for the so called lowest dregs of humanity, living in almost poverty, squalor and degradation, Anand, like the Bakha who boldly carried him to his mother, decided to carry the crores of Bakhas to the sensitive souls of this nation, giving them dignity and heroism. It is with this aim that he created the heroes, Bakha in *Untouchable* and Bhikhu in *The Road*. Perhaps Anand's reading of the Russian writers like Gogol, Tolstoy and Gorky which he had perused in India before going to London, strengthened his determination to create heroes even from the untouchables in India.

Untouchable (1935)

It was with *Untouchable* that Anand made his debut as a major

1. Anand, Mulk Raj: "The Story of My Experiment with a White Lie", In : *Critical Essays on Indian Writing in English*, ed: M.K. Naik, S.K. Desai, G.S. Amur. Madras: The Macmillan Co., of India Ltd., 1977, p. 6.

novelist. As such, he knew that only by maximum effort in the utilization of one's inherent artistic gift one could achieve greatness and therefore he directed his head and heart towards it.

The novel was the result of several incohate and wild urges that pressed the mind of Anand such as "the vanity of youth wanting recognition, the departure from abstract philosophical theories towards the search for philosophical insights based on the lives of the human beings whom one knew in the flesh and the blood; the urge to express oneself at all costs in an absolutist manner so as to expose the ugliness of death in life by deliberately dramatising, even through distortion, the non-human realities which impinged on one from all sides".[2]

While his mind was saturated with the creation of *Untouchable*, one day by chance he happened to see James Joyce's *Ulysses*. The technique in *Ulysses* taught 3 important things to Anand:

> (1) that the unities of time and space were possible all in one day of the life of a character; (2) that the disturbed, restless and paranoiac stream of consciousness of the people of our time could be reproduced, not as Joyce had done it, as so much raw material, but in the same kind of direction, so as to suggest value judgements about the characters; (3) that the 19th century novel, with a beginning, a middle and an end, was over, and that one could make a novel out of anything so long as there was a pattern. As E.M. Forster was to say later: "The story, the story — oh, what is story?"[3]

That Mulk Raj Anand's mind was very much influenced by the technique in *Ulysses* is obvious specially in the long reverie sequence of Bakha after he has been slapped on the face by a high-caste man and also from the duration of the story. The action of both *Ulysses* and *Untouchable* lasts only sixteen hours. This helped both the novelists to put their novels into a fairly neat framework for the dramatisation of their heroes' inner experience.

The novel as it is available to us underwent several changes before it got published in 1935. The 'untouchability' the author himself had experienced in several occasions in life urged him to modify his manuscript. He gives a clear instance of it in his essay, "The story of my experiment with a white lie": As a result of

2. *Ibid*., p. 6.
3. *Ibid*., p. 7.

Mahatma Gandhi's advice to make necessary amendment to the novel Anand decided to return to India. So he raised the money for his passage to India through donations from kind friends and took the P & O boat, *S.S. Multan* to Bombay. On board the ship, the British passengers, particularly the Assam tea planters, treated the Indians with contempt, except for the Maharaja of Alwar who was travelling first class. Anand began retouching his novel *Untouchable* from the new anger he felt about being an outcaste of the society of the ship.[4] This incident along with Anand's own understanding of the hardship his childhood friend Bakha faced in his encounters with the society helped him to identify himself with the hero of the novel.

Anand's life and experience in the Sabarmati *Ashram* proved extremely useful in realising the characters in the novel: For staying in the *Ashram*, Anand was asked to take a few vows. They included a promise to clean the latrines one day in a week, not to drink liquor and not to look at woman with desire.[5] Especially his cleaning of latrines in the ashram was a lesson in recognizing the dignity of labour. He realised that devotion to duty is the highest form of worship and all labour is a kind of creativity. With this new insight into work as worship Anand gave a new touch to the character of Bakha and we find him in the novel as a worshipper of God through hard work.

The periods of meditations in the *ashram* were often periods of recollections for Anand. He recalled how energetic and kind-hearted was his childhood friend, Bakha. He also recalled the feelings for devotion or '*bhakti*', which he had acquired as a young boy by seeing the personal love of his Sikh maternal grand father Nihalu, who used to tend the sick and the poor in his home. This recollection along with Gandhiji's exhortation to show devotion to the poor was a source of conversion for Anand. He began to dream of writing only about the poorest of the poor human beings like Bakha whom he had known and not very much about the orthodox and superior people of high caste, class, and status in the towns and villages where he had grown up.[6]

These passionate feelings and memories are reflected in every page of *Untouchable*.

4. *Ibid*., p. 9.
5. *Ibid*., p. 11.
6. *Ibid*., p. 13.

The novel describes one day in Bakha's life in Autumn. It begins in the early hours of the day and by the time dusk approaches, the author has been able to create round his hero (an eighteen year old sweeper boy named Bakha) a spiritual crisis of such proportion that it seems to seize the whole Indian subcontinent. 'Get up, ohe, you Bakya, ohe you son of a pig!'[7] calls out his father, and Bakha sadly abandons his fit of musings on the sahib's life that he wishes to lead himself and begins his work of cleaning the public latrines. He starts the work just out of the bed without even having a little hot water to warm his throat. Hence after completing five rounds of cleaning the latrines, he returns home with the hope of getting something hot to drink. But there is no tea and not even water. Hence his sister Sohini takes a pitcher and goes in search of water.

> She had a sylph-like form, not thin but full-bodied within the limits of her graceful frame, well-rounded on the hips, with an arched narrow waist from which descended the folds of her salwars and above which were her full, round, globular breasts, jerking slightly, for lack of bodice, under her transparent muslin shirt. Bakha observed her as she walked swaying. She was beautiful. He was proud of her with a pride not altogether that of a brother for a sister. The outcastes were not allowed to mount the platform surrounding the well, because if they were ever to draw water from it, the Hindus of the three upper castes would consider the water polluted. Nor were they allowed access to the nearby brook as their use of it would contaminate the stream......So the outcastes had to wait for chance to bring some caste Hindu to the well, for luck to decide that he was kind, for Fate to ordain that he had time — to get their pitchers filled with water. They crowded round the well, congested the space below its high brick platform, morning, noon and night, joining their hands in servile humility to every passerby; cursing their fate, and bemoaning their lot, if they were refused the help they wanted; praying, beseeching and blessing, if some generous soul condescended to listen to them, or to help them.[8]

On that morning, Sohini has been 'lucky' enough to return

7. Anand, Mulk Raj: *Untouchable*, New Delhi: Arnold-Heinemann, 1984, p. 15.

8. *Ibid*., p. 26.

home without waiting for long. Soon the mixture of tea-leaves, water, milk and sugar is prepared. Bakha feels very happy. The sharp, warm taste of the liquid sends forth a strange stimulus spreading into his flesh. He is soon out again to sweep the market road and the temple courtyard. On the way, he buys four *annas* worth of cheap sweetmeat after much speculation:

> 'Eight *annas* in my pocket' he said to himself, 'dare I buy some sweets. If my father comes to know that I spend all the money on sweets', he thought and hesitated, 'but come, I have only one life to live', he said to himself, 'let me taste of the sweets; who knows, tomorrow I may be no more'.[9]

Bakha being an untouchable, to avoid pollution by touch, the confectioner throws the packet of *jalebis*, like a cricket ball, for Bakha to catch. He catches it. He then places four nickel coins on a shoe-board near which the confectioner's assistant has been standing ready with some water to sprinkle and remove the pollution and then he walks away.

Bakha becomes extremely happy with the sweetmeat in his hand. He opens the packet with alacrity and puts a piece quickly into his mouth. The taste of the warm and sweet syrup gives him satisfaction and delight. He attacks the packet again and again with great excitement and continues to walk along the road, munching and looking at all the sights. This makes him forget to call out, "Posh, posh, sweeper coming", and he suddenly hears someone shouting at him:

> 'Keep to the side of the road, ohe low-caste vermin!'.....'Why don't you call, you swine, and announce your approach! Do you know you have touched me and defiled me, cock-eyed son of a bow-legged scorpion! Now I will have to go and take a bath to purify myself. And it was a new dhoti and shirt I put on this morning!'
>
> Bakha stood amazed, embarrassed. He was deaf and dumb. His senses were paralysed. Only fear gripped his soul, fear of humility and servility. He was used to being spoken to roughly. But he had seldom been taken so unawares.[10]

The Lalla who is 'polluted' continues to bombard abuses on

9. *Ibid.*, p. 51.
10. *Ibid.*, pp. 52-53.

Bakha. Soon he is encircled by men who have gathered to know what the uproar is about. The crowd which presses round him, is without a shadow of pity for him. When the Lalla is tired of shouting at the defenceless Bakha, he gives a sharp, clear slap at him as a punishment for his 'damned impudence', and 'ran away, like a dog with the tail between his legs'.[11]

Bakha recognizes with a shock his social position. It illuminates the inner walls of his mind. He realises that though he possesses like any human being, head and heart, and flesh and blood, he is in the eyes of the world an untouchable. Then conscious of his position, without failing he shouts aloud the warning words to announce his approach: 'Posh, posh, sweeper coming'. His pace quickens.

As he continues to walk he sees something strange in contrast to what has happened to him:

> A huge, big-humped, small-horned, spotted old brahminee bull was ruminating with half-closed eyes near him. The stink from its mouth as it belched strangely unlike any odour which had assaulted Bakha's nostrils that day, was nauseating. And the liquid dung which the bull had excreted and which Bakha knew it was his duty to sweep off, sickened him. But presently he saw a well-dressed, wrinkled old Hindu, wearing, like a rich man, a muslin scarf over his left shoulder, advance to the place where the bull was enjoying its siesta and touch the animal with his forefingers.[12]

Immediately he realises the wickedness of the society in which he is placed, which considers touching a human being like him as a malediction and touching a dirty bull like the one he has seen just then as benediction. He pauses for a few seconds and again resumes his steps shouting: 'Posh, posh, sweeper coming!' Within a short time he reaches the temple courtyard. He begins to sweep the area. He becomes suddenly curious to see what is happening inside the temple. The unfailing sense of direction of his inner impulse leads him through the temple steps towards the entrance door of the temple. Just then he hears a thundering sound:

> 'Get off the steps, scavenger! Off with you! You have defiled our temple! Now you will have to pay for the purification ceremony. Get down, get away, dog!'

11. *Ibid.*, p. 58.

12. *Ibid.*, p. 60.

Bakha ran down the steps, past the priest below him, to his sister. He had two impulses, that of fear for himself, for the crime he knew he had committed, another of fear for his sister, for the crime she may have committed, since she stood there speechless.

'You people have only been polluted from a distance', Bakha heard the little priest shriek. 'I have been defiled by contact!'

'The distance, the distance!' the worshippers from the top of the steps were shouting. 'A temple can be polluted according to the Holy Books by a low caste man actually on the steps at the door. We are ruined. We will need to have a sacrificial fire in order to purify ourselves and our shrine'.

'But I ...I .....' shouted the lanky priest histrionically, and never finished his sentence.

The crowd on the temple steps believed that he had suffered most grievously, and sympathised. They had seen the sweeper-boy rush past him. They didn't ask about the way he had been polluted. They didn't know the story that Sohini told Bakha at the door of the courtyard with sobs and tears.

'That man, that man!' she said, 'that man made suggestions to me, when I was cleaning the lavatory of his house there. And when I screamed, he came out shouting that he had been defiled'...

'Tell me, Sohini', he said, turning fiercely at his sister, 'how far did he go?'

She sobbed and didn't reply.

'Tell me! Tell me! I will kill him if....' he shouted.

'He-e-e-e- just teased me', she at last yielded. 'And then when I was bending down to work, he came and held me by my breasts'.

'Brahmin dog!' Bakha exclaimed. 'I will go and kill him!' And he rushed blindly towards the courtyard.

'No, no. Come back. Let's go away', called Sohini after him, arresting his progress by dragging hard at the lapel of his overcoat.[13]

---

13. *Ibid.*, pp. 69-70.

These incidents make his blood boil. He feels a wild desire to retaliate. And yet there is a futility written on his face. He knows that he will not be able to over-step the walls which the conventions of his superiors have built up to protect their weakness against him. The incident of 'touching' along with the attempt of the temple priest to induce his sister Sohini to surrender her chastity poisons all that happens subsequently, even such pleasant episodes as a hockey match, a country walk and a wedding. When the dusk approaches he finds three solutions to his problems: He may become a Christian with the help of Hutchinson, the Salvation Army Missionary. He has been happy to hear from Hutchinson that Christ receives all men and that *Yessuh Messih* makes no difference between the Brahmin and the *Bhangi*. But the missionary's talking of 'sin' and 'confession' and his failure to clearly tell who Christ is, confuses the mind of Bakha. The second solution is that he may take comfort in Gandhiji's chastisement of the caste Hindus and wait till the social conscience of the people is roused. Hard upon this comes the third solution: He may put his faith in the water-closet about which the positivist poet has talked. "It is prosaic, straightforward, and considered in the light of what has gone before in the book, it is convincing. No god is needed to rescue the untouchables, no vows of self-sacrifice and abnegation on the part of more fortunate Indians but simply and solely — the flush system. Introduce water-closets and main-drainage throughout India, and all this wicked rubbish about untouchability will disappear."[14] Bakha thinks of everything he has heard and returns to his mud-walled hut, with the desire to tell his father all what Gandhi said about them and what the clever poet said about the flush system.

In this sensitive portrayal of an individual, Mulk Raj Anand displays his penetrating thought and humane attitude in understanding the grim realities of the social life in India. It is a revolutionary novel in the sense that it has an outcaste as its chief protagonist. Anand's turning to the evil of caste system even at the very start of his writing career is understandable because it answers to his need to create in readers an urgent awareness of the dehumanising social evil, to stir the springs of tenderness in them, and to rally them for the removal of these evils in order that a desirable or a just social order may come into being. It is significant that this Indian novel in English first

14. E.M. Forster: "Preface" to *Untouchable*, New Delhi: Arnold-Heinemann, 1984, p. 10.

appeared at a time when social reformers in India were engaged in an earnest effort to remove casteism and untouchability.

It is more than half a century now, since the novel first appeared. Though social life in India has been revolutionized since then, still one cannot say with confidence that casteism is not with us. The Government itself is aware of its existence. Otherwise, why the government controlled media should come out with this message: "Untouchability is a crime against God and Man". Those who send or receive the postal Inland Letter Card are familiar with this message inscribed on it. In our social intercourse we often come across persons with caste-consciousness who are inquisitive to know a stranger's name for the sake of identifying his caste or creed. The caste taboos and discriminations do operate to a considerable extent in the rural areas. This is evident from the following newspaper item appeared a few years back in the *Newstime*:

Untouchability Still Prevalent in Bihar
– *Press Trust of India*

> *Patna*: The evil of untouchability is still prevalent in some parts of Bihar even after 38 years of Independence, according to a recent survey. The Survey revealed that 67 per cent people in rural areas confirmed that untouchability was very much prevalent overtly and covertly. This was evident at village wells, ponds, temples, eating places and at social functions. The survey was jointly conducted by the "Lalit Narayan Institute of Economic Development and Social Changes" and the "Bihar State Scheduled Caste Co-operative Development Corporation" in seven districts of Varanasi, Patna, Nalanda, Nawada, Gaya, Aurangabad and Palamau. The Survey revealed that 90 per cent people belonging to the Scheduled Castes were unaware of the civil rights provided in the Constitution. The Survey, mainly conducted in the rural areas, found that a majority of the people belonging to other castes were also unaware of the law against untouchability.[15]

Thus, despite the provisions of the law, untouchability is even to-day a social reality. Hence, the novel is relevant and has a perennial appeal to the reader.

15. "Untouchability Still Prevalent in Bihar", *Newstime*, Hyderabad: Vol. 3, No. 4, Tuesday, 28 January, 1986.

The novel begins with a vivid picture of the out-castes' colony :

> The outcastes' colony was a group of mud-walled house that clustered together in two rows, under the shadow both of the town and the cantonment, but outside their boundaries and separate from them.....The absence of a drainage system had, through the rains of various seasons, made of the quarter a marsh which gave out the most offensive smell. And altogether the ramparts of human and animal refuse that lay on the outskirts of this little colony, and the ugliness, the squalor and the misery which lay, within it, made it an 'uncongenial' place to live in.[16]

It looks as though the scavengers, leather workers, washermen, barbers, water carriers and grass-cutters – all these inhabitants of the colony are made to live a life of yahoos, huddled up together. The pity is that they are content to live in the gutter like worms only to be crushed by the superior caste people.

For the privileged, the colony of the untouchable is a forbidden place. That is why it is termed as "out-castes' colony". It reveals that the privileged people are totally indifferent to the welfare of the people who slavishly serve them. They treat the outcastes as their moveable, yet untouchable, property. They consider the sweepers dirty just because they clean their dirt. They make the untouchables lead a life of total dependence on them. Even for water, the basic necessity of human existence, the sweepers have to depend on the mercy of the caste Hindus. The novel gives a very ironic situation in which some untouchables collected at the foot of the well making a servile appeal to an illiterate sepoy who happened to pass that way:

> 'Oh, Maharaj! Maharaj! Won't you draw us some water, please? We beg you. We have been waiting, here a long time, we will be grateful', shouted the chorus of voices as they pressed towards him, some standing up, bending and joining their palms in beggary, others twisting their lips in various attitudes of servile appeal and abject humility as they remained seated separate.[17]

This is only one among the several instances of dependence the caste Hindus thrust on the untouchables to assert their authority over them.

16. Anand, Mulk Raj: *Untouchable*, New Delhi: Arnold-Heinemann, 1984, p. 11.
17. *Ibid.*, p. 30.

Bakha, the protagonist of the novel, is a dedicated worker. He begins his day even before dawn at the rude command of his father. The most beautiful aspect of Bakha is that he is very dutiful. While his father has often fabricated some sickness for himself to escape doing his sweeping work, Bakha avoids all such alibis accompanying idleness and goes about with strength and vitality. He finishes the fifth round of work even before he could have his morning cup of tea. His reverence for work makes him a Gandhi disciple without knowing it. But the society pays no credit to his devotion to duty: Cigarettes are flung at him as a bone is flung at an insistent sniffing dog. *Jilebis* are thrown at him, like the wastes thrown at a pig; and the thin paper-like pancake (given as food to the sweeper) flies down to him like a kite from the third floor. Wherever Bakha goes, he is belittled with such words as 'defiled' and 'polluted'. The privileged caste Hindus assert their superiority over the outcastes by inflicting pain on them. They state arrogantly: "They ought to be wiped off the surface of the earth!"[18] The mental depression of all untouchables finds its expression in Bakha's agonized interrogation: "What have I done to deserve all this?"[19]

"Dogs" is the name that normally comes to the mind of the privileged folk to identify the outcastes. The "touching incident" reveals the horror of being an untouchable. The people who gather around Bakha shoot abuses by calling him, "low-caste vermin", "swine", "cock-eyed son of a bow-legged scorpion", "dog", "brute", "dirty dog", "son of a bitch", "son of a dog", "offspring of a pig" etc.[20] These abusive words thrown on a lonely and helpless person are in opposition to the privileged folk's claim of being "twice-born". These words actually reveal their polluted mind.

Anand is a social critic. He often uses the tool of irony to expose social evils. Untouchability is particularly vulnerable to ironic treatment as its practitioners are satanic in their hypocrisy and pharisaical in their piety. In this regard what Saros Cowasjee says in his book *So Many Freedoms* is worth quoting:

> As irony is implicit in the theme, one finds it everywhere and even more pervasively than in any other Anand novel. The novel unfolds with a child of modern India shackled by age-

18. *Ibid.*, p. 56.
19. *Ibid.*, p. 133.
20. *Ibid.*, pp. 53-55.

> old traditions; the Hindus who pride themselves on their cleanliness gargle and spit in the stream and pollute the water while a person incomparably cleaner than themselves is treated like a dirt. There are Muhamadans walking about with hands in their pyjamas, purifying themselves in the ritualistic manner preparatory to their visit to a mosque, but infuriated when asked what they are doing; men squatting in the open to relieve themselves, earning from the Tommies well-deserved abuse; the rich Hindu businessmen overfeeding idle priests but grudging dry bread to those who sweat for them; the pretty merchant-cum-money-lender whose prices go up for the poor, and the sweet-meat seller who deftly manipulates the scales to cheat the outcastes. There are orthodox Hindus who worship a bull emitting foul smells but will not touch a human being; there are temples whose doors are closed to those who keep its ground clean; we see the queer Hindu notion of "pollution by touch" and "pollution from a distance"; and the hypocrisy of Hindu women who treat the sweepers as pariahs but want to be called "mother" by them.
>
> The ruling class too comes in for criticism. Englishman, after years in India, learn only some useful imperatives and swear-words such as 'acha' (good); 'jao' (go away); 'jaldi karo' (be quick); 'sur ka bacha' (son of a pig); 'kute ka bacha' (son of a dog).[21]

In the same book, Cowasjee says: "The Hindu religion is responsible for this fiendish segregation of humanity."[22] This is not an acceptable view. This reveals rather an insufficient understanding of what Hindu religion means or stands for. Casteism is a social practice and no Hindu religious leader of any merit and significance would admit it as part of his religion. Giving a place to casteism in Hindu religion is done by certain wolves in sheep's skin for certain privileges and advantages. As Gandhi says at the end of the novel, if the Hindus oppress the untouchables, "they should understand that the fault does not lie in the Hindu religion, but in those who profess it".[23]

---

21. Cowasjee, Saros: *So Many Freedoms: A Study of the Major Fiction of Mulk Raj Anand*, New Delhi: Oxford University Press, 1977, p. 55.
22. *Ibid*., p. 51.
23. Anand, Mulk Raj: *Untouchable*, New Delhi: Arnold-Heinemann, 1984, p. 165.

The priests of every religion know that the concept of untouchability is highly irreligious. As most of them are enveloped by a kind of spiritual emptiness, they lack the moral strength to fight against it. In fact some of them are even happy to fish in the troubled waters in which the untouchables are struggling to float. A typical example is Pandit Kali Nath. He typifies gluttony, hypocrisy and falsehood. We see him for the first time at the public well. He is cogitating on the rice he ate a day ago which caused constipation. Next he thinks of the *jilebis* he ate with milk at the confectioner's shop. Then the food he consumed at the residence of Lala Bansari Dass brings to his mind fresh feeling of pleasure and he recollects the taste of the various kinds of food with which he was honoured: the rice, pudding, 'kara-parshad' and so on. His mind is mostly preoccupied with the various delicacies he loves. This reveals his gluttony. As the action in the novel develops, we see him standing in front of the temple and shouting, "Polluted! Polluted!" with his accusing finger on poor Sohini. The great Pandit's misbehaviour with Sohini and his shameless accusation that she made physical contact with him and defiled him is a typical illustration of the general hypocritical behaviour of the white-washed guardians of religion. It also shows that lust knows no untouchability. Pandit Kali Nath's lustful behaviour with Sohini is only a human frailty whereas his accusation that she pollutted him with her touch is beyond doubt diabolic. Pandits like Kali Nath, are pilots leading the Indian society to a sure crash. Anand's exposure of them is intended only to avert it.

Throughout the novel Anand has been able to embody in Bakha a genuine person that attracts our attention. As E.M. Forster tells, "Bakha is a real individual, lovable, thwarted, sometimes grand, sometimes weak, and thoroughly Indian. Even his physique is distinctive; we can recognize his broad intelligent face, graceful torso, and heavy buttocks, as he does his nasty jobs, or stumps out in artillery boots in hopes of a pleasant walk through the city with a paper of cheap sweets in his hand."[24] Anand has with remarkable skill entered into Bakha's soul and exposed Bakha's helplessness, frustration, anxiety and agony to the degree that he has become an embodiment of Bakha himself. The author's struggle to extirpate his own personality and ideas, in order to give scope for the character to express himself, was very hard. One person who hoenstly helped the author in this

24. E.M. Forster: "Preface" to *Untouchable*, New Delhi: Arnøld-Heinemann, 1984, p. 9.

respect was Dr. K.S. Shelvankar. "Once when I explained to him", Anand tells us in 'The story of my experiment with a white lie', "the terms of reference of the novel, he was ruthless and sat down with me to cut all the projections which might intrude the author's personality on the characters. This made for a certain resilience and established the necessary distance to exclude sentimentality."[25]

However, the quick of Anand's own passion for Bakha and his full engagement with the destiny of this and other untouchables of India, stood as an obstacle for him to accept all the suggestions given by Dr. K.S. Shelvankar.[26] This is very much recognizable in the concluding section of the novel. E.M. Forster, it appears, must have seen in advance, the adverse comments the conclusion of the novel would invite, and in his preface defended it in these words:

> Some readers may find this closing section of the book too voluble and sophisticated, in comparison with the clear observation which has preceded it, but it is an integral part of the author's scheme. It is the necessary climax, and it has mounted up with tripple effect. Bakha returns to his father and his wretched bed, thinking now of the Mahatma, now of the Machine. His Indian day is over and the next day will be like it, but on the surface of the earth if not in the depths of the sky, a change is at hand.[27]

Though some reviewers agreed with Forster's remark many rejected it. *The Evening News* simply called the ending "unconvincing". *The Star* thought it "so simple as to seem almost comic"; and the *Glasgow Herald* said that, "It is an ending that might have been dispensed with."

Mahatma Gandhi's visit to the Goal *Maidan* near Bulasah leads the novel to a climax. The effect of the novel would have been better had the novel ended with that incident. After the Mahatma has left the *Maidan*, a group of people stays on there discussing the Mahatma's views. The arguments steal away some amount of the greatness of the novel. Their discussion on *Vedas* and *Upanishads*, *Maya* and *Nirvana*,

25. Anand, Mulk Raj: "The Story of my Experiment with a White Lie", In: *Critical Essays on Indian Writing in English*, ed: M.K. Naik, S.K. Desai, G.S. Amur, Madras: The Macmillan Co. of India Ltd., 1977, p. 16.
26. *Ibid*., p. 14.
27. E.M. Forster: "Preface" to *Untouchable*, New Delhi: Arnold-Heinemann, 1984, p. 10.

Machine *versus* Man, etc., have no satisfactory convergence. They could have been briefer. For the greater part of the time, a young poet dominates the stage, but Bakha is too much under the Mahatma's spell to listen to anyone. But the mention of a "machine which clears dung" and which may enable a sweeper to change his profession so that he may no longer be thought of as an untouchable grips his attention. It also catches his fancy. Of the three solutions given at the end of the novel, Bakha seems to be slightly inclined towards the flush system over the other two. It may be due to the fact that it makes no demands on his religion, as against the solution given by the Salvation Army Pastor and it is something revolutionary unlike the non-violence of Mahatma Gandhi. The machine which can clear the dung is of great use to the society. It can also replace the label pasted on some sections of society as scavengers. Hence it falls within Anand's concept of controlled introduction of Machine.

The defects in the novel are negligible compared to its great artistic merits. When it first appeared in 1935, the reviewers R.A. Scott James, V.S. Pritchett, Storm Jameson, Edward Thompson and Bonamy Dobree reacted with adulation.[28] E.M. Forster called it "an excellent work".[29] Jack Lindsay discovered "the kaleidoscopic movement of colour, sight, touch and sound"[30] in the novel. "Much of the power of *Untouchable*", says K.N. Sinha, "derives from its solidity of specifications. Anand creates here a dense web of actualities, so that the created universe in the novel, bears a direct resemblance to the actual one."[31] It is a tragic poem of an individual caught in the cross-roads of social hypocrisy. At the same time the novel has a tragic beauty of its own. The very structure of *Untouchable* and the classical purity of its form, brings Bakha's drawing inwardness and loveliness into sharp relief. His inner urge to revolt and his awareness of the inability of successfully doing so makes him stoically placed. In fact it is his failure to revolt that gives fidelity to the novel.

Untouchable closes on a note of faith and idealism. As Bakha returns home his mind is raised with the hope that soon the age of

---

28. Anand, Mulk Raj: "The Story of my Experiment with a White Lie", In: *Critical Essays on Indian Writing in Engliish*, edited by: M.K. Naik, S.K. Desai, G.S. Amur, Madras: The Macmillan Co. of India Ltd., 1977, p. 16.

29. See: blurb, In: *Untouchable*, New Delhi: Arnold-Heinemann, 1984.

30. Lindsay, Jack: *The Elephant and the Lotus – A Study of the Novels of Mulk Raj Anand*, Bombay: Kutub-Popular, 1965, p. 8.

31. Sinha, K.N.: *Mulk Raj Anand*, New York: Twayne Publishers, 1972, p. 29.

flush system will come when "the sweepers can be free from the stigma of untouchability and assume the dignity of status that is their right as useful members of a casteless and classless society".[32]

Certainly Anand's maiden novel, *Untouchable* is a masterly work, because it evinces a happy harmony between his social preoccupations and artistic gifts.

***The Road* (1961)**

The British Imperialists' concern expressed now and then on the social evils in India was shrewdly motivated, as I have hinted in the 'Introduction', to keep the Indian Intelligentsia busy with social reform and thereby to keep them away from interfering with statecraft. The British rulers patronised the activities of Dayanand Sarasvati, Raja Ram Mohan Roy, Swami Vivekananda, Sri Narayana Guru, Dr. Ambedkar as well as the reformatory movements led by Mahatma Gandhi. To show their support for the Indian reformists they enacted laws against two top social evils: Sati and Untouchability. The Introduction of the Indian Penal Code by the British Raj in 1860 stated that all men were equal before the law and that the nature of the wrong was not affected by the caste, the person committing it or against whom it was committed. The British as far as possible, maintained a policy of non-interference with the social and cultural life of Indians. Despite the Indian Penal Code of 1860, and its relatively strict enforcement in British India, it did little for the alleviation of the sufferings of untouchables. No Bakha dared to go along the road without shouting "Posh! Posh! Sweeper coming!"

The Road (1961) is based on an actual incident. When Saros Cowasjee asked Mulk Raj Anand why he wrote this novel, since he had covered much the same ground in *Untouchable*, he replied:

> Well, it was kind of shock to me when I went to live in Haryana, 20 miles from Delhi in the human empire of Jawaharlal Nehru, to find that the outcastes not only in the South India, but in the mixed North were still confined to the limbo of oblivion. There was something tragic comic to me in the fact that the caste Hindus would not touch the stones quarried by the untouchables to make the road, because the stones had been touched by the untouchables. I mentioned this to the great Nehru. He did not believe me.

32. Anand, Mulk Raj, *Untouchable*, New Delhi: Arnold-Heinemann, 1984, p. 173.

> He was quite angry at my mentioning this awkward fact. I said I would prove it to him by showing it to him in the "enchanted mirror".[33]

The "enchanted mirror" Anand created is *The Road*. The outlines of the story of the novel is as follows: The people in the village of Govardhan produce plenty of cattle milk and large amount of vegetables. But selling them to their city, Gurgaon, is a big problem as there is no transportation facility. The government, aware of this serious problem faced by the villagers, decide to fulfil their aspiration by building a road connecting the city to Govardhan. The work is started. The villagers are very happy that soon vehicles would be able to visit their village and they would have an era of economic prosperity. Bikhu and other untouchables also get chance to work in the road construction. The landlord Thakur Singh who has become rich by exploiting the untouchables, cannot tolerate the idea of Bikhu and other untouchables drawing wages just like the caste-Hindus for taking part in the road construction. The caste feeling soars up. The upper-caste Hindus refuse even to touch the stones quarried by the untouchables. But the village headman Dhooli Singh, inspired by the teaching of Gandhiji decides to treat the untouchables as children of God or Harijans. He courageously joins hands with the untouchables in the road construction. The landlord Thakur Singh becomes furious. By his instigation, the village priest excommunicates Dhooli Singh. Soon the landlord's son, Sanju, a merciless 'goonda', translates into action his father's fury with the untouchables, by burning their huts. Dhooli Singh's son Lachman, who is in love with the landlord's daughter Rukmani, also joins hand in the arson organised by Sanju against the untouchables, in the hope that it would please Thakur Singh and one day he would be able to marry Rukmani. On the other hand, the contre-temps lacerates the magnanimous heart of Dhooli Singh with sorrow and he decides to help the untouchables to build their huts. He generously permits them to occupy his own house till their huts are built. Dhooli Singh's wife becomes angry at his behaviour of freely mixing with the untouchables and getting "polluted", and so she leaves him. But Dhooli Singh stands all these ordeals with fortitude. When the government authorities come to know that the road, instead of uniting people, divides families, threatens friendships,

33. Anand, Mulk Raj, *Author to Critic: The Letters of Mulk Raj Anand to Saros Cowasjee*, ed: Saros Cowasjee, Calcutta: Writers' Workshop, 1973, p. 124 (letter dated: 12 Dec. 1971).

spoils marriage contacts and is responsible for the burning of the huts of untouchables, they send an official to instruct the people that untouchability has been legally abolished and anyone perpetuating it can be punished under the law. Soon reason prevails over emotion in Dhooli Singh's son Lachman and he joins the untouchables in the road construction. Sanju also behaves with repentance for some time, but soon the feudal blood he has acquired wings him to pursue his crusade against the untouchables. Hence the understanding that Lachman would marry Rukmani and Sanju would marry Dhooli Singh's daughter Mala ends. Meanwhile the construction of the road continues. Finally, when the road is ready, Bhikhu "did not go towards home. Instinctively he went in the direction of the road he had helped to build. And in his soul he took the direction out of the village, towards Gurgaon, which was the way to Delhi town, capital of Hindustan, where no one knew who he was and where there would be no caste or outcaste...."[34]

Untouchability has always provoked the intelligent heart of Mulk Raj Anand into action. He finds that legislation as a means of social change does not work in the case of untouchability, since untouchability is deeply rooted in the Indian psyche. He realises that this social evil can be removed only by appealing to the hearts of the privileged people who unscrupulously perpetuate it. He understands that untouchability can be abolished only through a literarcy of feeling. Hence, Anand, the angry young man who protested against untouchability in the 30s tries his hand on the same theme after 25 years, in *The Road*. His coming back again to the same social evil in this novel reveals his emotional involvement with the problem of untouchability.

The era of *The Road* is not very different from the social milieu of *Untouchable*. The law of the land has not influenced the attitude of the society. As in *Untouchable*, so in this novel, we find the caste Hindus ill-treating their outcaste brothren: They are not allowed to come into physical contact with the 'twice-born', or permitted to enter the temple for coming into contact with the God of all. Just like in *Untouchable*, in *The Road* also Anand introduces a lecherous and hypocritical priest. In both the novels we come across the "slapping scene". In *Untouchable*, it is a highly dramatic situation, the pivot of the novel, but in *The Road* it is a mere contrivance. On the last but

34. Anand, Mulk Raj: *The Road*, Bombay: Kutub-Popular, 1961, p. 110.

one page of the book we come across the slapping incident. The thirsty Bhikhu accepts a brass tumbler of water from Rukmani, the beautiful daughter of Thakur Singh. Her brother Sanju, who hates all untouchables sees this and rushes towards Bhikhu and slaps him for defiling the tumbler. Like his prototype Bakha, Bhikhu for a moment thinks of retaliating but common sense warns him of the perilous sea in which he and the other untouchables struggle even after 14 years of Indian Independence.

The upper caste's intransigent attitude to the changed social situation is evident in their refusing to touch the stones quarried by the untouchables, while enjoying the yield of the fields tilled by them. Pandit Suraj Mani in this novel reminds us of Pandit Kali Nath of *Untouchable.* He, Pandit Suraj Mani, moves about carrying with him a little earth to avoid pollution by treading on what has been 'soiled' by the untouchables. At the same time, he gladly accepts the mangoes plucked by the untouchables saying, "Sweet is the fruit of Lambardar Dhooli Singh's grove".[35] It shows his cunning and hypocrisy. Pandit Kali Nath of *Untouchable* and Pandit Suraj Mani of *The Road* are black-marketeers of their religion for selfish ends. As they have not received the divine light, they are incapable of the Gandhian realisation that untoucables are children of God or Harijans. In their shallowness, they mix up religion, politics and social life and vehemently preach on pollution by touch, pollution from distance or on the *karma* theory which says that the suffering of the untouchables is only a punishment divinely ordained for their bad deeds in their previous births and that they should submit themselves to every blow and kick the upper castes give them at every step of their lives with humility for the sake of caste-promotion in their next birth. Mulk Raj Anand's anger with such guardians of religions seems to echo the fiery words spoken by Swami Vivekananda:

> Priestcraft is the bane of India.... Do you think our religion is worth the name? Ours is 'Don't touchism', only 'Touch me not'. Good heavens! A country, the big leaders of which have for the last two thousand years been only discussing whether to take food with the right hand or the left, whether to take water from the right-hand-side or the left.... if such a country does not go to ruin what other will? A country where millions of people, live on the flowers of the *Mohua*

35. *Ibid.*, p. 82.

> plant, and a million or two of Sadhus (monks) and a hundred million or so of Brahmanas suck the blood of these poor people, without even the least effort for their amelioration — is that a country or hell? Is that a religion or the devil's dance?[36]

The Road portrays not only the suffering of the untouchables but also of the magnanimous caste Hindus who try to awaken the conscience of the members of their own community against the evils of untouchability. To be honest is a dangerous thing where the rule of hypocrisy dominates. That is what led to the assassination of Mahatma Gandhi, Abraham Lincoln and Martin Luther King. Socrates had to drink hemlock, Christ to hang on the cross and Joan of Arc to burn at the stake for being honest to society. Dhooli Singh, in *The Road* is a social reformer and a staunch disciple of the Mahatma. His following of his Master's footsteps was a hard task. His single handed fight against untouchability in a society where casteism is interpreted in terms of religion is considered as a challenge to the religion itself. But he represents the true religion; he personifies the author's vision of an ideal Hindu.

Anand's *The Road* (1961) has interesting similarities with Raja Rao's *Kanthapura* (1938). There is every reason to believe that Anand imitated certain aspects of *Kanthapura* in *The Road*. Both take place in caste-ridden villages where untouchables are exploited. Moorthy, the hero of *Kanthapura* is an *alter-ego* of Dhooli Singh. Both are Gandhians. Both treat the untouchables as Harijans or children of God and as such both freely mix with them and work for their social upliftment. Dhooli Singh welcoming the shelterless untouchables to stay with him may be as shocking to the caste-conscious people as Moorthy's visiting a pariah house and having tea there. Both earn enemies for adhering to the truth taught by Mahatma Gandhi and become victims of priestcraft and its tool, excommunication. The landlord Thakur Singh in *The Road* who is responsible for the misery of untouchables is similar in character to the landlord Bhatta in *Kanthapura*. They resist any social reform and they consider social reformers as their enemies. Both the novels are dominated by symbolism. The names and nick-names of people in *Kanthapura* bear the real flavour of the rustic ways of speech such as

36. Swami Vivekananda: *Caste, Culture and Socialism* (Published by Swami Ananyananda), Calcutta: Ashutosh Lithographic Co., 1983, pp. 40-41.

Temple Rangappa, Post-Office-House Chinnamma, Front-House Suranna, Four-Beamed-House Chandrasekkarayya, Waterfall Venkamma, Nose-scratching Nanjamma and Concubine Chinna. In *The Road* also we see such symbolic names created with the purpose of infusing life to the people by the impressionistic technique, such as Tomato-Face Thakur Singh, Dampling-Nose Dhooli Singh, Fox-Face Daya Ram, Cowherd Mahesh and Cock-eyed Ram Nivas. The symbolic names in *Kanthapura* are skilful creation and they give dramatic effect to the old grand mother's narration of the rustic life. But the names in *The Road* are to a great extent irrelevant. The fun and symbolic significance desired from the names are not realised and one may be right in asserting that the frequent use of these names does not in any way keep the reader delighted.

There are also other defects in the novel. It is difficult to say who is the real hero of the novel. Bhikhu the hero, does not hold on to the cynosure of the novel. Dhooli Singh seems to usurp it. Bhikhu remains shadowy. Anand's effort to infuse in him some of the qualities of Bakha makes Bhikhu a caricature of the hero of *Untouchable*.

The ending of the novel has captured the attention of many reviewers. The ending "makes Anand's views quite ambiguous"[37], says Premila Paul. After the construction of the road, instead of celebrating it, the hero makes an escape. He coolly disappears through the road and heads towards Delhi, the capital of the Nation. The action is confusing. If the rulers are not concerned about the welfare of the untouchables, then, the 'road to Delhi town, Capital of Hindustan' remains a path offering no solution and so the hero's action hardly has any symbolic significance. Perhaps Bhikhu must have reached the conclusion that even if prosperity and modernity embrace the village, the attitude of the villagers will not change and untouchability is bound to haunt and harass him and therefore the solution to his problem may be found in his anonymous mingling with the multitudes in Delhi. However, his decision is not in conformity with his character. He is defiant by nature. This is indicated at the very beginning of the novel, in his reply to his mother who pleads with him not to fight against the upper caste youths who block their entry into the temple:

'Son, we are at fault', Laxmi said.

---

37. Paul, Premila: *The Novels of Mulk Raj Anand: A Thematic Study*, New Delhi: Sterling Publishers Pvt. Ltd., 1983, p. 24.

> 'Join hands to them all and obey them. Dont fight....! And she turned to the superior ones, saying: 'Have pity on Bhikhu. He is a hot headed boy!.... And we will not go to the temple if you think we will pollute it....!
>
> 'Ma–what are you saying?' Bhikhu protested.
>
> 'Son, we are *chamars*', she tried to persuade him.
> 'And they are twice-born!'
>
> 'One is a leather worker by profession and not by birth!' Bhikhu shouted and he proceeded.[38]

Bhikhu is portrayed throughout the novel as a defiant person who faced the realities of life boldly and with determination. Hence his escapist action at the end of the novel is not in conformity with his character.

Another defect in the novel is the element of love introduced in it, namely the attraction of Lachman towards Rukmani and of Sanju for Mala, and a kind of undefined attraction between Rukmani and Bhikhu. It is a diversion from the focus of the novel and it is not dexterously handled. M.K. Naik's comment on this grafted romantic bit in the novel is worth quoting:

> Anand has falsified his vision by a gratuitous introduction of the love motif. He resurects the hoary romantic convention of the children of two adversaries being attracted towards each other, even providing the two adversaries — Dhooli Singh and Thakur Singh — with a son and a daughter each; and make matters still worse by dragging in the attraction felt by Rukmani and Bhikhu, thus destroying whatever authenticity his latter day vision of the outcaste has.[39]

"A new broom sweeps clean", says the proverb. Though Anand's first novel *Untouchable* could sweep the literary world off its feet, his novel on the same theme written 25 years after its publication, namely *The Road,* due mainly to careless characterisation, fails to attain the sovereign quality of the first novel. However, since the novel is told largely in dialogue and through inner monologues, its reading is highly interesting.

---

38. Anand, Mulk Raj: *The Road*, Bombay: Kutub Popular, 1961, p. 4.
39. Naik, M.K. : *Mulk Raj Anand*, New Delhi: Arnold-Heinemann, 1973, pp. 37-38.

III

COOLIE AND *TWO LEAVES AND A BUD*

In pre-British India, caste hierarchy to a great extent reflected economic disparity: The highest caste were as a whole, the richest and the lowest caste, the poorest. But the Indian society experienced a qualitative structural transformation during the British rule. It generated forces which directly or indirectly gave a mortal blow to the caste system and created basis for the emergence of new social classes, strata and associations and thereby laid the foundation for modern India.

If caste system is cruel enough to create untouchables among human beings, class system is no less cruel to humanity as it makes the rich, richer and the poor, poorer. It turns the poorest one in society a mere 'brother to an ox'. It segregates and enslaves thousands of people into endless misery and eventual extirpation. Class system is a greater evil than caste system. This is obvious from the fact that the rich low-caste is better placed in society than the poor high-caste. The caste victims can at least draw sympathy and support from members of their own caste whereas the class victims have no such consolation and have to suffer perpetual deprivation.

Coolie (1936) and *Two Leaves and a Bud* (1937) are artistic works depicting the widening gap between the haves and the have-nots, the exploiters and the exploited, the rulers and the ruled. The action of these novels takes place in the pre-independent India and as such they include characters both British and Indian. The British characters in the novel reveal the role of the West in contaminating the Indian society with the evil of class system. The problem of class is a universal phenomenon but Anand's interest lies in exploring the stresses and strains generated in Indian society as a result of the basic economic transformation brought about by various acts of the British government (such as the new type of land reforms), the penetration into the Indian society by commercial and other forces from the outside capitalist world, and the establishment of modern industries in India, which necessarily demanded new class arrangements in society.

In *Two Leaves and a Bud*, Buta is a barber by birth, but the abjectness traditionally attached to his low caste is rarely thought of, and he is greeted as Buta Ram by the poor coolies of high-caste origin, as he is a Sardar in position and as he is not reduced to penury like them. Though Munoo in *Coolie* and Gangu in *Two Leaves and a Bud* are *Khatriyas* by birth, their belonging to the wealthless class compels them to greet and obey people like Buta of the barber caste. The two novels, *Two Leaves and a Bud* and *Coolie* may be regarded as proletarian novels as their heroes belong to the unpropertied class who must sell their labour in order to exist. They focus on the inhuman attitude of the capitalist system which ignores the manhood in labourers and treats them as mere 'hands' in the machine of profit.

Coolie portrays the sufferings of an individual coolie in a class-ridden society while *Two Leaves and a Bud* pictures the same problem as a group experience in the framework of a leviation capitalistic set-up. Both are stories of crushed humanity, of sighs and tears, of what man has done to man.

Coolie

Just as Anand's childhood friendship with a sweeper boy named Bakha helped him to write *Untouchable*, his awareness of the sufferings of his childhood playmate, Munoo, who was compelled to labour in a pickle factory and who accepted his lot with a fatalism peculiar to the Indian peasantry, urged him to write *Coolie*. The novel was written in three months and was published in 1936 by Lawrence and Wiskart.

Coolie is one of the most popular works of Anand. It is translated into more than 38 languages of the world. Thus it shares with *Untouchable* (1935) not only the author's social rage, but also its immense popularity. It has been widely praised by readers, scholars and critics alike. It has been called an 'epic of misery', the 'epic of modern India' and the 'odyssey of Munoo, the Coolie'. Anand calls it 'a Whitman poem'.[1] V.S. Pritchett praises it in the following words: "I got more out of *Coolie* than out of any other novel I have read for

1. Anand, Mulk Raj: *Author to Critic: The Letters of Mulk Raj Anand to Saros Cowasjee*, ed: Saros Cowasjee, Calcutta: Writers Workshop, 1973, p. 22 (letter dated 3 Feb. 1968).

a very long time indeed. There is so much talk about political novels in these times but so few of them to me to be works of any high order. In fact *Coolie* is the only political novel I have read which profoundly satisfied me."[2]

The novel presents a chain of adventures in a picaresque manner. But Munoo the hero is not a rogue. He is only a victim of the world's rogueries. His search for bread, in a world where poor man's flesh and blood is treated as cheaper than bread, makes him restless and it forces him to move from place to place.

Munoo is an orphan boy. In the opening scene of the novel, he is fourteen years of age. He is ill-treated by his uncle Daya Ram and Aunt Gujri, but still remains happy in his native village of Bilaspur. His uncle, Daya Ram, finds him to be old enough to earn his living and therefore he is asked to get ready to go to town in search of a job. A quiver shoots through his belly. In spite of the fact that his aunt Gujri "beat him more than he beat his cattle, he really did not want to go to the town".[3] But he knows that he has no choice. His uncle makes him walk miles and miles barefoot without even giving the boy time to rest, and even slapping him for getting tired. Finally when they reach the town of Sham Nagar, Daya Ram contacts Babu Nathoo Ram, Sub-Accountant, Imperial Bank, Sham Nagar, as the latter wanted a servant. Soon Munoo is employed as a domestic servant of the Sub-Accountant at Rupees three per month, with the understanding that the amount should be paid not to him but to his uncle. The Babu's wife, Bibiji, treats Munoo like an animal and always shouts of curses at him. Everyone in the house treats him like a monkey. He gets human treatment in that house only from the Accountant's brother, a doctor, whom Munoo calls 'Chota Babu'.

"Life in the Babu's house soon resolved itself, for Munoo, into the routine of domestic slavery. He did not settle down to it easily. The wild bird of his heart fluttered every now and then with a desire for happiness."[4] One day, seeing the Babu's daughter Shila and her friends playing, Munoo joins them and tries to make them happy by performing a monkey dance. Shila tries to drag him and Munoo unconsciously bites her on the cheek. That leads to the culmination of his misery in that house. Baboo Nathoo Ram "slapped Munoo on

2. V.S. Pritchett's letter to Anand, dated 12 March 1937.
3. Anand, Mulk Raj: *Coolie*. New Delhi: Arnold-Heinemann, 1985. p. 11.
4. *Ibid*., p. 46.

the cheek with his thin, bony hand and kicked him with his shiny black boots, the boots which had been the dream of Munoo's life....And kicking the boy again, ferociously he made towards the corner where a thick stick lay".[5] He rushes to the boy again and strikes him blow after blow. Munoo slips out of the Babu's house, in the twilight, immediately after the family withdraws into the kitchen and leaves him in disgrace. He runs down the hill and reaches the railway station and sleeps in the floor of a train.

In the train, he is discovered lying under the bunk by a passenger named Seth Prabha Dyal, who owns a pickle-factory. He becomes compassionate towards the boy and takes him to his place, Daulatpur.

Unfortunately for Munoo, his benefactor Prabha is deceived by his partner, goat faced Ganpat. They clash each other and as a result, the partners begin the business separately. As ill luck will have it, Prabha's business breaks, his creditors protest with the accusation that he is hiding huge amount of money somewhere and he is arrested, ill-treated, and thoroughly beaten by the police and all his things and stocks are sold to pay the dues.

Munoo becomes a coolie in the Grain Market of Daulatpur and a porter at the station. One day he accidently reaches the place where a circus is going on. There he comes into contact with an elephant-trainer. He gives Munoo the work of fetching water for the elephant. Munoo requests the elephant-trainer to help him to go to Bombay when the circus party will move to that city.

On the day the circus party moves to Bombay the elephant trainer secretly arranges a place for Munoo in the goods wagon. However, the elephant trainer cautions Munoo not to expect too much from Bombay:

> 'The bigger a city is, the more cruel it is to the sons of Adam', the elephant driver said crawling under the buffers of the train. 'You have to pay even for the breath you breathe.'[6]

The train moves on and finally it comes to a standstill by an outlying platform of the huge central station.

He walks down the pavement and to his surprise he sees "at the edge of a foot-path in a corner a coolie lay huddled, pillowing his head

5. *Ibid.*, p. 73.
6. *Ibid.*, p. 177.

on his arm, shrinking into himself as if he were afraid to occupy too much space. Munoo's heart sank at the recognition of the labourer lying about so precariously. 'So even here the coolies sleep in the street!' he suddenly realised."[7] Now he realises the words of the coolie in Daulatpur that in Bombay "One could earn anything from fifteen to thirty rupees a month"[8] is totally false. He continues to walk with the grim fear where he will sleep at night. However, he is lucky to meet an old man, Hari and his wife, going in search of a job in Sir George White Cotton Mills. With them are their two children. Munoo joins them in the direction of the Cotton Mills. But the mill is too far from them and the night has been advancing. Hence they look for an unoccupied place on the pavement to spend the night.

In the early morning, before the arm of the law with baton in hand comes to clear the pavements, they all get up and the cavalcade moves on. When they reach the mill, they beg for jobs to Jimmie Thomas, the head foreman of the mill. Finally they are given job at the rate of Rs. 25 each for Hari and Munoo, Rs. 5 for Hari's wife and Rs. 2 $\frac{1}{2}$ each for children per month. And then Jimmie Thomas says: "And now I suppose you have no money. Well, I will advance you ten rupees at four annas in the rupee, which sum I will add to the regular monthly commission you give to me. Agreed? I will go and fetch the money."[9]

Jimmie Thomas is employer's agent to engage workmen, supervisor of the labourers while at work and the intermediary between the employer and the worker. "Because of all this he charged every worker in the factory a price for the gift of a job, a price which went up if there were more men about than there were vacancies to fill; and that, incidently, he ran a money-lender's business; that lastly he was a landlord who owned hundreds of straw huts in the neighbourhood and rented them out to the coolies."[10]

When Jimmie Thomas has returned with money, they are also allotted a hut at the rate of Rs. 3 per month. They go to their hut whose "mud floor was at a level lower than the pathway outside, overgrown with grass which was nourished by the inflow of rain-

---

7. *Ibid.*, p. 179.
8. *Ibid.*, p. 163.
9. *Ibid.*, p. 200.
10. *Ibid.*, p. 201.

water. The cottage boasted not a window nor a chimney to let in the air and light and to eject the smoke".[11]

They settle there and join the work force. On the day of payment, when Hari's name is called by Jimmie Thomas, he comes forward and makes his thumb impression on a register. Then Jimmie giving Rs. 40 to Hari says:

> 'Ten rupees you owe me in cash. A rupee interest on the loan. Three rupees rent for the hut for one month. One rupee for repair of hut. Five rupees cut for damaged cloth. The remainder you receive for you, Munoo, your wife and children'.
>
> Hari knew these phrases well from long experience: 'Loan interest, rent, damaged cloth'. And though he resented them, he had learned to respect them. He accepted the forty rupees, salamed the foreman, and withdrew.
>
> His heart sank as he came towards Munoo. His eyes were full of tears. His face was knotted and pale, and half told the grim tale.[12]

Munoo, Hari and other coolies continue to work in the factory suffering patiently all the exploitations and atrocities committed by their employers. But the crowded dwellings, dirty latrines, regular cuttings made from the low-pay given to them on one pretext or another and the dismisal of Ratan, who has been a member of the trade union, compel the Trade Union leaders to be active in the cause of labourers. Soon Munoo hears the speeches made by the leaders of Red Flag Union. Particularly Munoo is impressed by Sauda's speech:

> There are only two kinds of people in the world: the rich and the poor, and between the two there is no connection. The rich and the powerful, the magnificent and the glorious, whose opulence is built on robbery and theft and open warfare, are honoured and admired by the whole world and by themselves. You, the meek and the gentle, wretches that you are, swindled out of your rights, and broken in body and soul, you are respected by no one, and you do not respect yourselves.[13]

---

11. *Ibid.*, p. 202.
12. *Ibid.*, p. 234.
13. *Ibid.*, pp. 266-267.

Sauda's speech reminds Munoo that long ago at Sham Nagar, he too has had similar thought about the rich and the poor. With the fiery speeches of the leaders of Red Flag Union, the situation turns dangerous for the factory owners. So they cleverly convert the labour meeting into a Hindu-Muslim communal riot. Munoo realises the danger and takes to his heels. As he runs up Malabar Hill to escape the hectic police action, he is knocked down by the motor car of an Anglo-Indian lady, Mrs. Mainwaring. She feels compassion for the wounded boy and takes him to Simla, where she wants to go. She, as narrated by the author, is a woman of vast pretensions and no morals. In Simla, Munoo is employed as a servant in her house and he used to pull her in a rickshaw up and down the road. Munoo gradually grows weaker, catches T.B. and "in the early hours of one unreal, white night he passed away".[14]

Such is the story of Munoo, the coolie. "The magic of the book is", as Saros Cowasjee comments, "in Munoo's innocence, in his naive warm heartedness, his love and comradeship, his irrepressible curiosity and zest for life. He belongs with some of the most endearing juvenile characters in modern literature: with Victor Hugo's Gavroche and Dicken's David Copperfield. And through him the whole misery of India speaks."[15]

The main concern of the novel is the anathema of the new caste system, on the basis of the purchasing power of the individuals. This power can corrupt a man so much that he may even purchase a fellow human being and totally subjugate him. Munoo certainly serves as a symbol of Anand's dissatisfaction with a society whose utilitarian concern unscrupulously massacres social morality.

The coolies as depicted in the novel are united by a common feeling of misery and hunger. It makes them forget the sophistication of religion, caste system and untouchability and helps them to live in fraternity. Munoo is excited to see in Bombay, Muslim, Hindu and Sikh coolies freely mixing up, enjoying the common bed of pavement and sharing hookah and water. He feels that there is nothing wrong in them. He himself had one day bought a pot full of mutton curry with swollen bread from a Muhammadan cook-shop. "He had not felt there was anything strange in violating the prevailing custom, except

---

14. *Ibid.*, p. 318.

15. Cowasjee, Saros: "Introduction" to *Coolie*, New Delhi: Arnold-Heinemann, 1985, pp. 6-7.

the guilt of having tasted a dish which the Muhammadans cooked better than the Hindus."[16]

The nucleus of the novel is present in Chapters Three and Four, depicting Munoo's experience in Daulatpur and Bombay. In this part, the angry young man in Anand is also a forceful social critic. In it, the social criticism is focused on the exploitation of the poor by the rich. Everything that happens in the pickle-factory at Daulatpur and in Sir George White Cotton Mills is directed towards the same focus.

The pickle factory at Daulatpur is modelled on the British utilitarian organisations. The unbearable amount of work given to the employees in the factory shows that the employers' only concern is profit: The slow death the labourers face in the factory for the sake of fattening their employers is only returned with a mere subsistence wage. Ganpat, the goat-faced partner is devil-like in his dealings with the labourers. He rushes about in the early morning hours saying, "We need a log of wood to awaken a log of wood"[17], and thoroughly thrashes any labourer found sleeping. The author presents us the misery of all the factory workers through Munoo's own misery:

> It was a dark and evil life. He (Munoo) rose early at dawn before he had his full sleep out, having gone to bed long after midnight. He descended to work in the factory, tired, heavy-lidded, hot and limp, as if all the strength had gone out of his body and left him a spineless ghost of his former self.[18]

The bullocks that plough the field or pull the cart, the elephants that lift huge log of wood in the forest, the asses that carry the large bale of clothes of the washerman, even the machines that work for hours in a factory are given rest. But the labourers in the pickle factory get no such respite from their employers. For the employers, time is money and therefore giving time to the employees to rest is like giving away their money. Hence as the author tells us:

> They worked from day to day in the dark underworld, full of intense heat of blazing furnaces and the dense malodorous smells of brewing essences, spices and treacle, of dust and ashes and mud, which became kneaded into a sticky layer on the earth of the passage with the overflow of water from the

16. Anand, Mulk Raj: *Coolie*, New Delhi: Arnold-Heinemann, 1985, p. 141.
17. *Ibid.*, p. 94.
18. *Ibid.*, p. 107.

> barrels of socking fruit, and plastered the bare toes of the labourers. They ran about bare-foot and naked except for loin-clothes, emptying the boiling water which hummed ceaselessly in the cauldrons, refilling them, joining the receptacles to tin tubes with smears of sticky clay and rags: cooling the flasks; transporting them; then coming back to wash the fruit; doling it out to the women and helping them to peel it, till the next flasks of essences were ready, drawing water out of the well or helping the bosses in the intricate business of making jams and pickles. They worked long hours, from dawn to past midnight, so mechanically that they never noticed the movements of their own or each other's hands. Only the sweat trickled down their bodies and irritated them into an awareness that they were engaged in a strenuous physical occupation.[19]

The life of coolies in the colonial enterprise, Sir George White Cotton Mill, is worse than the life of labourers in the pickle factory at Daulatpur. Here the coolies work eleven hours a day for a mere subsistence allowance. Jimmie Thomas' exploitation of the miserable and skeleton-like coolies in terms of loan interest, rent, damaged cloth and price for giving job and so on shows their degradation. To him and other Whitemen, the coolies are only swine. This is obvious from the swear word, "swine" with which the Whites refer to the coolies, the kicks and thrashes administered on them, and the filthy latrines and pigsty like huts allotted to them. To the poor coolies who live from hand to mouth, the idea of strike or the fiery speeches of the well-fed All India Trade Union leaders make no sense. Instead, the company's declaration of short-work as a response to the strike plan, causes a volcanic eruption in their belly. They rush at the Sahib and beg him with entreaties and prayers not to declare the factory on short work. But the Sahib abuses and threatens to strike any native who dares come near him or touches him with his dirty hands. Hence,

> The coolies of the Sir George factory crept like ghosts, through the waste-lands of the mills that afternoon. They seemed to have died all of a sudden; that little spark of life which made them move about willingly had died, and left them a queer race of men, dried-up, shrivelled, hollow-chested, hollow-cheeked, hollow-eyed. Their wretchedness

19. *Ibid.*, p. 110.

> had passed beyond the confines of suffering and left them careless, resigned.[20]

The sahibs who exploit the coolies can be compared to the blue-black crow that Munoo sees, within a short time of his arrival in the city of Bombay, sitting on the head of the marble statue of Queen Victoria. It caws defiance to the world as it hops and flutters after relieving itself. Then suddenly it swoops down and snatches away the food, the only worthy possession Munoo has, a gift from the elephant driver.[21]

The Charter, the trade union leader Sauda asks the coolies to repeat after him points to the prominent areas of capitalistic exploitation. It says that the coolies are human beings and not soulless machines; they want to work without having to pay bribes; they want clean houses to live in; they want to be saved from the clutches of money-lenders and so on – demands which are completely ignored by the company owners. The Chapter epitomises Anand's social criticism against capitalistic exploitation.

The communal riot that has occurred during the strike is also part of the capitalistic exploitation. It is cunningly engineered by the capitalists by their money power, knowing fully well that the conflagration of communal violence will not consume them and that the victims will be the poor coolies or wretched destitutes whose home is the pavement or the street. The British capitalists' "divide and exploit" policy is crystal clear in this situation. The company owners have exploited here the religion of orthodoxy or fanaticism which has firm and ineffable grip on the minds of the people and which provides sustenance to the forces of communalism. The shouts that resounds in the air, 'Allah ho Akbar' or 'Shivaji Ki Jai' and the pandemonium and butchering of the helpless human beings that accompany it are purely based on rumour that some Hindu children had been kidnapped by Pathans. Rumour-mongers are everywhere. What some invent others enlarge and the volcano of social hatred erupts. Anand's touching and realistic portrayal of the Hindu-Muslim riot is intended to give a prophetic vision to the nation which was about to become independent so that it may follow a true secular ideal, making no compromise to fanaticism. It also foreshadows the horrible happenings during partition.

---

20. *Ibid.*, p. 261.
21. *Ibid.*, p. 178.

According to Anand's narration, the riot and murder continues for many hours. The author, in many pages covering the narration of the riot, it seems, deliberately avoids the presence of police, to show that very often police inaction is the cause of the spread of communal violence. If the police force is not absolutely secular, it may side with one group or the other during communal violence and may make the situation worse. A country like ours where religious fanaticism frequently turns into violence, an effective, well-trained police force of secular outlook is essential. The author is, certainly not satisfied with the attitude and approach of the police to communal violence. The police which is supposed to preserve and protect the law, is often seen siding with the rich and the powerful in their oppression of the poor and the helpless. This is obvious in the arrest and torture of Prabha for non-payment of debt. He is arrested by police without a warrant. The person responsible for the arrest is sub-inspector Ram Nath, whose father, Sir Todar Mal had some quarrel with Prabha. Though Prabha pleads that he has become bankrupt, the police continuously beat him so that he may 'confess the truth'. The police "struck him blow after blow in wild orgy of excitement, his face set, his lips stiff and his body towering over the poor man's frame".[22] Making a truthful man like Prabha, 'confess the truth' in this manner is the weakness of our police force. A police officer with a bit of humanity would not have ordered to beat Prabha, after hearing his touching admission with folded hands: "*Huzoor*, I have no money buried anywhere. But I have stock. I only crave your forgiveness and I will pay up every *pice* that I owe to my creditors".[23] Anand's social criticism here is directed upon the callousness of the police.

Coolie takes us round on a guided tour of India. It is as Anand says, a Whitman poem; "A Passage to India". Its action moves from the North to the South, and then back again to the North. In it we get not only the panorama of the physical features of India, but also of her society in all its varied nuances. In it we come into contact with the people who have plenty of appetite but no food to eat as well as the people who have plenty of food but no appetite; the rich who are restless on their Dunlop beds as well as the wretched ones who enjoy peaceful sleep on the bed of stone slab and pillow of brick; the long-robed priests with huge beards, attending the dancing parties at the Viceroy's residence as well as *yogis* lifting their hands with a

22. *Ibid.*, p. 132.

23. *Ibid.*

deliberate saintliness and spiritual grace uttering 'Shanti! Shanti!', and in the secret hours of night shamelessly working for the births of 'sons of god' to the wives of merchant class, causing shock to innocents like Munoo.

Coolie and *Untouchable* are the most popular works of Anand. A Comparison of these two novels can help us to know the drawbacks of *Coolie*.

Unlike *Untoucahble, Coolie* lacks compactness: The action of *Untouchable* is limited to a single day in the life of Bakha and this helps the author to select and control the episodes and knit them together with great care. But in *Coolie* the action is diverse and it is spread over several months with the result that what Anand gains in breadth tells adversely upon the form.

The character of Munoo, unlike that of Bakha is not precise and sharp: In *Untoucahble* there is less action and more analysis and this helped the author to go deep into the inner soul of the hero. But *Coolie* is dominated by action and the too many scenes and episodes introduced in the novel prevent the author from concentrating on the characterisation of Munoo. But the weak characterisation of Munoo is a less serious mistake than the lack of a sense of proportion in dealing with the other characters in the novel. The most striking illustration of this is the presentation of the detailed history of Mrs. Mainwaring, the lady who employed Munoo as her servant in Simla. According to the narration of the author her father, William Smith, was born of one John Nicholson's union with a Muslim washer woman. He, William Smith, grew up and became a sergeant in the British Indian army. The sergeant, all of a sudden, became a colonel by joining the Nawab of Zalimpur's army. He then got married to the daughter of an English engine-driver. After the birth of May (Mrs. Mainwaring) her mother left the colonel, as she was expecting another child by some one else. May was looked after in her childhood by the wife of a catholic missionary and then sent to the convent of the Sacred Heart at Simla. During her school days, she "developed a tremendous inferiority complex about her origin".[24] As she grew up she became "a bitch to all the dogs that prowled round her bungalow".[25] Before she got married to her present husband Guy Mainwaring, she was the wife of a young German photographer,

24. *Ibid.*, p. 286.

25. *Ibid.*, p. 288.

Heinrich Ulmar and later of Captain Aga Raza Ali Shah in the Nawab's army. Thus the author goes on for five pages describing her shady past and present and the worst of it is that her actions in the novel do not substantiate the label of prostitute the author has pasted on her. What surprises one most is that Anand who earlier used to simplify his characters to their bare minimums has devoted so much time and attention to this minor character. Usually Anand's characters are modelled after individuals whom he knew intimately. His detailed and vindictive description of Mainwaring may be a deliberate attempt to find an outlet for his bitter feelings against a woman similar to her. Whatever may be the reason, the characterisation of Mainwaring is prejudicial and is vulnerable to criticism. In fact the novel would have been more appealing to the reader if it ended without the last chapter dealing with Mrs. Mainwaring. Two of Anand's most sympathetic critics, Jack Lindsay and C.D. Narasimhaiah are of the same opinion. They feel, and I agree with them, that the last chapter is not an organic part of the total pattern and could be dispensed with.[26]

A careful study of characterisation in the novel may convince a critic that the English characters in the Bombay chapters are caricatures. The reviewers of *The Times Literary Supplement* and the *Manchester Guardian Weekly* also blame Anand for his caricatures. As Alaister Niven points out in his book, *The Yoke of Pity*, "The cotton-mill episodes show Anand's sustained attempt to write off the European character. He fails because Jimmie Thomas, the factory foreman, is so clearly a figure from school-room melodramas, — 'a massive man with a scarlet bull dog face', who spoke 'with another twist' to the edges of his moustache."[27]

Another defect that is noticed in *Coolie* by some critics is the novelist's predilection for propaganda. "In *Untouchable*", says Paul C. Varghese, "this is done a little subtly, but in *Coolie* it is open and blatant."[28] It is true that in *Coolie* the author's social concern has at times got the better of his artistic concern. But in it there is certainly no 'blatant propaganda' as stated by Paul C. Varghese. The arrival of

26. See: Jack Lindsay's *The Elephant and the Lotus: A Study of the Novels of Mulk Raj Anand* (Bombay: Kutub-Popular, 1965) and C.D. Narasimhaiah's *The Swan and the Eagle* (Simla: Indian Institute of Advanced Study, 1969).

27. Niven, Alastair: *The Yoke of Pity (A Study in the Fictional Writings of Mulk Raj Anand)*, New Delhi: Arnold-Heinemann Publishers Pvt. Ltd., 1978, p. 61.

28. Varghese, Paul, C. : *Problems of the Indian Creative Writer in English*, Bombay: Somaiya Publications, 1968, Chapter 9.

the Trade Union leaders in the novel is not an incredible incident, especially after the labourers are diabolically exploited and Ratan, a member of the Union, is dismissed. If the Union leaders speak things which the author wants to speak, we must remember that it is a clever connivance as that is the only way they can and they ought to speak. Thus, their fiery speeches do not appear odd in the given situation. Sauda's solution that all workers should go on strike is riddled with irony as that cannot be a solution to them whose only concern in life is, how to earn some money for their next meal. Thus in *Coolie*, as in *Untouchable*, Anand has no simple solution to offer. "And it is primarily because the author does not explicitly offer a solution that the novel cannot be called propagandist in intent."[29] The exploited millions may not be able to read the novel. But, will they call the novel a propaganda, after seeing it on the silver screen? Certainly not. They would see in it only the photographic fidelity of the hard realities of their sub-human existence. "If there is propaganda in the novel, it is, as V.S. Pritchett points out, 'digested completely'. or, at its worst, as Peter Burra comments, it is 'propagandist' only in the sense that any frank statement of such facts is bound to appeal for their correction."[30]

"If *Untouchable* is a microcosm, *Coolie* is a macrocosm, that is Indian society"[31], says K.R. Srinivasa Iyengar. It is a passage to India, a country made weak by capitalism and religious fanaticism and seen by Mulk Raj Anand through a telescope made in the pink decade. It is the sweetest song of the coolies that tell of their saddest thoughts with the chorus: "We belong to suffering! We belong to suffering! My love!"[32]

Two Leaves and a Bud (1937)

The novel takes its title from the simple refrain, which the tea leaves gatherers recite as they pick two leaves and a bud:

> I will make a good sheaf
> Plucking, plucking, plucking

29. Cowasjee, Saros: *So Many Freedoms: A Study of the Major Fiction of Mulk Raj Anand*, Delhi: OUP, 1977, p. 79.

30. Quoted by Saros Cowasjee, In: "Introduction" to *Coolie*, New Delhi: Arnold Heinemann, 1985, p. 7.

31. Iyengar, K.R. Srinivasa: *Indian Writing in English*, Bombay: Asia Publishing House, 1973, p. 265.

32. Anand, Mulk Raj: *Coolie*, New Delhi: Arnold-Heinemann, 1985, p. 247.

> Two leaves and a bud
> Two leaves and a bud.[33]

Most of Anand's social concerns voiced in *Coolie*, are introduced also in *Two Leaves and a Bud* which is, in a way, an extension and enlargement of the scenes and affairs relating to the Bombay cotton mills of the former novel. *Two Leaves and a Bud* is to a great extent *Coolie* written in a thicker strain as it makes an aggressive attack on the dehumanising effects of imperialism, of capitalist economy and its corollaries such as exploitation and harassment of helpless labourers.

Gangu, the hero of the novel is an older version of Munoo. The innocence Munoo displayed in *Coolie* is replaced here by experience. Munoo who travelled from North to South and back again to North, it seems he had only a phoenix-like death and is born again to make a *pis aller* travel to the East with the hope that his unfulfilled aim to preserve his family from starvation may be realised. This journey of Gangu and his wife Sajani, with their daughter Leila and son Buddhu has been arranged by Buta, the Sardar and coolie-catcher of Macpherson Tea Estate, Assam. As Gangu sits beside Buta in the moving train he feels that life is like a journey, a journey into the unknown. With the desire to know the unknown, he enquires: "Are the sahibs kind, brother Buta Ram?"[34], and the Sardar replies, "Just like *mai-bap* (mother and father)"[35], and he explains how they would help the coolies. But "the insistent overtone of his speech did not hide the obvious insincerity of its content. And Gangu, though broken and defeated, was a shrewd enough peasant whose bitter sufferings had inclined him to measure every particle of speech even as the *sahukar* of his village weighed every grain of wheat: He knew somehow that he was being deceived."[36] This he is able to confirm within a few hours of his arrival in the Tea Estate from his neighbour in the line, named Narain:

> 'You will soon know, brother', said Narain, 'First water, afterwards mire! This prison has no bars, but it is nevertheless an unbreakable jail. The chowkidars keep guard over the plantation, and they bring you back if you should go....The

33. Anand, Mulk Raj : *Two Leaves and a Bud*, New Delhi: Arnold-Heinemann, 1983, p. 110.
34. *Ibid.*, p. 4.
35. *Ibid.*
36. *Ibid.*, p. 7.

> chowkidars go round at night with a lamp and open every door to see if we are all at home. There used to be a roll call every night before I came."[37]

After a week of hard labour in the Estate, the amount given to Gangu's whole family is less than 8 *annas*: three *annas* for him, two *annas* for his wife and daughter, and three *pice* for his child. It reminds him that in his village he alone used to earn 8 *annas* a day by working on the land-lord's land. This make him sad with the thought what a liar Buta has been in all his talk about high wages, about the free-gifts of land and so on.

Within a week of their employment in the Tea Estate, Gangu becomes a victim of malaria. "I shouldn't die", he muttered under his breath, "till Leila is married, and Buddhu has grown up"[38]. The next morning he is all right but the fever which has left him catches Sajani. Soon the news spreads that the cholera which took away the lives of 200 coolies in the previous year has visited them again. The coolies become panic-stricken. The Medical Officer of the Tea Garden, John de la Havre promptly visits Gangu's hut and checks Sajani. He then sadly declares that she is dead. "Gangu fell upon Sajani with a howl. Leila shrieked and went towards Buddhu."[39] Gangu's sadness is augmented by the worry that he had no money to buy a red cloth and to make a bamboo hearse. In any case, he does not want to borrow money from *sahukar* as that had been the cause of his ruin in his native village. He then recalls what Buta had told him that .the Manager Sahib is a sort of *mai-bap*, who lends money when the coolies are in need. So he goes and beseeches the Babu of the Estate, Shashi Bhushan Bhattacharya to talk on his behalf to the Manager Sahib in 'angrezi' to get the loan. Since the Babu wants commission for this service, Gangu says:

> 'Babuji, I promise to give you some of the money which the sahib may give me if you talk to him in *angrezi* and get me the loan I want ......My wife died last night. And I have been ill. Take pity on me.'[40]

This tempts the Babu to contact the Manager Sahib, Croft-Cooke. But when the Manager comes to know that Gangu who was

37. *Ibid.*, p. 38.
38. *Ibid.*, p. 83.
39. *Ibid.*, p. 88.
40. *Ibid.*, pp. 112-113.

under segregation is the one who has come for loan, he becomes furious, kicks him and asks him to get out of his premises.

Gangu leaves the place deeply chagrined and humiliated. The next day he approaches Buta with the request: "Can you give a loan of money for the cremation? I have not a *pice* and the body has been lying in the house for two days."[41] Buta, the barber-turned-sardar, comes up with all manners of excuses. Since Gangu does not get any help from Buta, desperately he goes to the *Bania* breaking his vow, and borrows 20 rupees from him for the cremation. As he knows that it would be impossible to pay back the loan and the interest on it, he pleads with the Doctor Sahib, John de la Havre, to make a recommendation for him to the 'Burra Sahib' for land, so that he may do some part-time cultivation to clear his debt. The doctor agrees. Soon Gangu is given a strip of land. He cultivates rice. But as ill-luck would have it, the torrential rain on the slopy hill that follows, washes away the tender shoots of rice.

Gangu is afraid that other coolies will make vulgar comments on how he has managed to have a strip of land. The coolies normally get land for cultivation by offering their wives or daughters to Reggie Hunt, the assistant planter. He, at the age of twenty-two, possessed tremendous emotional energy and he has been keeping with him always three coolie women. He gives Neogi Gurkha, the sardar of the women coolies five acres of land and many other gifts for his wife's generosity towards him. This causes jealousy in the coolie women Chambeli, who used to stay before with Reggie Sahib. A quarrel starts. Murder takes place. The crowd turns uncontrollable. "I will shoot you all"[42], Reggie shouts. He orders the chowkidars to strike some of the coolies. Soon the coolies march towards the doctor sahib, shouting, "Dilawar Sahib, ki jai", and request him to talk a few words to the Manager Sahib and save them from the anger of Reggie Sahib. De la Havre asks them to take courage and proceed to meet 'Burra Sahib' for demanding justice. The coolies proceed shouting, "Dilawar Sahib, ki jai".

> 'Shirrup, complaining fool', Reggie Hunt shouted, rushing forward. 'Step back, or I will shoot you dead! Let de la Havre mind his own business. Back you go, swine, back you go to the lines"...... 'Get back! Swine', roared Croft-Cooke, roused

41. *Ibid.*, p. 118.
42. *Ibid.*, p. 193.

> out of his deliberateness by Reggie's impetousity, and advancing under cover of the warders. 'Get back to your lines. And I can deal with de la Havre Sahib'.[43]

The crowd get frightened and take to their heels and immediately John de la Havre is dismissed from service. The planters do not know the purpose with which the coolies have marched towards the 'Burra Sahib". They believe that the coolies are trying to attack them. They expect more problems and probably a mutiny. So they contact the R.A.F. bombers to come to their aid. When the steel birds fly over the lines of coolies, the poor coolies realise that their marching towards the 'Burra Sahib' to appeal for a fair economic deal is misunderstood and it is treated as a mutiny and that they should run to the valley and hide if they valued their lives. They all run in different directions just to protect their existence. And then the soldiers march through the road facing no opposition from any one and the authorities declare that the mutiny had been crushed.

Croft-Cooke, Reggie Hunt and the other big men of the Estate who earlier used to spent their days going to the club, playing polo etc., now realising that the coolies will not disturb them again, return to their habitual enjoyments. They also organise a special hunting expedition for the entertainment of His Excellency, Sir Geoffrey Boyd, the Governor of Assam. The coolies are engaged, at great risk of their lives, in the elaborate hunting arrangement. Before the Royal Guest leaves the Estate, to stimulate goodwill between the sahibs and the coolies, His Excellency pardons those who had created the "riot" and half their fines remitted.

Reggie Hunt, who is habituated to hunting coolie-women, is fascinated one day to see Leila's "slim young body defined by the narrow girth of her skirt and the fine stretch of her bodice, her whole demeanour like a bird that would flutter in the hands of the *shikari*".[44] So he asks her to come to his bunglow. Leila refuses and slips into her hut. Reggie pursues her and asks her to come out. She again refuses. He then asks Buddhu to tell his sister to come out. Buddhu gets frightened and shouts "Father, Father", and rushes towards Narain's hut where his father is. Reggie wants to run away but he was face to face with Gangu at a distance of two yards. Maddened by frustration and fear he indiscreetly fires resulting in the murder of Gangu. This

43. *Ibid.*, pp. 205-206.

44. *Ibid.*, p. 271.

is followed by a trial lasting three days. In the trial, Mr. Justice Mowberley and a jury of seven European and two Indian members find Reggie Hunt not guilty on the charge of murder or culpable homicide and he is discharged.

That is the story of *Two Leaves and a Bud*, a story which takes us to the luxuriant forests of Assam and reveals to us the horrid plight of the labourers in a tea plantation there. Its central character Gangu, an unheroic hero, is a typical farmer facing debt, hunger, malaria, insult and even death with a strange natural dignity. After he is kicked and chased out from Croft-Cooke's premises (when he went there to request a loan for Sajani's burial), he reacts with the resigned indifference of the Hindu saying, "It was only one more reward for the misdeeds of his past life".[45] Though the author does not share Gangu's belief in *Karma* and his superstitious belief "that to bring a piece of iron home on Monday was the sure harbinger of an impending tragedy"[46], and which urges him to ask his son Buddhu to throw away the nail he has joyfully picked up from the ground, Anand introduces them in the novel to make Gangu's portrayal realistic. However, the author does not maintain this detachment throughout the exposition of Gangu. The author's interference with Gangu, the peasant, is clear in some of his philosophical pronouncements. A typical example of it can be Gangu's comment about God to his daughter Leila: "There was no God. There were only men and life and death fulfilling their purpose through cross-purposes, as in a play. It was all a play, Leila."[47]

Anand is involved in a certain philosophical speculation illustrated by the following questions raised by Gangu:

> 'Did all the sahibs who came to own this land get their labourers by letting lies pass for truth, did they make deceit a virtue and exalt the worst to the best, make every pushful duffer like Buta into a sardar, and liberate all the selfishness that any charlatan could use for his own purpose? Do all good men die here, and others live on?'[48]

Gangu only very rarely makes such utterance. They momentarily turn the illiterate peasant into a brooding philosopher exposing the author's inconsistency in the characterisation of him.

45. *Ibid.*, p. 115.
46. *Ibid.*, p. 116.
47. *Ibid.*, p. 68.
48. *Ibid.*, p. 65.

Comparing *Two Leaves and a Bud* with the previous novels, K.R. Srinivasa Iyengar says: "If *Untouchable* has a sort of piercing quality that is akin to the lyrical, if *Coolie* with its enormous range and multiplicity of action and character has an almost epic quality, *Two Leaves and a Bud* may be said to be essentially a dramatic novel."[49] It is a tragic drama as its loveliness arises from the clash of characters and their interests. As we go through the novel, we see the coolies falling on the thorns of life and bleeding. The painful truth presented in the novel brought Anand into conflict with the ruling class who always boasted of their human right record. In a review of this novel, Goronwy Ree lauded the author for exposing with "great skill, and without insistence.....the Indian coolies, exploited, starving, cheated, dirty, diseased as the true heirs of one of the world's great civilizations."[50] He further commented: "I have no doubt that Dr. Anand's account of the tea-planters is true."[51] The last remark provoked protests from the planters:

> Angry letters were exchanged in *The Spectator* between Mulk Raj Anand and one Mr. L.J. Godwin of the Monabarie Tea Estate in Assam. Possibly encouraged by Ree's review, Anand wrote in *The Spectator* of 11 June 1937 that the ghastly conditions he had exposed in the novel were still prevalent. Mr. Godwin challenged Anand's conclusions in the 20 August 1937 issue of the magazine and stated that Mr. Whitley, who chaired the Royal Commission of Labour, had in fact commended the British planters for their humane treatment of the labourers in a personal conversation with him. Anand, answered back in *The Spectator* of 3 Sept. 1937, quoting from Mr. Whitley's Report itself to show how the coolies were being abused, over-worked, and kept in a state of serfdom.[52]

As the tea-planters found difficult to silence Mulk Raj Anand, the then President of Indian Tea Association contacted and influenced the India Office to keep the novel among the list of proscribed books

49. Iyengar, K.R. Srinivasa: *Indian Writing in English*, Bombay: Asia Publishing House, 1973, pp. 268-69.

50. Ree, Goronwy: In, *The Spectator*, No. 5679 (30 April 1937), p. 832.

51. *Ibid.*

52. Quoted by Saros Cowasjee, In: *So Many Freedoms: A Study of the Major Fiction of Mulk Raj Anand*, New Delhi: OUP, 1977, p. 84.

in India. This was a blessing in disguise for the author. When India became Independent, the novel acquired a resurrected dignity.

In his 'Preface' to the second edition of *Two Leaves and a Bud* Anand remarks:

> What I had to say in it was deep in me from the days when I lived for a while near a plantation in Assam and visited Ceylon, and saw the inhumanity and barbarism prevalent there, with the consequent dehumanisation of the colonials involved in the process. (I can never forget the painter George Keyt telling me of an evening he had spent on an estate near Kandy, where the sozzled assistant managers played cards and swore and boozed in company with their coolie women mistressed whom they abused, physically and verbally, with the vulgarity of the old buccaneers in Africa). In the light of that and my own evidence, I would say that the descriptions in *Two Leaves and a Bud* are comparatively under-estimates. Only the decent Englishmen at home will not easily believe that their representatives in the Empire could be guilty of such excesses as are familiar to most of the subject races![53]

Anand's claim that "the descriptions in *Two Leaves and a Bud* are comparatively under-estimates" can be confirmed from the Report of the Royal Commission on Labour. Anand has collected much of his information from the above mentioned report, and instead of magnifying he has minimized the crimes of the English planters and the cruelties inflicted on the coolies.

There are many works dealing on the sub-human existence of the tea plantation coolies in Assam. Among them are, a doctoral thesis by S.M. Akhtar entitled *Emigrant Labour of Assam Tea Gardens* submitted in 1932 to the University of London and a novel by Dr P.H. Daniel titled *Red Tea* (1969).[54] These underscore the authenticity of *Two Leaves and a Bud* . From 1941 to 1965 Dr P.H. Daniel worked in a group of Assam tea gardens as Chief Medical Officer. During that period he interviewed a number of workers and also collected signed statements from them. He made use of them

53. Anand, Mulk Raj: "Introduction" to *Two Leaves and a Bud*, Bombay: Kutub Popular, 1951, p. 7.

54. See: Saros Cowasjee's *So Many Freedoms: A Study of the Major Fiction of Mulk Raj Anand*, New Delhi: OUP, 1977, pp. 85-86.

in his novel *Red Tea*. The inhuman treatment Daniel's coolie Karuppan and his wife Valli received from the General Manager Mr. White is much more terrifying than anything inflicted on Gangu and his family. The doctoral thesis of S.M. Akhtar shows the Whitemen shamelessly exporting their sadism and lust on the coolie women even in the presence of their men. At night the coolies are locked up just like cattle. From the day they are employed they are treated as prisoners: they are guarded by *chowkidars* and any one trying to escape is thrashed almost to death and brought back by savage hill men only to receive further torture from the *chowkidars*. Taking these into consideration there can be no doubt that the novel *Two Leaves and a Bud* is absolutely based on facts. But in fiction, straight facts are useless, unless they are made artistically necessary to plot and character.

The characters in the novel can be divided into three groups: (i) exploiters, (ii) victims, and (iii) social commentators. Reggie Hunt, Croft-Cooke, Tweetie, Hitch Cock, Major Barbara, Shashi Bhushan Bhattacharya and Buta belong to the group of exploiters. They not only exploit but also glorify their exploitation. This is evident in Reggie Hunt's angry words to the coolies, "The *angrezi log* civilize you"[55], or in the over-zealous words of Buta, "wonderful this *angrezi* race! They have spanned rivers and conquered the spirit of the Forests!"[56] The English exploiters have no love for the Indians. As faults are thick when love is thin, they find the Indians lazy, born liars, shocking barbarians in point of intellect and civilization, and the coolies sub-human creatures, contemptible and bare.[57] It is their prejudiced and rude attitude to the Indians that makes the East-West conflict unavoidable.

The victims in the novel are Gangu and other coolies. In the scenes where the author brings together the exploitors and victims to face each other, the novel acquires a special charm and the story moves forward making the situation interesting and exciting. This is clear in the scenes of Gangu's encounter with Croft-Cooke, the coolies marching towards the Manager and the events that follow it and Reggie Hunt's hunting of Leila. The scenes where the exploiters are seen alone, namely the polo game, the club scenes and the

55. Anand, Mulk Raj: *Two Leaves and a Bud*, New Delhi: Arnold-Heinemann, 1983, p. 194.
56. *Ibid.*, p. 11.
57. *Ibid.*, p. 31.

hunting expedition, the nolvel remains uninteresting and dull. The scenes where the victims are seen alone are also boring, though less boring than the scenes where exploiters are alone crowded together.

The social commentators in the novel are mainly John de la Havre, Miss Barbara and Narain, the coolie. It is mainly through them that the author presents his social criticism on the evils of capitalism. The three look at capitalism from three different angles. John de la Havre exposes with anger the exploitation of the poor Indians by the English capitalists. Miss Barbara reveals with annoyance the hypocrisy and shallowness that has penetrated in the day to day life of the British society in India. Narain narrates with sadness the story of misery experienced by the victims of capitalism like himself.

To John de la Havre, a cup of tea is nothing but, "The hunger, the sweat and the despair of a million Indians".[58] He sadly asks, "Why do these swarming, under-nourished, bleary, worm-eaten millions of India suffer so?"[59] After seeing the sordid side of the tragic existence of the coolies he realises the necessity of revolution: "The black coolies clear the forests, plant the fields, toil and garner the harvest, while all the money-grubbing, slave-driving soulless managers and directors draw their salaries and dividends and build up monopolies. Therein lies the necessity of revolution in this country."[60] To John de la Havre, the coolies are "prisoners of so many chains, bearing the physical signs of grief, of lassitude, even death".[61] According to his observation, "The coolie spends practically the last of his monthly wages on his rice. The clothes or rather rags, worn by the Indian coolie, occupy but an insignificant positions in his budget."[62] He says, "The position of the plantation coolies in India is, in many respects, similar to that of the cotton plantation slaves of the Southern States of North America, of whom Harriet Beecher Stowe wrote in *Uncle Tom's Cabin*. "If there be any difference, I think that actual inquiry would prove that the present economic condition of the Indian coolies is worse than was that of the negro slaves in America."[63] Thus John de la Havre goes on, giving arguments and statistics, thereby

58. *Ibid.*, p. 22.
59. *Ibid.*, p. 122.
60. *Ibid.*, p. 123.
61. *Ibid.*, p. 37.
62. *Ibid.*, p. 126.
63. *Ibid.*, p. 124.

overpowering the author and tilting the direction of the work from a novel to a thesis. The technique the novelist adopts to voice the opinion of de la Havre is not artistic enough to receive applause. Most of the utterance of the doctor quoted above are from his writings Barbara found lying on his table. She reads, skips some pages, and again reads all that the angry young man in Mulk Raj Anand prepared in the name of John de la Havre.

John de la Havre is a caricature as he lacks the normal qualities of the English blood, namely shrewdness and tactfulness. When Gangu requests de la Havre to make a recommendation for him to the 'Burra Sahib' for land, the doctor, without any English blood in him, tells Gangu:

> 'Yes, I will do that.... Certainly you ought to get land; it is in the contract of every labourer that he will get land to grow rice on when he comes here. I will see that the contract is enforced.'[64]

No one will believe that an intelligent doctor will speak in such a plain and honest manner to an insignificant coolie. It is obvious that the author created the doctor with the sole aim of exposing the monstrous crime against humanity committed by the capitalist planters. The doctor's obsession with blood and thunder ideas makes even the love scenes between Barbara and he something dull and lifeless. The reader may feel a sense of relief when he bids her the final good-bye.

Miss Barbara, a young and attractive girl, would have been a source of pleasure to the reader if she were kept away from the uninteresting John de la Havre and given some other meaningful role. Her self-disgust against the graceless antics of the club members does not appear natural. It only helps to expose the author's disgust with the European exploiters "displaying themselves to each other in their evening dress, Sunday after Sunday, trying to look beautiful and important, and putting on airs, talking pompously about politics and business, or cracking jokes, telling stories and singing songs that meant nothing to them, and hiding their real emotions....not perceiving that they became even more ridiculous in so doing."[65]

---

64. *Ibid.*, p. 133.
65. *Ibid.*, pp. 101-102.

Of the three social commentators, only Narain seems to play a natural role in the novel. Like an old man narrating a folk tale to young ones, Narain narrates to the new comer Gangu the brutality let loose by the planters on the poor coolies:

> "Bless your fate, brother", said Narain to Gangu. "He (Reggie Hunt) is a very *budmash* sahib. He is always drunk. And he has no consideration for anyone's mother or sister. He is openly living with three coolie women!.... Nobody's mother or sister is safe in this place." [66]

As the novel develops, Gangu comes to know from Narain how the coolies are able to get land. His story telling faculty is clearly shown in his description of how Neogi Gurka managed to have five acres of land. Narain's jealousy is here balanced by his sympathy for Neogi:

> 'But the Regi Sahib is a *budmash* and Neogi had no choice. He would have lost his job and been lashed as Ranbir, the coolie from Ranchi was lashed, because he refused to give his wife to the *Ashastant* planter. The Sahib had Ranbir imprisoned, and took his wife. The bitch was living at the bungalow for months, till the Sahib turned her out and sent her back to the lines a few days ago! [67]

The author's social criticism on the evils of capitalism presented through Narain is free from artificiality and it has no enervating effect on the novel. Anand portrays Narain convincingly but he does not provide enough flesh and blood to John de la Havre and Barbara. They are robots operated by the author. They are given extreme benevolence as if to strike a balance with the extreme malevolence given to the British planters. By portraying the English characters in the novel as exemplars of extreme goodness or badness the author has undermined the credibility of his characterisation. John de la Havre and Barbara are pegs on which the author openly hangs his criticism of the English. Though much of what he says is true, his presentation of the English remains inartistic, unconvincing and stereotype. Worse still as Stephen Spender points out, "They are too flatly portrayed and, although they act a great deal, they do not develop."[68]

---

66. *Ibid.*, p. 42.
67. *Ibid.*, p. 171.
68. Spender, Stephen: In, *Life and Letters To-day*, Vol. 16, No. 8 (Summer 1937), p. 155.

The novel is by and large a failure and the best reason for it can be found in Anand's own confession given in the 'Preface' to the Second Edition of *Two Leaves and a Bud:* "I confess that, as I got into the book, I was biased in favour of my Indian characters and tended to caricature the English men and English women who play such a vital part in this book."[69] If Anand were to treat the characters he created, as his own children, with affection and without any prejudice or impartiality, they would have had a natural growth in the novel, making *Two Leaves and a Bud* a wonderful work of art.

69. Anand, Mulk Raj: "Introduction" to *Two Leaves and a Bud*, Bombay: Kutub Popular, 1951, p. 6.

IV

"*THE VILLAGE*" TRILOGY

The Village, Across the Black Waters and *The Sword and the Sickle* are three novels written as a continuous story and yet each of these in itself is a complete unit. Together, they constitute a Trilogy. The three novels depict in three parts the life, adventures, escapades and struggles of the same hero, whose magnetic personality binds the three works together, though each novel explores different and unrelated themes. The illuminating cynosure in these novels is a dynamic and amiable hero Lal Singh, a young man from the village of Nandpur in Punjab, whose progressive views in an ultra-conservative society, where religious fanaticism, superstition, meaningless rituals and landlordism have reigned, make it impossible for him to survive, and compels him to take refuge under the soldier's uniform only to pine at the end that the uniform and the hardships it has enveloped would not help him to hold even his own plot of land after his return from the army. Lal Singh, as presented in these novels is an existential figure, 'condemned to the liberty of choosing his own destiny' in a single handed manner, in a society unwilling to grant individual freedom. He stands alone and struggles alone with great concern for man's being, in a world where superstitious practises and rituals have replaced the real God. It is his existential drift that accounts for his escape from home into the army.

The three novels together in Paperback edition run into 960 pages and Anand's three-decker achievement is admired by most of the critics. S. Menon Marath calls the Trilogy "the finest and the most balanced of Anand's works"[1], while Meenakshi Mukherjee avers: "Anand's achievement in the first two volumes of the trilogy has not yet been surpassed by an Indo-Anglian novelist".[2] A study of the

1. Marath, S. Menon: "Three Indian Novelists", In: *Life and Letters*, Vol. 59 (Dec. 1948), p. 190.
2. Mukherjee, Meenakshi: "Beyond 'The Village': An aspect of Mulk Raj Anand", In: *Criticial Essays on Indian Writing in English*, edited by: M.K. Naik, S.K. Desai and G.S. Amur (Karnatak University, Dharwar, 1968), p. 195.

pilgrim's progress of Lal Singh from the village to the contonment, and from there to Festubert in France and back to Uttar Pradesh as presented in *The Village*, *Across the Black Waters*, and *The Sword and the Sickle* is essential to the understanding of Anand's art and his social concerns.

The Village

Anand had spent some of the happiest days of his childhood, boyhood and youth in his mother's village in Central Punjab, among the tribesmen of the North-Western Frontier, and in the Kangra Valley. The Punjabi poetry he had heard, specially the 'Baramasa' poem of Guru Nanak had filled him with images of the beauty of the Northern earth. The proverbs, the folk tales, and the epic poems had been distilled into his consciousness through the recitals of his three maternal uncles. His fellow students at the Khalsa College, Amritsar, who came mostly from the villages, talked of harvest and drinking *lassi* and sugarcane juice. These pleasant thoughts mixed up with his disgust with the ritual-ridden social life, religious fanaticism and superstitious belief of the villagers and his awareness of their painful life of toil from dawn to dusk only to pay back the claims of the money-lenders, the absentee landlords and the revenue hunting sarkar. Anand found such social situation a spontaneous, striking and excellent background in presenting the lonely struggle of his hero, Lal Singh, to liberate himself from the malice and manipulations of the society.

When Nihal Singh reaches Nandpur station after selling cotton and maize at the town of Manabad, his youngest son Lal Singh is there to welcome and accompany him in his homeward journey. The old man (aged seventy) curses the Devil like train, considers it as the sign of the arrival of the age of darkness and speaks of the advantages of going by bullock carts. He is sad that the cotton and maize he sold did not earn enough even to pay the rent that was due. As the old man does not want his son to carry the luggage, Lalu (Lal Singh) takes a pathway to collect the mended hoe from the power house.

As Lalu strikes the earth hard with the newly mended hoe, his mind is preoccupied with the thought of how to go to the Fair at Manabad. He wipes the perspiration pouring down his forehead, and expresses his annoyance with his religion which demands its followers to wear long hair.[3]

---

3. Anand, Mulk Raj: *The Village*, New Delhi: Arnold-Heinemann 1948, p. 28.

In the evening, when he returns home after a day of hard labour, his eldest brother tells him to go to the Mahant taking a parcel of gift his father (Bapu) has bought for him. So taking the parcel Lalu goes towards the monastery. After reaching the Mahant's chamber, he goes up to the 'holy man', kneels before him, touches his feet with the right hand, and lays the things he has brought before him. Then, after putting up a show of reverence to the Mahant, he goes out of the chamber and soon finds himself in the company of his two friends, Gughi, son of the yekka driver Jhandu and Churanji, the money-lender's son. They scrable up to the top of a strawladen cart belonging to the landlord, Sardar Bahadur Harbans Singh. They start playing cards. The household of the Sardar have been travelling in the bullock cart ahead. But the landlord's little child and his sister Maya are travelling in the cart on top of which Lalu and his friends are playing cards. Lalu finds it a wonderful chance to come into contact with Maya, a maturing girl of fourteen.

When they reach the fair site, Lalu loses sight of his friends. He feels very hungry. He enters a Muhammadan shop from where a palatable smell is spreading. He orders an earthen saucer of curry and satisfies his hunger. Then unaware of the sacrilege he is committing he enters 'King George Vth Haircutting and Shaving Saloon' and has his hair shorn. When he returns home, his eldest brother Sharm Singh notices that Lalu's turban descended lower than the nape of his nick. He asks Lalu what has happened. Lalu coolly tells that he paid a visit to the 'King George Vth Hair Cutting Saloon' in the town and had an hair cut.[4] The situation suddenly becomes tense. "Nihal Singh sprang forward and dealt him a resounding slap on the face. With the fury of an old tiger, he fell upon his son, digging his claws into the boy's neck, while Sharm Singh ground his teeth with an, 'ohe, rape-mother!' and struck him hard on his head, his neck and on his body".[5] The news soon spreads around the village and a crowd gathers in front of the house. Hardit Singh, the elder son of the landlord rushes at Lalu and blackens his face. Then, Arjan Singh, the priest of the Sikh temple brings forward a donkey and Hardit Singh with great force lifts Lalu and puts him on the back of the animal. Without any delay, the donkey is sent forward among the shouting, bawling, hysterical, blood-thirsty men and women and children who have run ahead into the lane. Lalu struggles hard to free himself from

4. *Ibid.*, p. 90.
5. *Ibid.*, p. 91.

the grip of his enemies and at a lucky moment manages to deal blows right and left, forward and backward and slips away. The crowd chases him but he has escaped.

After this shocking incident Lalu keeps up a low profile in his house. He hardly talks with any one. However, he obeys his mother's request and goes with his father and brother in their pursuit for loan to the shop of the money-lender Chaman Lal, as Chaman Lal's son Churanji is his friend.

Soon, Lal Singh's family is seen busy preparing for the marriage of his elder brother, Dayal Singh. The house is in a merry mood. One day a group of children come to play the dholki and sing. To Lalu's surprise Maya, the landlord's daughter with whom he came into contact during his travel by bullock-cart to the Fair, is among them. And he pales to find her there, so beautiful, soft and tender. They start playing. When their playful pandemonium is at its height, Maya falls upon Lalu "with a lovely helplessness, beating him, scratching him, digging her fists into his sides and he laughed and shook from side to side to ward her off".[6] Just then Sardar Bahadur appears in the hall. Seeing their play, the landlord becomes outrageous, abuses Lalu, takes hold of his daughter and drags her away.

The next day the police Havildar Napoo Singh comes to Lalu's house with a summon to arrest him on the charge of theft. Lalu realises that the charge was fabricated by the landlord to punish him for playing with his daughter. So he takes to his heels and reaches Manabad. There he hears an army Havildar bawling at the top of his voice, enumerating the advantages and asking young men to join the army. Lalu realises that by joining the army perhaps he could escape arrest and so he, without any hesitation, expresses his willingness to join the army.

Lalu and other recruits are taken in the evening by the Karachi Mail to the 68th Rifles of Ferozepur. Though a Sikh by birth, on account of his short hair, Lal Singh is enlisted as a Hindu Dogra as Recruit No. 12444 to Platoon, B Company in the 68th Rifles. The new recruits have had intense training. The capricious, blood-thirsty drill instructor, Lance Naik Lok Nath dislikes Lalu from the very beginning. He slaps and abuses Lalu for every slight mistake during the drill. As against the cruelty of Lok Nath, Lalu receives compassionate treatment and affection from Kirpu, the orderly of the Subedar Major, who has

6. *Ibid.*, pp. 154-55.

been nick-named 'uncle' for his age and eccentricity, Daddy Dhanoo, older and even more fatalistic than uncle Kirpu and from Havildar Lachman Singh. He has been in the army for nearly five months when one day he receives a telegram informing that his father is seriously ill. He is allowed to go home. After a quick journey from Ferozepur by rail he reaches his home.

After reaching home, Lal Singh is drawn to his father with a pitying affection. His father has been receiving medical care from Muhammad Ali, the Mulah who has been practising a mixture of the indigenous and the Greek system of medicine.

On the day his leave has expired, Lalu packs his luggage and with reverence touches his father's feet. The old man blesses his son and asks him to be brave. His friends quarrel for the privilege of carrying his belongings. Almost the whole of the village follow him in a procession to see him off. When Lalu reaches Ferozepur he is able to confirm the rumour he had heard earlier that a war has started between Germany and England. Soon orders arrive for the 68th Rifles to get ready as part of the Ferozepur Brigade to go for war. The only topic of conversation for Lalu and his friends is the exact date of departure and their destination. "But the sepoys had been left completely in the dark on both these counts and the range of conjecture had become limitless".[7] And finally the exact date of departure arrives and they march towards the sea-shore where their ship is anchored. While Lalu and his companions wait for their chance to enter the ship, Havildar Lachman hands Lalu a telegram which reads: "Baba Nihalu passed away. Harnam Singh". Tears, the silent language of grief appear on Lalu's face. Uncle Kirpu, Daddy Dhanoo and Havildar Lachman console him. "Then he shrugged his shoulders and ran along the decks towards the forming sepoys –".[8]

Lalu, as presented in the novel is a non-conformist. His reason for cutting his hair is this :

> The *katch, kara, kirpan, kesh* and *kanga* might well have been necessary when Guru Govind was fighting Aurangzeb. Then it was said he enjoined his men to wear shorts, because he couldn't get clothes, bangles and swords for symbols, and long hair because he couldn't get barbers to shave them, and

7. *Ibid.*, p. 240.
8. *Ibid.*, p. 253.

> combs to tidy their hair. Such provisions were dictated by necessity and common sense. But as everyone with a grain of intelligence said, what was the use of observing these conventions now that there was no further need for them? There was no religion in doing so.[9]

The non-conformist Laul' s common sense has clearly gone against the conscience of his community. So, the society looks upon him as a dissenter and pervertor of truth. His own affectionate family condemn his action: Ajit Kaur exclaims, "Oh. The Shame! It is the most shamefullest shame that could be for a Sikh to have a single hair of his body shorn", and she further adds, "It is the most terrible insult to our religion of the five K's."[10] Lalu's Brother Sharm Singh becomes uncontrollable. He shouts at Lalu, "You are a dirty contaminated dog, a pig."[11] Lalu's mother turns deeply sad and deplores, "Oh, all is lost! We shall not be able to show our faces in the brotherhood."[12] Soon the news spreads around the village. The Priest of the Sikh temple becomes furious, as he is aware of the danger in allowing anyone within the faithful fold to exercise private judgement and conscience. He shouts, "Look, oh, people. This rogue has spoiled our religion, disgraced the village !......."[13]

The sound and fury of the society does not alter Lalu's conviction. The priest's accusation that he 'disgraced the village' by his hair on his head shorn is something absolutely absurd for Lalu, the existential seeker of his own destiny. He firmly believes that all those who have persecuted him did him wrong for his doing the right thing of cutting oppressive long hair on his head. The question of hair as presented in the novel was something unacceptable to the staunch believers. They found the novel a book of sacrilege and in 1968, under their pressure, it was banned by the Punjab Government.

Closely connected with Anand's criticism of religious fanaticism is his laughter provoking presentation of religious parochialism. Muhammad Ali, the Mulah of Nandpur Mosque, who treats Lalu's father more by prayer than by medicine, though free from malice, is not prepared to see the manifestation of God in religions other than in his own:

---

9. *Ibid.*, p. 28.
10. *Ibid.*, p. 93.
11. *Ibid.*
12. *Ibid.*
13. *Ibid.*, p. 95.

> 'According to my religion, you will soon have to stand before God on the Judgement Day', said the Maulvi. 'And since you are an infidel, the prophet cannot intercede on your behalf. The first Guru, Guru Nanak, was an admirer of Muhammad, however, and that may count in your favour'.
>
> 'But each day in life is judgement day', burst Lalu, impatient at the Maulvi's words. 'And surely there is no favouritism shown to men in heaven, if there be such a place, just because men belong to one religion or another.'[14]

Lalu's protest seems to be Anand's own protest against religious intolerance. Religious intolerance is intolerable to Anand. It is the religious intolerance which makes Gujri indignant about the Maulvi's entrance into the barn through the kitchen and makes her lift the shoes, which the Maulvi has discarded at the door, by means of a stick and throw them into the courtyard. It is the same social attitude which provokes a Hindu merchant, who has a booth at the Fair next to the Mohammadan stall in which Lalu enters, to shout at him:

> 'Sardarji, have you left your senses that you are eating at a Muhammadan shop? But probably they have left you, since the hour of twelve o'clock has struck. At this hot hour, I suppose it is impossible for your head loaded with hair to think at all.'[15]

Intolerance is the root of religious fanaticism and mankind can destroy this root only through goodwill. Anand's humanism insists that religion should be humanised. This he illustrates through an incident in the novel. Lalu goes with the Maulvi to collect a potion he promises to give which will ease the pain on his father's back. On their way they hear from the mosque by the waver's line the deep musical cry: "Allah ho Akbar! Allah ho Akbar!" and immediately "Maulvi Muhammad Ali lifted his hind feet like a duck out of water and rushed through the gateway without a word to Lalu, as if he would miss his chance of entering the kingdom of God if he tarried".[16] Lalu has to wait there, till the Maulvi ends his prayer to collect the promised potion, leaving his dying father in the meanwhile to continue to suffer the pain. Piety is good but piety at the expense of an urgently required

14. *Ibid.*, p. 218.
15. *Ibid.*, p. 80.
16. *Ibid.*, p. 205.

help to follow human being is something contradictory in essence. Our zeal for God should not eat away our common sense.

The life in the villages in India is plaited with superstitous practices. Not only Lalu's old mother Gujri who is foolish enough to believe that it is a good omen to meet a sweeper or a black dog before one begin's one's journey, but also the entire village community is in the grip of superstition. Superstition is the religion of feeble minds; it retards progress; it eclipses and spoils the true aspects of religion. Superstitious beliefs are continued to be honoured in India, as every new generation of Indian society submissively adjust themselves to the older generation and its irrational values and traditions. It is unfortunate that superstition is still an integral part of the general Indian set up. A person like Lalu who has the courage to challenge superstitious practices is treated as an outcast of the society. The risk involved in rebelling against superstition is enormous and so every one in this country dances to the old tune leaving India, a land of incorrigible superstition. People who justify superstition may justify anything and Anand through his character Lalu, ridicules such people. In the situation referred below, Lalu is getting ready to go with his eldest brother and father in search of a loan for his elder brother's marriage:

> 'Let us go then and see to the rent as well as the marriage', said Lalu sardonically, emphasizing his last words in half-mocking, half-serious manner.
> 'Wait, wait my son', Gujri cried. 'I will go to the well and meet you with a pitcher of water on my head so that your visit may be auspicious.'
> 'God suits the burden to the strength', said Lalu cryptically, and headed towards the door.
> 'Wait, wait my son', Gujri cried out impatiently.
> But luckily Kesari was just entering with a brass jug full of Ganges water which was given to devotees at the monastery.
> '*Acha*, now you can go' Gujri said.
> Lalu stood near the hall waiting for his father and Sharm Singh to issue forth. He cast a glance at his mother who was mumbling prayers as the two men passed ahead, laughed and followed the elders submissively.[17]

---

17. *Ibid.*, p. 110.

Most of the farmers in Nandpur are poverty-stricken, miserable looking 'slave of the wheel of labour', like Lalu's uncle Harnam Singh who had to mortgage the whole of his six acres to the money-lender Chaman Lal to pay the land rent to the Sarkar and to have a little money on hand for seed. Most of what they grow goes to the money-lender as interest and there is no question of paying back the capital for years. Yet poverty never teaches the villagers to be frugal. Instead, the empty illusion of prestige induces them to spend money on feeding, ungrateful brotherhood and the 'holy men' who are embodiments of hypocrisy. Lalu is irritated with such a social attitude. Lalu's annoyance and anger with the Mahant of Nandpur who has indicated his desire for a dearer variety of silk than that his father has bought for him from his meagre saving is in fact an anger with the whole society which is foolishly generous:

> Lalu felt a violent revulsion againist Nandgir now. That the wretch should make it a point to remind the old man about the cheapness of the cloth. And his father had said that the harvests were not fetching much. Why couldn't the family learn better than to waste money on gifts for these charlatans? Why? The man hadn't done anything for them for years, but came in at the end of every harvest for his share of the grain and the gift of clothes! The lecher! He ate sumptuous food, dressed in yellow silks, smoked charas and drank hemp, and, if reports were true, whored and fornicated. And he was a holy man, the Guru of the community.[18]

The main obstacle to the progress of a society is its unwillingness to accept modernization. The society's adherence to the old and the tried with an allergy to the new and the untried makes economic stagnation inevitable. Anand wants India to be modernized and he knows that the enemies of modernization are the people themselves who are unwilling to give up their old ways of life and who protest against anything new and more advantageous. The old dog's unwillingness to study new and more efficient tricks is presented in the very opening chapter of the novel where Lalu and his father enter into an argument on the modernity brought about by train. Nihal Singh's comment about the train, "This machine is like the Devil. How it made my heart jump! *Wah Guru*! *Wah Guru*! And the smoke

18. *Ibid.*, p. 45.

it emits is so bad for the fields...."[19], makes Lalu protest, which in turn creates an amusing clash of opinion between the father and the son, the conservative and the progressive:

> 'And whatever you say, Bapu, you know you would not like to be carrying all those sacks of grain to Manabad and Sherkot on your back. The bullock-cart drivers stop twenty times, to smoke and to feed the bullocks, and they often get drunk and take two days and a night sometimes. But you can send anything to town in an hour by the goods train!'
> 'You are a fool', snorted Nihal Singh impatiently. 'You don't think of the hire and the bribes you have to pay to the Babu at the godown each end, and the difficulty of smuggling anything past those fiends of the customs. You can take a bullock cart into town by a hundred devious ways...'[20]

To Nihal Singh, "Men are their own devils, drinking *angrezi* wine and constructing evil machines".[21] It is his hatred for machine, borne out of dreadful anachronisms, that makes him prefer bullock cart to train. He is like some of the characters of Hardy or Dickens who are opposed to "the dark, satanic mills", the "iron-horse" — in short, the modernization. He fights to the very end of his life, in his own limited way, against the introduction of machines. In his conversation with Lalu during the latter's home visit from the cantonment to see his dying father, the old man speaks,

> about the time when the seeds of their present misfortunes were sown, of when the *ferungis* came with their *railgadis* which took away the grain from the villages at the lower prices. The *ferungis*, the *ferungis*. For he could never forgive the *ferungis* for all the new-fangled machines they had brought in, the heavy taxes they levied and their bad justice. Lalu told him of how kind the *Ajitan* Sahib of his regiment had been to him, and said that some of the machines he had seen were wonderful.
> But the old man was not interested in his son's praise of all these toys, regarding his words as the impetuous talk of a

19. *Ibid.*, p. 2.
20. *Ibid.*, p. 2.
21. *Ibid.*, p. 11.

> youngster who had been seduced by the superficial amenities of city life.[22]

The above passage clearly illustrates the generation gap between the father and the son, the adolescent and the adult world. Lalu, like Bakha in *Untoucahble* or Munoo in *Coolie*, is an admirer of machine. Lalu's comment 'some of the machines he had seen were wonderful', implies that not all the machines he had seen were wonderful for the prosperity of the nation. Lalu's comment tallies with Anand's recommendation for the nation to have controlled introduction of machine which would produce a healthy balance between tradition and the amenities offered by industrial progress.

The novel could have had sharper focus if the evocation of the village life had not been marred by the lengthy description of the life in the cantonment and the troop movement for the war. It is true that the hero of *The Village*, Lal Singh, is very much alive in the contonment and is able to return in memory to his village and parents but that alone cannot satisfy the requirement of the title of the novel. Out of the 253 pages of the novel, 64 pages, that is, slightly more than one fourth of its length, deal exclusively with cantonment, quite away from the village. This shift in the direction of the novel is made to stand out further by the loquacity of Daddy Dhanoo and Uncle Kirpu and the vulgarity of *Lance Naik* Lok Nath. But for this weakness in the plot, *The Village* is a highly interesting novel, leaving the reader with an irresistable urge to know more about its hero, Lal Singh, who is seen at the end of novel on board the ship to begin the voyage across the Black Waters.

Critics who accuse Anand of being a propagandist, will not find a chance to make such an accusation in *The Village*. As G.S. Balarama Gupta wrote:

> The entire novel bears the stamp of naturalness and authenticity, and Anand hints at the changes he wants in rural society by giving a convincing picture of the intelligent hero's reactions to the *status quo*, and not by directly sermonising about them. Thus the novel escapes from being stigmatised as a work of art marred by obtrusive propaganda.[23]

The descriptive passages in the novel are particularly possessed

22. *Ibid.*, p. 217.
23. Gupta, G.S. Balarama: Mulk Raj Anand – *A Study of his Fiction in Humanist Perspective*, Bareilly: Prakash Book Depot, 1974, p. 58.

with a charm and melody. It is not difficult to discover poetry in passages like the one given below:

> And walking along this road, Nihal Singh sensed a kinship with the familiar earth. He felt the invisible warmth of the sheltered lives in the village where he was respected. He sniffed the air as if it were nectar and gazed upon the landscape as if it were heaven full of the ineffable bliss of life, full of men and women and children and animals and fruits and flowers.[24]

The Village in fact depicts every village in India and Anand's rural roots certainly explain his roubustness and sensibility in the novel. The extortionate government, unscrupulous landlords, greedy money-lenders, fleecing lawyers, orthodox religion ossified through years into mere rituals, social life saturated with superstitious practices etc., as presented in *The Village* hold a mirror up to the situation of every Indian village. The novel is a panorama of the inner India, a work giving an imaginatively vivid picture of Indian rural life in pre-war days. As Alastair Niven wrote, "*The Village* is perhaps the most rounded portrait of village and rural life that the Indian novel in English offers us."[25] In the very opening chapter of the novel, the atmosphere is created with remarkable skill, for the reader to feel that he is already in a village. The singing of robin, the twittering of sparrows, the chattering crows, the flowers of thorny bush, the paddy fields, the timorous breeze, movement of domesticated donkeys, the village black dog of name Kalu, the bullock-cart whose driver everyone knows and above all the typical way people talk adding blessing or cursing as presented in the opening scene of the novel fixes the reader's mind to feel that he is in a village. The novel is replete with lively description, as of the Fair in the town. The prose is of an easy spontaneous type, flowing flawlessly, adaptable and capable of fine suggestiveness. There is a blessed lack of exaggeration in style as in conception and above all the fine fusion of art and idea in the novel makes it an excellent and enduring work of art.

Across the Black Waters

One year after the banning of *The Village*, the Punjab Government in 1969 banned the second novel of the trilogy, *Across the Black*

24. Anand, Mulk Raj: *The Village*, New Delhi: Arnold-Heinemann, 1984, p. 12.
25. Niven, Alastair: *The Yoke of Pity – A Study in the Fictional Writings of Mulk Raj Anand*, New Delhi: Arnold-Heinemann, 1978, p. 65.

Waters. In his letter to Saros Cowasjee, dated 22 Oct. 1969, Anand expresses his irritation with the Chief Minister who ordered the banning of it without even knowing its content: "It seems the Chief Minister rang up a friend of mine to ask her if she had a copy of the novel *Across the Black Waters* because he wished to read it. Of course, true Sardarji style, it was after he had banned the book".[26]

Whatever may be the reason for the Punjab Government to ban it, the novel remains to be the best Indian war novel. *Sainik Samachar* calls it "a classic"[27], and Alastair Niven found it to be Anand's "best novel since *Untoucahable*, for it exactly communicates the claustrophobic tension of man in the front line, the imminence of death and the pervading sense of inevitability.....[28]

The novel is based on Anand's own experience in trench warfare in Spain. Anand says that the book was sketched in a rough draft in Barcelona and Madrid during the Spanish Civil war between January and April 1937, and entirely re-written in Chinnor, Oxen, between July and December 1939.[29] The scenario of the novel is the battlefields in France during World War I, When Indian troops landed in Marseilles, made their way by train and by road and engaged in hand-to-hand fighting with the Germans. It is a book of great interest, since we believe it to be the first book written by an Indian about an Indian regiment in the First World War, and since it shows the Indian troops in action at Messines and Festubert in 1914 and 1915 from their own point of view.

Lalu's friends in the Ferozepur cantonment who appeared in *The Village*, re-appear in this novel in greater depth, and better realised as they are forced to seek "the bubble reputation even at the cannon's mouth".[30] Apart from Lal Singh, the rustic Indian adolescent reaching manhood in the School of suffering at the cold, wet trenches of France, we come into contact in the novel with Falstaff like Uncle Kirpu, Hotspur like Lachman Singh, superstitious and eccentrically

---

26. Anand, Mulk Raj, *Author to Critic* : *The Letters of Mulk Raj Anand to Saros Cowasjee*, Ed. Saros Cowasjee, Calcutta : Writers' Workshop, 1973, p. 76 (letter dated 22 Oct. 1969).
27. See: Blurb, In: Anand, Mulk Raj : *Across the Black Waters*, Delhi: Orient Paperbacks, 1980.
28. Niven, Alastair, *The Yoke of Pity* : *A Study in the Fictional Writings of Mulk Raj Anand*, New Delhi: Arnold-Heinemann, 1978, p. 72.
29. Anand, Mulk Raj, *Across the Black Waters*, Delhi, Orient Paperbacks, 1980, p. 4.
30. Shakespeare, *William, As You Like It*, Act: II, Sc. (vii), lines: 52-53.

pious Daddy Dhanoo, Power-greedy and arrogant Lok Nath, the young Subedar Subah who got promotion through his father's influence and goes drunk on patrol, the considerate English officers and many others who originated in *The Village*.

The very opening of the novel tells us that the soldiers, Lalu and his companions, have completed a long voyage and the ship which carried them has reached Marseilles. Even then, those poorly paid but highly esteemed soldiers meant for active participation in war are not told where they have to fight. But suddenly they hear the thundering sounds of the gun from the land. They feel that they have arrived at the front. A Sikh N.C.O. tells the ignorant sepoys that they are "the guns of the Fracsici warships saluting us".[31] Then the news has gone round that the sepoys will enter the shore there, rest for a day or two and afterwards go by train to the front as soon as possible. As they have alighted from the deck, they see Pathans, Sikhs, Dogras, Gurkhas, Muhammadans in khaki, blue jacketed French seamen and porters and English Tommies. They hear a babal of voices, shouts, curses, salams and incomprehensible courtesies. Then, obeying the orders they march up the hill amidst the French people's greetings of 'Vievelesallies! Vive...'. The Indian regiments response by shouting 'Long Live the Francisis', 'Wah Guruji ka Khalsa!', 'Bolo Sri Ram Chander ki jai!', 'Allah ho Akbar!' and so on. After the march past and short speech of the General of Lahore Division, the sepoys go to the newly erected tents.

After a few days, the Indian troops are transported to Orieans. At Orieans, the corps practise route-marching during the next few days. On the evening of October 17th, 1914, orders come for the Lahore Division to entrain the next day to go to Flanders. They get ready with "a strange sense of fellowship, as if they felt that they ought to hang together because they were going farther into the unknown".[32] Lalu in the company of Uncle Kirpu, Daddy Dhanoo and other sepoys gets inside the unlit cattle truck, which is to be their compartment. The train starts. In the moving train next to Kirpu sits a French soldier. The sepoys talk with him using their heads and hands profusely. After some time, the song of soot and fire which the train has been singing subsides. They reach Rouen. There, they are caught by a grim silence. They see a train standing in the opposite

31. Anand, Mulk Raj: *Across the Black Waters*, Delhi: Orient Paperbacks, 1980, p. 10.
32. *Ibid*., p. 62.

direction of their train with red crosses on them and full of wounded soldiers.

The unending tortuous journey into the unknown continues and the train reaches Calais. They see hordes of European soldiers standing by cattle-truck trains, who lift their hands and cheer the sepoys: 'Viveles Hindus!' The sepoys rush to the doors and cheer back in the only English greeting they have known: 'Hip Hip Hurrah!' The train shrieks and groans out of Calais. After some time it slows down and finally halts at Lillers. Havildar Lachman Singh asks the sepoys to form up on the platform for the roll call. Then the regiment is ordered by Colonel Green to march to the camp, in the village of Arques, a few miles away. After resting there for a day the 69th Rifles are taken by buses to Wulvergham near Ypres and from there, they are ordered to march to the trenches. They hardly pass the dugout when the bullets come whistling over their heads. Now each moment seems to Lalu to be his last. He suddenly gets frightened by seeing some corpses. There are eight in number, eight dead men. Lalu struggles eagerly through the ditches, keeping as close to Havildar Lachman Singh as possible. The runner angrily tells the sepoys to go steady keeping their heads down. And when they reach the location, Havildar Lachman Singh, Uncle Kirpu, Daddy Dhanno, Lalu and others adjust their rifles into the hole in the sandbags. But the expected offensive has not come for many days. So they settle down grimly to routine, like repairing the barbed wire in the no-man's land, fetching ration, bearing away the wounded to the ambulance etc.

Then on a rainy day orders come for the sepoys to attack the enemy. At the instance of the order, they rush forward. A hail of bullets scatter them and Lachman Singh shouts at them to lie down and crawl. The smoke of the gun has mixed with the curtain of rain. The detonations seems to throw up great clouds of earth and limbs and smoke along the line. Lalu does not know what to do or where to go. He lies down and begins to crawl. Another crash and a whirlwind of earth and smoke fly up from an explosion near him, while rifle and machine gun fire pour down like rainstorm. No one is able to go forward in the face of that fire. And the orders come to 'turn back'. In this encounter many sepoys and many Tommies have fallen dead.

During the next three days the Germans have kept up a heavy bombardment to which the English guns, inferior in strength, have replied now and then. More orders arrive. Half the 69th Rifles are ordered to march with the 4th Calvary Brigade to new trenches. The sepoys "did not even complain about the inconvenience of changing trenches and this red-hot reception they were getting from the enemy as if after the hardships of the first attack they were now prepared to accept anything".[33] The enemy has been "prodigal of lead", for their artillery continues to fire without any break. In response, Lalu keeps firing round after round, as if he has been intoxicated with a passion for violence. After many days of restless attacks and counter-attacks, the No. 2 Company of the 69th Rifles are allowed to be relieved and to go to billets. They are moved to a large dusty barn for rest. When their roll call is made they discover that out of the strength of seven hundred and fifty, only two hundred and fifty are left.

That night the No. 2 company sleeps on beds of straw in the large dusty barn near the farm house by the brook. In the clear running waters of the brook, Lalu and other sepoys have a dip and there Lalu meets a boy, Andre, and his sister Marie. He is enchanted by Marie's beauty. He comes to know that they are the children of the farm house owner with whom the regimental officer and the British Officers are billeted. Lalu's friendship with the farmer's children Andre and Marie steadily increases. The farmer and his wife also treat Lalu with affection.

When the two days of rest given to the sepoys ends, though they still remain in billets, they are subjected to a succession of fatigues, parades and inspection. But Lalu is taken on to help in the office to write letters home for the illiterate sepoys.

On one occasion, *Jamedar* Subah Singh sees the attractive Marie showing affection to Lalu. The young *Jamedar* gets excited. As he is not able to get an opportunity to come into contact with her, the *Jamedar* asks Lalu to bring her out on some pretext so that he can take her into a field. Lalu says that he will have to ask Babu Kushi Ram's permission to leave the office. Subah does not understand Lalu's position. So he leaves the place with great anger and the next day Lalu receives orders to attend parade.

After a few days, the sepoys are ordered to march to Festebert. It is an extremely cold place. In spite of their use of many blankets and warm clothes, they shiver and are not able to sleep in the trenches. Some of them have to be heaved out of the clay holes by means of ropes, as they were frozen at night.

---

33. *Ibid.*, p. 166.

At Festebert, along with *Jamedar* Subah and *Lance Naik* Bikhi Ram, Lalu is given the hard and risky task of spying on the sap built by the enemy. The party is led by an young officer, Lieutenant Hobson. They crawl towards the German trenches. *Jamedar* Subah who was fully drunk, remains far behind the others. Suddenly the *Jamedar* comes running up, crunching the snow and throws himself down by the side of Lalu.

Just then a German machine-gun begins to speak the language of death and Lalu is pained to Lieutenant Hobson lying flat. Unable to succeed in the mission and with the shock of the lieutenant's death, they crawl back. *Lance Naik* Lok Nath, who had a grudge against Lalu since the Ferozepur days, does not tell the sentries to look out for the patrol party and they keep up an intermittent fire mistaking the patrol for the enemy. They are nearly cut off in no-man's land between the two fires, but sheer luck helps them to survive.

All day preparations for a final offensive has been going on in a quiet manner. Suddenly, the German machine guns spray the entire sector with a deadly ferocity and sepoys fall headlong, or back over the parapet into their own trenches. Just then a bullet goes through the calf of Lalu's left leg and he falls face forward. Immediately a lion-mostached German drags him and two other sepoys into the trench. When he opens his eyes, he realises that he has become a captive.

Across the Black Waters is Anand's definitive statement on the evils of war. The scattered corpses we are presented within the action scenes of the novel give us the impression that it celebrates the religion of death. The only reality in the novel is the reality of death. It is this sorrow that permeates the whole novel and one can't help being affected by it. The soldiers in the novel are churned up in the war machine, in the bogs, mud and slush of France. They are drilled to commit organized violence for Rs.11 a month, plus uniform. The brutality expected from them is evident in the advice given to the sepoys by *Lance Naik* Lok Nath just before they are set to action.

> Now you show them some of your savagery. All brave men like hand-to-hand fighting. And I have always tried to instill in you the fact that as brave sepoys you must charge the enemy without fear with your bayonets, wherever you find him, and hit him in a vital spot. Aim at the heart, remember the belly or the testicles of the enemy! If he has the

> advantage in attack, swiftly fell him with a blow from the butt end of your rifle and trample upon him and drive the bayonet deep into the body and draw it out so that he bleeds and dies.[34]

Bravery at war is nothing but barbarism. It is beautifully expressed by Lalu in one of his chit-chat with Daddy Dhanoo: "...if one who slays one is a murderer then he who slays a thousand is not a hero."[35] The cruelty of war is stressed throughout the novel. The sepoys are treated like yoked bullocks kicked and thrashed by the ploughman to make them go round the field making deep scratches on it. Orders to march or attack are the only words that the sepoys hear from their higher officers. They are merely food for the enemy's powder. No excuse is given to their inability to march. In a horrifying scene in the novel, a sepoy named Hanumant Singh suffering from fever is ordered to get up and march. He refuses to get up and the officers who gather around him shower abuses. Then come the horrible deal:

> 'I shall deal with him', said Suchet Singh, taking out his revolver. 'If you don't get up while I count three... one, two....three'. And he shot at Hanumant so that the sepoy shrieked and doubled over with a 'Hai, hai, oh my...'.[36]

The cruelty of war re-bounding on themselves turns the sepoys dazed and wooden. Though they have admired the shrewdness and wealth of the sahibs they cannot understand why the sahibs are killing each other and making a large graveyard of their land. Most of the sahibs think that they are in war with the Germans to save the cause of civilization. Whereas is reality, as stated by Captain Owen, they are victims of civilization. To Lal Singh, war is a holocaust of men, beasts and houses and he wonders why the people of so-called high civilization involve in this:

> ...he (Lal Singh) could not believe that ordinary men and women of good sense, and the Government of France, England and Germany, which were saner and wiser than the ordinary people over whom they ruled, could be engaged

34. *Ibid.*, pp. 141-42.
35. *Ibid.*, p. 137.
36. *Ibid.*, p. 178.

> in a war in which men were being wounded and houses shattered.[37]

The saddest aspect of the war described in the novel is the suppression of even the necessary information required to give the sepoys emotional involvement, and a sense of participation in war. The officers fail to realise that they are giving orders to human beings similar to them with emotion, feeling, anxiety and curiosity. So they never bother to explain the orders they give. As uncle Kirpu puts it: "The sarkar is like a bitch, son. It barks its orders and does not explain."[38] As they are not told where they are to fight and why they have to fight, they feel that their thoughts and feelings are not fed with the right spirit required to fight and that they are only treated as mere instruments in the war and not as human being. This makes them dull and indifferent. So they move about with a resigned attitude towards the whole business:

> no one asked where the war was or why it was being fought and how it happened that they were going there. For there had been no answer to such queries in the past and now they took it for granted.[39]

Thus, the poor sons of Indian peasants who have joined the army to earn a little ready cash to pay off the interest on the mortgage of the few acres of their land or to solve their other pecuniary problems are caught by Fate and they are in France condemned to fight. Their only concern is to save five or six rupees out of the eleven rupees of their monthly pay and thereby relieve the suffering of their family. The following passage in the novel summarises why stoicism and militaristic tepidity has taken hold of the Indian soldiers during the war:

> A passionate people, prone to sudden exaltations and depressions, more faithful than any other if they believe, they were neutral in this war, because this was not a war for any of the religions of their inheritance, nor for any ideal which could fire their blood and make their hair stand on end. Ordered about by the Sarkar, they were as ready to thrust their bayonets into the bellies of the Germans as they

---

37. *Ibid.*, p. 83.
38. *Ibid.*, p. 103.
39. *Ibid.*, p. 177.

> had been to disembowel the frontier tribesmen, or their own countrymen for the pound a month which the sahibs paid them. But they were like conscripts, brutalized and willing to fight like trained bulls, but without a will of their own, soulless automations in the execution of the army code.......[40]

The much required tragic relief in the novel is provided by Uncle Kirpu's sullen humour and citation of pain-petalled proverbs. As the author tells us, "The reputation of Uncle Kirpu as a humourist made the very sound of his voice infectious with light-heartedness."[41] Though he is stubborn and independent every one has known him to be harmless. His words to Owen Sahib, "So, Sahib, we brave lions have come just in time to stop the enemy...."[42], reveal his natural disposition. He speaks to his friends casually calling them "watchdog of the Sarkar", "wooden owls", "the son of land" etc. He speaks to them in fitting proverbs like, "A dog is a lion in his own street", "The master asks the dogs to go hunting when they are dying and they must go", "The dogs must bark early in the morning to show their master that they have been keeping watch all night", "Make yourself a sheep and the wolf will eat you", "Black clouds frighten, grey are the rain-givers", "A leper has got the itch, and when a man has got the itch, he wants a companion" and "The angry man listens to no counsel". His frequent comparing of sepoys with dogs is based on his understanding of the treatment they actually receive from their superiors.

The laughter-provoking repartee between Lalu and Uncle Kirpu reduces the scathing bitterness in the novel. In their visit to the farm of Papa Labusiere at Ypres, they see hefty, small horned, well-polished cows raising their snozzles at them and staring. So Uncle Kirpu asks Lalu what they are saying:

> 'Praying to God that they might be transported to Uncle Kirpu's village', mocked Lalu, 'so that they can roll about in the mud, eat grain out of their dung and be under no obligation to give milk.'[43]

These humorous words of Lalu are not devoid of truth. Anand criticises the way, we in India look after our domestic animals.

---

40. *Ibid.*, p. 133.
41. *Ibid.*, p. 117.
42. *Ibid.*, p. 177.
43. *Ibid.*, p. 195.

Though we are willing to give a kind of 'divinity' to our cows, most of the people in India don't care much for the dignity of animals and the welfare they deserve.

Uncle Kirpu, after his promotion to Lance Naik, addresses the sepoys with a mockery of his best N.C.O. voice and manner, blowing an imaginary particle of dust off the stripe on his shoulder and pretending to be very respectful to himself. Behind his sardonic humour, Mulk Raj Anand is eloquently protesting against the army code which provides a lot of comfort to the officers at the expense of the ordinary soldiers. Anand must have observed the dog-like treatment the ordinary soldiers receive from their officers and he, through the words of his mouth-piece Uncle Kirpu criticises the slavery to which the sepoys are subjected by the officers, without any official or moral sanction. Anand's intention here is clear. He wants reformation in the army set-up which would permit even the lowest in rank to live with dignity:

> 'A soldier must not question an order given by a superior', he (Uncle Kirpu) now began to fool with a hyperbolic exposition to the army code. 'He must obey promptly and willingly, if possible by crawling before the officer or by tying the officer's shoelaces. For an officer is like the king, father and mother, though he has no beard like *Jarj Panjam*.....if you are not still convinced of the importance of an officer's position, as issuing from the king's instructions, then you have only to look at me!' And he made a wry face, put on a scowl and began to twist his moustache at the tips with deliberately heroic efforts to make them stand.[44]

Lalu who has been enjoying the foolery of Uncle Kirpu interrupts his lecture by calling him 'Holdars!' with exaggerated politeness and says: "I have not been to a kit inspection and the sepoy who showed my clothes at parade for me when we came back to rest said that I shall have to have new socks".[45] *Lance Naik* Kirpu replies:

> You will have to be polite to the quarter-master *holdar* and call him a *subedar*, even as you have called me a *holdar*, and go and complete any deficiency that there is in your kit to-day. If you get nothing but abuse from the quarter-master

44. *Ibid.*, p. 230.
45. *Ibid.*, p. 231.

> then that is what you deserve, for kit is meant to be kept in store or to be given to favourites and not to the fighting sepoy. If you are told off at the next inspection parade by myself or another N.C.O. for not having made good the deficiency then don't grumble but regard it as a law of the army that a soldier is the donkey who must bear all the burden of the army on his back![46]

Denunciation of war is the central theme, the key element of social criticism in *Across the Black Waters*. In this connection, it is worth recalling the speech made by Bonar Law before World War I started: "There is no such thing as an inevitable war. If war comes it will be from failure of human wisdom".[47] In war people kill one another to win 'honour' and the greatest murderer is given the highest 'honour'. Uncle Kirpu's 'Falstaffism' towards honour and war appears in many parts of the novel. When *Havildar* Lachman praises the bravery of sepoy Usman Khan of Pathan company, Uncle Kirpu's reaction is interesting:

> 'Bravery', said Lachman: 'What a bravery! Sepoy Usman Khan was hit by rifle fire. He was hit a second time but he stood like a Bahadur. A large piece of flesh was blown away from both his legs by a splinter and he had to be carried back. *Karnel* Sahib has recommended him for a medal....'
> 'He can hang it on his .....', said Kirpu, 'now, that he has no body left to decorate'.[48]

The soldiers are encouraged to indulge in crime for the reward of medal and promotion. Uncle Kirpu's mockery of medal for bravery is clearly seen in his words of ridicule to his friends who are discussing on the possibility of getting it:

> 'Boys, it is my duty as a *Lance Naik* to tell you that there are some gold medals being given by the women in the Red Lamp shops......'.[49]

The linking of *Across the Black Waters* with *The Village* is achieved not only by the role of the hero, Lalu, and his companions

46. *Ibid.*, p. 231.
47. Quoted from, *Best Quotations for all Occasions*, arranged and edited by Lewis C. Henry, London: Premier Publishers Pvt. Ltd., 1968, p. 243.
48. Anand, Mulk Raj: *Across the Black Waters*, Delhi: Orient Paperbacks, 1980, p. 120.
49. *Ibid.*, p. 208.

Uncle Kirpu, Daddy Dhanoo, and his superiors Subah, Lok Nath, Owen Sahib etc. who figure in both the novels but also by the hero's recurrent recollection of the trials, tribulations and happiness of his life in his village of Nandpur. When he sees in the distant France a few Sikhs of No. 4 Company standing and combing their long hair, he "recalled the brutality with which the fanatics of his village had blackened his face and put him on a donkey when he had his hair cut. The humiliation had bitten deep into him. They must look odd to the Europeans, he thought".[50] His love for his parents and home makes him see dreams at night. In one of his dreams "his mother was crying over the body of his dead father, and his brother, Dayal Singh, was rebuking him for running away when they most needed him."[51] He recalls his love for Maya and its consequence, the landlord and the police coming with a warrant for his arrest and his escape and so on. These flashbacks of the events in *The Village* to *Across the Black Waters* and the involvement of the same characters of importance in both the novels effectively knit together the first and second volume of the trilogy.

Just as *The Village, Across the Black Waters* too, is free from the elements of propaganda. The author's criticism on the evils of war in this novel is not presented through any vehement, direct slogans against it but through a suggestive description of the agony and tension the soldiers suffer as they are fighting loyally and dying nobly for the Sarkar. However, the novel suffers from the defect of having no conventional plot. It is made up of a series of passing incidents. Apart from many trivial incidents, the novel has many tedious conversations. "Though this novel deals with trench warfare", as Saros Cowasjee wrote in *So Many Freedoms*, "the soldiers do not go into action until we are through one-third of the book. The earlier chapters are given to showing the Indian soldiers' reaction to Europe".[52] In the same book, Saros Cowasjee accuses Anand's striving for effect: "Anand seems to be striving for effect; and the cliches such as 'the sepoys sat in the bottomless pit of misery', 'the black hell of the trenches', and 'the God of Death was about with his hosts', strike no terror in us".[53]

50. *Ibid.*, p. 19.
51. *Ibid.*, pp. 9-10.
52. Cowasjee, Saros: *So Many Freedoms: A Study of the Major Fiction of Mulk Raj Anand*, New Delhi: OUP, 1977, p. 106.
53. *Ibid.*, p. 108.

On artistic ground though the novel may not be appreciated by all critics alike, it does certainly possess a special significance as a novel of protest and both Englishmen and the Indian readers find the novel interesting. It is a book of extreme interest to the Indian readers since it (in the words of Meenakshi Mukherji), "captures certain aspects of the Punjabi spirit with remarkable success. Their extrovert fellow feeling, their broad humour, their simplicity, their attachment to land rather than to country or nation, are all conveyed through the reactions and conversation of the sepoys who are all peasants at heart".[54] Another reason why it fascinates the Indian readers is the fact that it is perhaps the only major war novel under Indian writing in English. The best reason why it is interesting to the Englishmen can be found in Maurice Collin's review of it in *Time and Tide*:

> Every honest man will warm towards these poor fellows who came to England's help with such simple, open and brave hearts. They were rough, coarse, loving creatures; they spilt their blood far from home in another's quarrel. Too uncouth for us to understand, we treated them coldly when their hearts, were full of affection.[55]

The Sword and the Sickle

The original plan of Mulk Raj Anand was to give the third volume of the trilogy the title "All Men are Brothers", based on a slogan Lal Singh asks the peasants to repeat.[56] George Orwell who made one of his characters in his fable *Animal Farm* says, "All men are enemies. All animals are comrades", advised Anand to give a more direct and forceful title than the ironical one he intended to give and suggested to him the title *The Sword and the Sickle*, taking his cue from the lines of William Blake:

> The sword sang on the barren heath,
> The sickle in the fruitful field,
> The sword he sung a song of death,
> But could not make the sickle yield.
>
> (from Gnomic Verses–Merlin's Prophecy).

---

54. Mukherjee, Meenakshi: "Beyond *The Village*: An aspect of Mulk Raj Anand", In: *Critical Essays on Indian Writings in Englis*, edited by: S.K. Desai, G.S. Amur M.K. Naik, Madras: The Macmillan Co., of India Ltd., 1977, p. 239.
55. Collins, Maurice: "Review of *Across the Black Waters*" In: *Time and Tide*, Vol. 21 (30 Nov. 1940), p. 1167.
56. See: *The Times Literary Supplement* (3 Jan. 1942), p. 4.

Anand accepted Orwell's suggestion and the third volume of the trilogy was published in 1942 as *The Sword and the Sickle*. The title of the novel is quite apt as it depicts the struggle of the sickle-force of India, namely the peasants, not to yield to the song of death sung by the holders of sword, namely the landlords and their agents.

The Sword and the Sickle is the continuation of the story of Lal Singh. When World War I ended in 1918, Lal Singh, a prisoner of war in Germany is set free. He returns to India. As he proceeds to the Lahore cantonment by Bombay-Peshawar Mail, he is full of hope that he will be given a medal, promotion and some land for his meritorious service to the Sarkar. Hope envelops him with happiness. But after his meeting with Peacock Sahib at the cantonment, Lalu's hope and happiness evaporates as he is accused of seditious behaviour in the German prison camp and is demobilized without the promised gift of land. He returns to his village. There, he is shocked to know about the death of his mother two years ago and the auctioning of his home and land by the machiavellion machinations of the money-lender Chaman Lal. As he has nowhere to go, he accepts the hospitality of his friend Gughi, now a bus driver, and stays with him. One evening, when Lalu is alone in Gughi's apartment, the landlord's daughter Maya, now a widow, visits him and narrates how she has been waiting for him. She promises Lalu that she is prepared to go anywhere with him.

A few hours later, Gughi returns to his room with a Professor named Verma whom Lalu had noticed the previous day going with the *Jatha* of landless agitators led by his uncle, Harnam Singh. Prof. Verma tells Lalu that he has come to fetch him, to offer him the job of organizing *Kisan Sabhas*, on behalf of the Count of Rajgarh, Kanwar Rampal Singh, whom Lalu had heard of in Berlin.

Lalu agrees to go with the Professor to Rajgarh if he would be permitted to take with him his beloved, Maya. The Professor agrees and after a hectic elopement and the rush to catch the train, Professor Verma, Lalu and Maya are in Rajgarh. At Rajgarh, Lalu and Maya are given a room well equipped in English-Indian style in an old house, overlooking the river.

The revolutionary forces of Rajgarh are only a handful in number. They are gathered in the Count's *diwan*. The Count introduces his secretary Ram Din, hunter Nandu, Comrade Gupta and Pandit Ram Kumar Misra, Manager of the printing works of

Rajgarh estate to Lalu. Then they start discussing their plan to start the paper called 'Naya Hind' for propaganda among the peasants.

On the day of eclipse festival, the comrades arrange a function to make the peasants aware of their rights. Lalu winds up his speech by saying,"....to-day, the gates of a new life will begin to open to you. For, in far land called Roos, too, the peasants once suffered as you do, and then they set up their own Raj....And now the peasants and workers are ruling there, and all men there live like brothers....So give a shout: 'All men are brothers!' The peasants answered....".[57] The other comrades also give speeches. As the gathering grows in strength, there starts a disturbance, and a group of policemen appears on the scene and scatters the crowd.

One day, the Count and the comrades happen to meet a group of men standing by a corpse ready to be borne away by a boat into the Ganga. They come to know that the deceased is the son of a tenant of the Nawab of Nasirabad who was ordered to do forced labour. The deceased boy, "Chandra, had refused to get up from the bed, where he lay ill, to go and do forced labour, whereupon he had been fetched before the Manager of the estate, and flogged till he collapsed. But he had been dragged out and forced to cut wood. He had hardly climbed the tree when he had fallen and died".[58] Lalu, seeing the brutality, suggests that they carry the dead body in a procession to Allahabad, in order to open the eyes of the national leaders on the cruelty of landlordism. Ram Din, Nandu and Gupta support Lalu's suggestion. The Count agrees. He donates the price of several pitchers of 'Tari' to enliven the procession on its way to Allahabad.

Comrades Lal Singh, Ram Din, Nandu, Gupta and One-eyed Sukhua along with twenty evicted peasants including the father of the deceased, Bhupendra, begin their procession carrying the dead body of Chandra in a coffin to Allahabad. On their way, they successfully face the challenge of the Nasirabad Estate watchman Bhoori Singh and his two bull-dogs, George and Mary, and they proceed only to face the gun shots of Sheikh Hadayat Ullah, the Manager of the estate. One of the bullets hits Nandu's head and his history tragically ends. The panic-stricken peasants and comrades rush along the river side carrying the dead bodies of Chandra and Nandu, and they spot

57. Anand, Mulk Raj: *The Sword and the Sickle*, Delhi: Arnold-Heinemann, 1984, p. 133.

58. *Ibid.*, p. 169.

an unoccupied boat. They jump into it. As the body of Chandra starts to give out foul smell, they realise that they cannot carry the body upto Allahabad and so they offer it and Nandu's body to the Mother Ganga. Soon a police party chase them. They row the boat with all their strength and finally reach the "ancient Prayag, outside Allahabad, where the snow white Ganga meets her darker sister, the Jamuna".[59] They steer the boat to the banks of Prayag. Then comrades Lal Singh and Ram Din go to contact Kanwar Rampal Singh, Verma Sahib and the leaders of the Congress. They come to know from Ganga, the personal servant of the Count, that Mahatma Gandhi, the great Congress leader is in Allahabad to attend a feast given to untouchables at the house of Pandit Moti Lal Nehru, and that Kanwar Sahib and Verma Sahib have gone there. So they go to Anand Bhavan in search of them.

Though it was difficult, somehow the Count manages to arrange for Lalu an audience with the Mahatma so as to present the grievances of the peasants of Partapgarh district and to invite him to visit their district. In that solemn meeting Gandhi preaches non-violence and the merit of suffering to Lalu. The meeting ends with the Mahatma asking Lalu to invite the peasants on his behalf to come and join in the feast at night when their untouchable brothers will dine with the caste Hindus.

Lalu leads the peasants to the feast. After the feast, on the same night itself the peasants and the comrades return to Rajgarh by train.

Lalu collects all the evicted *kisans*, who have nowhere to go but the charity houses attached to the Rajgarh temple, and tells them of the plan to build a new house for the victims of the landlordism, which is also to serve as the headquarters of the *Kisan Sabha*. They are happy with the plan. The work is started earnestly. When the headquarters is about to be ready, a wire from Jawaharlal Nehru arrives informing that the next day he will be at Rajgarh. The rumour of the expected arrival of Panditji spreads from shop to shop and house to house. Apart from the evicted tenants at *Kisan Nagar*, even, the gentry of the estate and other 'big men' of the place are at the station to welcome the great young leader.

The Count plans Panditji's itinerary of tour to the villages. On hearing the rumour that Panditji is to speak at *Kisan Nagar*, peasants in big numbers rush to the location. Unfortunately, a telegram which

59. *Ibid.*, p. 192.

has summoned him to urgent business in Allahabad, prevents his programme at *Kisan Nagar*.

After this terrible disappointment, the Count and the comrades continue their revolutionary activities. One evening, the Sub-Inspector of the local police station meets the Count and hands over a paper. It is an order asking the Count and his comrades to leave Rajgarh and remain interned in *Kisan Nagar* where the police can have a watch on them. The Count, Ram Din and the student leader Razwi immediately go to see some high officials at Rae Bareilly to get the Court of Wards' Order cancelled. But they cannot get any help from the officials, and instead they are arrested. When Lalu comes to know this, he rushes to meet the Count in the jail at Rae Bareilly. Meanwhile the news of the arrest of the Count and others spreads far and wide and thousands of *Kisans* begin to move towards Rae Bareilly to protest against the arrest. When Lalu reaches Rae Bareilly, he finds it under curfew. He sees police pickets at every corner of the streets. Soon Lalu gets the information that multitudes of peasants have been gathering beyond the river, outside Rae Bareilly as police have not allowed them to enter the town. So he struggles through the curfew bound streets of Rae Bareilly to reach the spot. After escaping through the streets of the town, he rushes through a cornfield and then crawls like a giant snake through the last stems on the field and jumps across the road. He has been panting. As he raises his head, the peasants notice him and shout, 'Comrade Lal Singh! Comrade Lal Singh!' Hearing the noise made by the peasants, the soldiers shout, 'Silence....' And then a volley of shots rings out. The peasants shrieking with pain and terror run towards Lalu. Lalu realises that in order to stop the soldiers from further shooting, the only way is to show himself up and surrender. So he gets out of the cornfield and surrenders to the soldiers.

Lal Singh and the peasants who have been arrested, are crowded into the barrack cells. One day, after the evening roll call, one of the assistant jailers informs Lalu that a son is born to Musamat Maya Devi. Lalu eagerly waits in that mosquito filled, unhygienic prison cell for the day to break open so that he can send "a message to Maya to ask her how their new-born son was getting on, though from her answer to his previous inquiries during her pregnancy, he knew what she would say: Sardar Lal Singh, your child is alive and kicking!"[60]

---

60. *Ibid.*, p. 386.

In *The Sword and the Sickle* the novelist uses the novel form to express his views on political matters. Hence, for proper understanding of this outright political novel, it is necessary to know the National movements of the 1930s. In the 30s there was an ideological clash between Mahatma Gandhi and Pandit Nehru, the most prominent leaders of Indian National Congress and freedom movement. If Gandhi could be called the leader of the right wing faction of the Indian National Congress, Nehru could be identified as the leader of its left wing faction. The Indian National Congress was mainly dominated by the middle class of the Indian society who had no sympathy for the poor peasants and the proletariate. Nehru wanted the Congress to become the true representative of the masses of India by ensuring the active participation of the basic organizations of workers, peasants, trade unions and *Kisan Sabhas* to the Congress. He criticised the then dominant tendency to subordinate completely the social struggle to the political struggle, or, much worse to postpone the social struggle to a future period in order to focus attention on national unity and national struggle. The reason usually offered was that the national issue must be settled first. But there could be no honest struggle which did not incorporate the social struggle of the masses.[61] In December 1933, in the speech made at the All India Trade Union Congress, Pandit Nehru assured the workers that, if they participated wholeheartely in the national struggle as well as in their own social struggle, they would help bring about not only "political freedom in India but social freedom also".[62] In his letter of 13 August 1934 to Gandhi, Nehru spoke with deep disgust on the triumph of opportunism in the Congress and put part of the blame on the Working Committee which had "deliberately encouraged vagueness in the definition of our ideals and objectives".[63] He was angry with the Working Committee particularly because it had passed a resolution on 18 June 1934, while he was in jail, indirectly condemning socialism and socialists for practising "the necessity of class war".

It is interesting to note that several pages of the *Autobiography*, written during 1934-35 and published in 1936, were an open challenge to Gandhian ideology though they were presented in a gentle,

61. Nehru, Jawaharlal: *Recent Essays and Writings*: Allahabad: 1934, p. 4-17.

62. *Ibid.*, pp. 131-32.

63. Nehru, Jawaharlal: *Bunch of Old Letters*, Bombay, 1958, p. 115.

amicable, even reverential tone. There could be no doubt that they were intended to give Indian nationalism a new ideological direction.

Thus it seemed by the middle of 1936 that Nehru was formulating a left political alternative to the Gandhian leadership – an alternative that would challenge the latter in all basic aspects: programme and ideology, social nature of the movement and of its leadership, and the strategy of its struggle. He was moreover beginning to emerge as the leader of a broad socialist bloc, which was as yet loose and even incoherent, but which was getting formed around his personality. Nor did Nehru limit his new orientation to his diary or debates in the Working Committee. He wrote extensively for journals and newspapers, both in English and Hindi and toured every part of the country spreading his message and attracting students and youth to himself.[64]

In this ideological conflict between Gandhi and Nehru, Mulk Raj Anand is clearly with Nehru, whom he reverentially calls 'Panditji' and the novel, *The Sword and the Sickle* is an open propaganda in support of Nehru's approach to the predicament the nation faced in the final one and a half decades of British Imperialism in India. A comparison of Nehru's ideas and views scattered in his writings with Mulk Raj Anand's *Apology for Heroism (A brief Autobiography of Ideas)*, shows their similarity of approach to many national problems. In this connection, the dedicatory words of Anand's *Apology for Heroism* is significant: "For J.L.N. with whom I share many ideas".[65]

Nehru's desire to affiliate the *Kisan Sabhas* to the Congress movement in contrast to Gandhi's relative lack of concern for the hardships of the evicted peasants is dramatically illustrated in the novel. At the end of Lalu's audience with Gandhi, the Mahatma invites the peasants to come and dine at the feast hosted by Motilal Nehru, intended to bring together the untouchables and the caste Hindus. In his short speech after a prayer at the party, Gandhi does not utter a word to console the evicted, miserable farmers. Lalu is in a state of panic as the Mahatma has not spoken a word about the peasants:

> 'He came as an autumn cloud, rained a few blessings and went away!' Lalu said, unable to repress his dismay.

64. Chandra, Bipan: *Nationalism and Colonialism in Modern India*, New Delhi: Orient Longman Ltd., 1979, pp. 186-87.

65. Anand, Mulk Raj: *Apology for Heroism*, Delhi: Arnold-Heinemann, 1975, p. 1 (Dedication).

'But we have the ardour of spring in store for you there', said the Count. 'Look! Jawaharlal, there, is going to speak to the peasants....'.

Lalu veered round and saw the solemn young son of the host, who was known to be a 'revolutionary', standing on the second step and speaking:

'Brothers, go on eating!'

There was laughter at this interruption. 'All I want to say is that we have a number of oppressed peasants from Pratapgarh district here, who have come to be our guests... they have come to invite us to their village..... Well, I want to assure them that I shall come to see them in their own homes in a few days.'

'*Bolo* Pandit Jawaharlal *Ki Jai*!' Ram Din burst out at this.[66]

The peasants under the leadership of Lalu request both Jawaharlal Nehru and Mahatma Gandhi to visit their villages. Nehru as quoted above accepts the invitation, but Gandhi's plan to postpone the social struggle in favour of National struggle prevents him from accepting the invitation. So he tells Lalu, "I have a very full programme."[67] As Alastair Niven rightly comments on this novel in his book *The Yoke of Pity*, "Gandhi is portrayed as the supreme egoist, smug in his own self-righteousness and bound in by the narrowest Hindu Orthodoxy. As Lalu is received into the 'sacred' presence, Gandhi is dictating an article for the poor of India on the sanctity of the cow."[68] He preaches to Lalu, something totally rejected by Anand in all his novels, that suffering is the mark of human tribe, an eternal law, an indispensable condition of our being. According to Gandhi, progress has to be measured by the amount of suffering endured by each man. He defines non-violence as the conscious acceptance of suffering. The Gandhi as presented in the novel is seen through the eyes of revolutionaries who have accused him of compromising with the Imperialists. Anand deliberately exposes through the 'Gandhi-scene' in the novel, the hypocrisy, subterfuges, "the bluff of moral grandeur

66. Anand, Mulk Raj: *The Sword and the Sickle*, Delhi, Arnold-Heinemann, 1984, pp. 208-9.
67. *Ibid.*, p. 204.
68. Neven, Alastair: *The Yoke of Pity (A Study in the Fictional Writings of Mulk Raj Anand)*, New Delhi: Arnold-Heinemann, 1978, p. 78.

and the egoistical concern for the self which he sees residing at the core of the ethos of many Gandhians".[69]

As the Count and other revolutionaries have not got support from Gandhi for the cause of the evicted peasants, they become disappointed and begin to expose their annoyance with him:

> 'The spinning-wheel! The spinning-wheel!', the Count parodied the Mahatma's voice with indifferent skill, 'I say unto you! ....The spinning-wheel is the cure of all our ills in this destructive machine age....As if the *Charkha*, itself were not a machine!'[70]

After this abortive expedition to Allahabad, as the comrades and peasants travel by train back to Rajgarh along with the Count, they join him in the criticism of Gandhi. They especially criticise Gandhi's rejection of the machine, his propaganda for *charkha* and condemnation of 'destructive machine age', which sounds similar to Lalu's father Nihal Singh's preference of bullock-cart over train. The sharpest attack comes from Professor Verma and Lalu:

> Professor Verma added: 'The Mahatma knows that the spinning wheel is a good slogan, though he knows that all the yarn necessary for the needs of the country cannot be provided by hand spinning. So he shuts a corner of his left-eye behind his glasses and winks at the factory-wallahs to go ahead with their plans. All that is necessary to cover up the double-dealing is a mystical phrase!...So to speak his right hand, the giver of blessing does not see what his left hand, with the bags of gold, is doing!'
>
> 'The man is talking religion when we want food!' shouted Lalu, thrusting another dagger into the remoteness of the Mahatma which he had not been able to penetrate during his interview. And then he set about to chop up the carcase like a butcher: 'His right hand is much longer than his left, his eyes dip inwards and are blind to what he doesn't want to see.'[71]

Though the novel has nothing much to say in praise of Gandhi,

69. *Ibid.*, p. 79.

70. Anand, Mulk Raj: *The Sword and the Sickle*, Delhi: Arnold-Heinemann, 1984, p. 210.

71. *Ibid.*, p. 212.

the left wing leader of the Congress movements Jawaharlal Nehru is presented as an admirable personality. The novelist calls him 'the great young leader'. The characters in the novel are made to talk of him in unrestrained eulogy:

> 'Panditji is a friend of the Prince of Wales', said Seth Wall Chand, the cloth merchant. 'I hear they were at the same college and played golf together'.
>
> 'Yes, it is a great sacrifice, indeed, for him to give up all his fine clothes and to wear home-spuns', said Mr. Sastri, the post-master.[72]

The novel takes care to mention that Panditji has travelled in 'a third-class compartment'. Nehru's real concern for and interest in the affairs of the peasants, unlike the hypocritical concerns of many nationalists, is excellently exposed in the scene describing the arrival of Nehru at Rajgarh station:

> Panditji's head showed up the window of a third-class compartment, a clear cut shy smiling image of ivory.
>
> '*Bolo* Pandit Jawaharlal *ki jai!*' Ram Din the slogan shouter yelled.
>
> And the evicted tenants, the gentry, the officials, even the other passengers travelling with Jawaharlal, echoed the call.... And, in the flash of a moment, all the populace on the platform ran towards the compartment in which the leader had been sighted, the gentry struggling to get ahead of the rabble, and bringing out garlands of marigold and white motia from wet towels to put round Panditji's neck, so that even stalwarts like Lalu were left behind...Panditji seemed to have noticed the cross-currents at a glance.
>
> And he cut through the stampede of the exalted, up to Lal Singh and the peasants, and had himself garlanded by them first.[73]

The novel stresses the need for a revolution against the growing polarisation of classes in agrarian areas and criticises the national leaders' negligence of responsibility in coming to the aid of the agrarian proletariat. The urgency of the revolution is the 'money

72. *Ibid.*, p. 245.
73. *Ibid.*, pp. 246-47.

famine' caused by the war described in *Across the Black Waters*. Though the war did not take place in India, the hero finds out on his return from the prison camp in Germany that it had nevertheless wrought havoc in India. The opening chapters of the novel present the post-war effect on the villages. Apart from war, the Gorgon Medussa of drought and famine kills the people in thousands. Those who have money, mainly, the money-lenders and landlords rejoice at the swelling situation as it is a boon for them to expand their territory. The labourers become street beggars; the small land holders lose their land to the landlords and money-lenders and end up as tenants, and many tenants are forced to become bounded labourers. Harnam Singh, a typical victim of war, cries out in fury and agony:

> They (the Sarkar) took away crores of rupees as free gifts and loans from the country to support their war and foodstuffs to help to stem the privations of the *Memnies* in *Vilayat*....They took our grain, our timber, our tea, why, even the skins of our buffaloes and the oil from the poor man's saucer lamp! And there are some people in the villages around here to-day who hide their nakedness in the clothes discarded by those who have died of plague while their children go naked![74]

The unbearable exploitation of the Sarkar and the cunning of landlords transform Harnam Singh, the patient sufferer in *The Village* into a fiery orator and leader of landless agitators in *The Sword and the Sickle*. His criticism of Imperial exploitation and fiendish landlordism is touching and picturesque:

> Oh, Hindustan! Hindustan! This country is like a lean bullock that has been reduced to the bone by the *Angrezi* lion, son. Each day the lion awoke and gnawed a chunk of flesh off the bullock's body and left it weaker but still standing. And then, the other beasts of the jungle came, and set to – the local jackals and the forces took their toll!.....There had been bad times before in this country, but surely no time so bad as the present. It is one of those ages during which all joy and hope seems to have fled and in their place remains only a pain, a disease, which you can't even diagnose...[75]

74. *Ibid*., p. 63.

75. *Ibid*., p. 64.

Thus, the war and the 'money-famine' that followed make many people revolutionaries. But they are like boats without rudder. They eagerly wait for the Mahatma to come to their aid, as "he would do in a day or two what will take us years. He could form a *Kisan Sabha* in no time, because so many thousands of people would come to take a 'darshan' of him. And then he has a genius for joining issue with authority."[76] But the Mahatma refuses to support their dream for revolution and he finds no time to visit the evicted peasants. The nationalists' disinterestedness towards these revolutionaries and a lack of efficient and widespread organization make the peasant revolt vulnerable to the Imperial force of police and the Count and his comrades end up in jail.

Though the main social concerns expressed in the novel are on war and its devastating effect, the cruelty of landlordism, the hypocritical attitude of our national leaders to the peasant revolt and the Gandhian attitude against the introduction of even useful machines, yet the novelist has also a significant criticism to make on the behaviour of peasants: one such criticism is the peasants' strict adherence to the belief in untouchability. In the feast organised by Motilal Nehru at Anand Bhavan and inaugurated by Mahatma Gandhi to bring together caste Hindus and untouchables with the intention of educating the masses on the 'assness' of untouchability, some poorest of the poor peasants from Pratapgarh like Bhupendra and Raghu, who have not eaten a tasty meal for years, instead of enjoying the platable meal freely provided, get up on seeing that they are actually dining with untouchables:

> ....not even the privations of the march, through which they had eaten only roasted gram, would make Bhupendra and Raghu touch the food, while others gobbled handfuls of the delicious rice mixed with gravies of different dishes, spiced with the tastiest condiments.[77]

Anand is obviously angry with the poor peasants who are brain-washed to such an orthodoxy that not even the example of rich and powerful persons partaking in the feast or the power and magnetism of Gandhiji can do anything to change their attitude, leaving them incorrigible, pathetic buffoons of their own foolish belief. Through

76. *Ibid.*, p. 212.
77. *Ibid.*, p. 209.

this incident, Anand laughs at the ridiculous caste consciousness of thousands of undernourished wretched people of our country.

When Lalu returns to Nandpur, after his captivity in Germany, the villagers are already agitating against landlordism. For Lalu, Nandpur is an ideal place to organize the peasant revolt. But Anand shifts the locale of the novel to Rajgarh in the United Provinces of Agra and Oudh for the sheer exigencies of the plot he planned. Anand wants to present in the novel the *Kisan Sabha* movement and the peasant revolt with historical realism. Since, they and Pandit Nehru's visit to the evicted farmers took place not in the Punjab but in the United Provinces of Agra and Oudh, Anand was compelled to shift the locale. It may be noted that every major incident in the novel starting from the peasants' march to Allahabad is based on historical facts as presented in Jawaharlal Nehru's *An Autobiography*.

Apart from the historical necessity, there is also another important reason which has urged the author to shift the scene of the novel from the Punjab. If the hero were to stay on in his native village, Nandpur, after his elopement with the landlord's daughter, he would have been either killed or imprisoned and the course of the novel ought to have taken a direction different from the author's plan of presenting the hero as leading the peasant revolt. So we can conclude that to give credibility to the peasant revolt as well as to the love theme, Anand shifted the scene from the Punjab to Uttar Pradesh.

However, the novelist's presentation of the hero as a lover as well as a political agitator puts the character to test. Lalu is made to oscillate from his role as a political agitator to a lover and again back to the political agitator, leaving him an interesting figure in both the roles. His revolutionary role often reminds him, his mistake of eloping with Maya and in his extreme moments, he is sorry that his role as an agitator is a hindrance to his happiness. But he has no other go. He is a paid agitator, bound to accommodate himself, sacrificing his own individuality, to the fantastic Count's comic aspirations. His dependence on the Count, no doubt, has pernicious effect on his strong appetite for existentialism, so eloquently displayed in the earlier volumes of the trilogy. Meenakshi Mukherjee who gave the highest praise among the Indo-Anglian novelists to Mulk Raj Anand for his achievement in the first two volumes of the trilogy has nothing to say in praise of the third volume. Her views on *The Sword and the Sickle* are generally shared by most critics:

> This is the longest volume of the three, nearly as long as the other two put together and the total effect is diffused. The canvas is large, the characters numerous, some of the characters and incidents touch upon historical reality, a strand of love and sex hitherto absent is woven unsuccessfully into the narrative, and the authenticity of the earlier volumes is dissipated beyond recall. Lalu is no longer an evolving individual, but becomes merely a mechanism for bringing together fresh situations and new characters. After having lost grip of the lifeline which held the first two volumes together, Anand has tried to make up for the loss by mere invention and accretion.....As long as Lalu was in his own element, whether in the village or in his battalion, the novels rang true; but from the moment Rampal Singh and his entourage are introduced, the story develops numerous cracks in its structure.[78]

"The Count", as the author tells us, "certainly liked to hear his own voice and his talks with his friends, had often been mere exhibitions of his own cleverness."[79] His frequent repetition of the proverb, 'The scarcity of men made my father a judge' (which the Count repeats seven times in the novel) and his repetition of some Punjabi proverbs produced by Uncle Kirpu in the earlier volumes of the trilogy reveal the unconvincing role the Count plays and also the weakness of the novel. The novel has many loose threads. The Sub-Inspector Thanedar's visit to the Count's place with the intention of arresting Lalu under a warrant from the Punjab police for eloping with the landlord's daughter, the story of what had happened to Lalu's friends at Nandpur and the arrest of the Count and others are simply introduced and afterwards totally ignored without any consequence. Towards the end of the novel the author seems to realise that he had not sufficiently cemented together the third volume with the first and second volumes of the trilogy and so he introduces the hero's reminiscences of *Across the Black Waters* and *The Village* days as a saving grace. In the final chapters, the novel

---

78. Mukherjee, Meenakshi: "Beyond *The Village*: An aspect of Mulk Raj Anand", In: *Critical Essays on Indian Writings in English*, edited by: M.K. Naik, S.K. Desai, G.S. Amur, Madras: Macmillan Co. Ltd., 1977, pp. 241-42.

79. Anand, Mulk Raj, *The Sword and the Sickle*, Delhi: Arnold-Heinemann, 1984, p. 357.

becomes a series of speeches and orations on the evils of landlordism, British Imperialism, Communism, Gandhism etc. The digressions in the novel are uncontrolled and the author appears as if he is unable to shut the mouth of some of his characters like that of the comrade Sarshar, the quarrelsome and toddy-thirsty one-eyed Sukhua and the snake devotee Raghu who preaches on Vasuki, Luxmi, Devi, Shiva and so on.

Though Anand does not always maintain in *The Sword and the Sickle*, the great artistic quality he has displayed in the first two volumes of the trilogy, the hero's unifying role and the author's dramatic exposition of "homo homini lupus est" (man is a wolf to man), through the experiences of the hero first in his native village in Punjab, and later in France and finally in Uttar Pradesh give to the three volumes the quality of a triumphant trilogy.

V

THE BIG HEART AND *DEATH OF A HERO*

Both *The Big Heart* and *Death of a Hero* have the same track and follow the same direction. They are works of exuberant imagination exemplifying the excellence of Humanism. The Hero of *The Big Heart*, Ananta, and the protagonist of *Death of a Hero*, Maqbool Sherwani are Christ-like figures who suffer greatly for their noble causes and ultimately sacrifice their lives in order to redeem their society from falling into the abyss of ignorance and social evils. Their struggle for the spread of humanism does not end with their death. In fact, they become more powerful in their mission after their death and so their message, after their death, spreads like a shaft of light across the land.

The Big Heart

The Big Heart (1945), has been acclaimed as a great novel by Margaret Berry, K.N. Sinha and M.K. Naik in their respective books on Anand. It deals with a small community of coppersmiths of Amritsar, who suddenly come face to face with machine civilization. Seth Gokul Chand, the *chandri* of utensil sellers' community, belonging to *Kasera* brotherhood establishes a factory in partnership with Lala Murli Dhar, the headman of the "thathiar" coppersmith brotherhood. Lala Murli Dhar's ambition to elevate his family of the *thathiar* caste to the higher sub-caste of *Kaseras*, impels him to ignore the welfare of his own community. Consequently most of the *thathiar* youths are not absorbed by the new factory. As the factory begins to produce most of the essential items required by the villagers, the *thathiars* fail to get piece-work for making utensils. They are thrown out of their hereditary profession and are rendered jobless. Starvation stares them in the face. The machine deprives them of their daily bread. Into this community Ananta, the coppersmith, the man with the big heart like Ratan in *Coolie*, steps in. He has been to Bombay and Ahmedabad and has participated in the Gandhian freedom struggle in those places before his return to his native place, the Billimaran Lane of Amritsar. He brings with him Janki, a young widow, whom he loves and who is now slowly dying of tuberculosis. He has little respect for tradition. He has lived with Janki in Bombay and she is here with him in spite of all the things that people say against them. In Amritsar, Ananta resumes his hereditary trade, but like most people of his *thathiar* brotherhood, he has difficulty in making a living. He has had glimpses of labour movements and trade unionist activities in Bombay and Ahmedabad. As he too is refused a job in the factory of Gokul Chand, he readily identifies himself with his dispossessed brothers, and he makes it his sole aim in life to help them out of their predicament. Ananta knows that revolution will be a far cry unless coppersmiths learn to unite. So he pleads for organized action and tries to bring together all the jobless coppersmiths into a union, so that they can in a fruitful manner bargain for their rights from the profiteers. In this endeavour he wins the support of a poet and scholar named Puran Singh Bhagat. But his efforts are thrown into disarray by the opposition he faces from men like Professor Mejid, Satyapal, an angry young student leader who preaches violent methods for the emancipation of the coppersmiths, Mahasha Hans Raj, an anti-machine *Arya Samajist* and also from his own men who are emotionally and mentally gripped by the fear of opposing the *Karma* and also skeptical of his motives. Many of his own friends fail to accept his ideas as his living openly with the young widow, Janki, is not acceptable to them. His open liaison with her deprives him of the moral hold expected of a leader in a tradition-bound society.

Though Ananta faces many hardships due to the introduction of the machine, he does not become blind to facts. He recognizes the reined horse-power of the machine as a must for modernization and progress. So he makes a lovely comparison between machines and dowry while talking to Janki: "Like the fashionable *Vilayati* bride we have accepted, we ought to accept the dowry of machines she has brought, and make use of them, provided we keep our hearts and become the masters."[1] He also agrees with the poet Puran Singh Bhagat that if we have the "controlling switch" of the machine in our hand, we can make the machine a slave rather than our master.[2]

In the afternoon of that single day in the life of Ananta

1. Anand, Mulk Raj: *The Big Heart*, New Delhi: Arnold-Heinemann, New Revised Edition, 1980, p. 40.
2. *Ibid*., p. 90.

described in the novel, Lala Murli Dhar's grandson Nikha's marriage takes place. The Lala's desire to assimilate his family with the superior caste of *kaseras* urges him to insist that Gokul Chand and other prominent *kaseras* should visit his home and honour his grandson's marriage. At the betrothal ceremony he offers his guests only soda water so that the *kaseras* may not be embarrassed in having to drink sherbat or whay made in the house of his *thathiar* brethren, whose lower caste status is looked down upon by the various exalted Hindu brotherhoods. Lala Murli Dhar's hope that soon his family will be taken into the *kasera* class, makes him proud and turns him arrogant towards his old community of coppersmiths and he invites only a few among them for the ceremony. So his community boycotts this ceremony as a protest and at the critical moment, as a symbol of apology, the old man has to put his turban at the feet of the elders of the bride to save the ceremony.

In the evening, the hot blooded *thathiar* youth, Ralia, whose hatred for the machine has been mainly due to the fact that he does not get employment in the factory, after hearing the fiery speeches inciting people to violence, made by the student leader Satyapal and Professor Mejid in front of the factory gate, breaks open the factory and starts hammering and destroying the machines, shouting abuses at them, with uncontrollable madness and fury. The police Sub-Inspector comes upon the scene a bit too late. When all others are helplessly watching the wanton destruction Ralia is carrying on, Ananta takes courage and tries to appeal to his sense. In the struggle that follows, Ralia strikes Ananta's head against a broken machine and kills him. Thus, in the very process of helping his brethren, Ananta, the defender of machines, is crushed between the machine and the oppressed craftsman. The Poet, Puran Singh Bhagat, appears on the tragic scene and lectures to Janki on the death of the old order and the birth of the new for which Ananta has lived and died. The poet extracts a moral from the catastrophic end of Ananta: "All stories end in death, Janki", the poet said, "but, childing, even if one is given a short life it becomes shorter if it is guarded selfishly. On the other hand, think of the beauty, the richness and the joy of living with others, of helping others...."[3]

In a letter to Saros Cowasjee, dated Nov. 1971, Mulk Raj Anand stated the purpose of writing this novel :

3. *Ibid.*, p. 229.

> I wrote this novel at the end of World War II in London when the machines of Western Civilization had nearly destroyed the world. I was convinced that if India also went the same way, after freedom, without controlling the machine, but allowed it to become instrument of exploitation, then we would also produce the same horrors.....I was thinking of Gandhi's natural rejection of machine. I wanted to show that though we can't reject the machine altogether, we have to control it, as a driver controls a railway engine.[4]

The letter clearly reflects Anand's attitude to the machine: He wants India to be industrialised but not at the expense of traditional pieties. The machine in Anand's fiction is a double-edged sword. Wide and rapid industrialization is one side of the sword that can affect society adversely and cut the throat of village artisans through unemployment and exploitation. At the same time total rejection of the machine is the other side of the sword that can jeopardise the growth and necessary modernisation of the nation.

Anand, according to the above mentioned letter, had seen in the English midlands the smoking towns when he had gone to Derbyshire to meet D.H. Lawrence once. He had experienced the misery, the tortures and the gray squalor of the lives of the coal miners in contrast to the vast estates of the Sitwells, when he was Osbert Sitwell's guest for a weekend. He recalled Rimbaud's disgust at the sordidness of the big heaps of towns built on machine shops. He had known the transformation of Amritsar, 'the ocean of nectar', the holy city of the Sikhs, into sweet shops in almost every lane. The emancipated hillmen coming from the beautiful Kangra valley and the widows earning a pittance on the foetid drains of narrow alleys from little businessmen seemed to him to be pictures of despair. The further complication of Capital investment churning their lives up portended a disaster worse than any invasion of the walled city by northern hordes.[5] The influx of cheap British and non-British machine-made goods into India and the transportational advancement which made it possible for these goods to reach the interior villages forced thousands of village artisans to unemployment. The newly started factories did not care to absorb the village artisans and so they

4. Anand, Mulk Raj: *Author to Critic: Letters of Mulk Raj Anand to Saros Cowasjee*, ed. Saros Cowasjee, Calcutta: Writers Workshop, 1973, p. 121 (letter dated, Nov. 1971).

5. *Ibid.*, pp. 121-22.

found no source of survival. Anand, though he wanted India to be industrialized, did not want modern industries to rob the meagre resources of village artisans like coppersmith, blacksmith, weaver, tanner etc. He wanted the modern industries to give alternate employment to the coppersmiths and other village artisans so that the introduction of the machine will not frighten them like a copper-head and drag them to poverty and misery. In short, *The Big Heart* is a trumpet of a prophecy: if the industrial policy-makers of the nation introduce machine without sound considerations, the blessings of the machine will turn into curses, the cures expected from it will fail to cure and the future of the nation will be dismal indeed.

The setting of the novel — Billimaran or the Cat-Killer's Lane — exposes the conflict between the East and the West, tradition and modernity, industrialization and the conventional way of life:

> It must be remembered, however that Billimaran is not a blind alley. Apart from the usual mouth, which even a 'cul-de-sac' keeps open, it has another which makes it really like a two-headed snake. With one head, it looks towards the ancient market, where the beautiful copper, brass, silver and bronze utensils made in the lane are sold by dealers called *Kaseras*, hence called the Bazar Kaserian. With the other it wriggles out towards the new Iron-mongers' Bazar, where screws and bolts and nails and locks are sold and which merges into the Book-seller's mart, the cigarette shops and the Post Office replete with the spirit of modern times.[6]

The iron-mongers' Bazar represents the machine, and thus modernity, while the Bazar Kaserian typifies tradition. The items available in the Bazar Kaserian — copper, brass, silver and bronze utensils – are made by village artisans. They are mainly meant for use in kitchen and have a homely touch. But the items sold in Iron-mongers' Bazar are full of sophistication. They – 'screws and bolts and nails and locks' – evoke a frightening picture of mechanisation. They are tools symbolic of the capitalists' oppression, suppression, imprisonment and exploitation of the proletariate. Though the 'screws and bolts and nails and locks' are in themselves frightening, yet if they are properly used with blocks of materials, they can

6. Anand, Mulk Raj: *The Big Heart*, New Delhi: Arnold-Heinemann, New Revised Edition, 1980, pp. 16-17.

produce attractive structures. Anand, while appreciating the loveliness and simplicity of tradition, does not ignore the merit of modernity, its potentiality to provide adequate structures to society. Society should move the world and also should move with the world. To move the world, good aspects of tradition are important; to move with the world, acceptance of modernity is indispensable. Though the author and his spokesmen Ananta and the poet, Puran Singh Bhagat, know the debilitating aspects of industrialism and the advantages of the old way of life, they realise that the old order is obsolete in a country on the verge of a gigantic social, economic and political change. The machine, however it may oppress the workers, is a necessity for the progress and prosperity of the nation. Perhaps, the solution to the exploitation of workers by the factory owners can be found in having well organized trade unions, which would fight for the welfare of the labour force. The workers should unite and form unions and with their collective strength, they must fight for their cause. As the hero of the novel, Ananta, tells his friends :

> A living, heart-to-heart appropriation of '*Vilayati* fashions' is what is wanted. The coming of the machine in England, brothers, wrought as much havoc there, a hundred years ago, as it is doing in Hindustan. The bones of millions were ground to dust by machines. Women and children were set to work for a few coppers, so Puran Singh Bhagat tells me – *Angrezi* woman and children, brothers. And there was such hunger as we see in our Hindustan today. The men of property were deaf to the cry of the victims of poverty..... But the working men of *Vilayat* themselves took their destiny in their own hands and banded themselves into the new brotherhood of unions. At first they were persecuted and penalized by the employers, and the Sarkar, which was behind the employers. The men stuck together, and struggled and struggled, until today there are few working men and women in factories who are not members of the union. They bargain together for higher wages, shorter hours, against bad conditions, for holidays with pay, and defend their rights by strike action....[7]

Just as Ananta wants the victims of industrialization in *The Big Heart*, Anand wants the Indian proletariate, to learn lessons from

7. *Ibid.*, p. 200.

their counterpart in England, lessons which are sure to yield comfort and happiness.

Anand's attitude to the machine is conveyed in the refrain of Ananta's song:

> This is the machine age, sons,
> This is the machine age,
> We are the men who will master it....[8]

Anand considers the machine as an indispensable vehicle for socio-economic transformation and is suspicious of people who oppose it simply because it has come from the West. The wiser thing to do would be to accept it and master it and enjoy its benefits. Ananta, the hero of the novel, is a crusador for the utilization of the machine for the general well-being of man. He has no doubt in the capacity of his fellowmen to master the machine and thereby revolutionize the social life. He says:

> When the *thathiars* begin to handle the machine, we shall soon show them!..... We need not to become slaves to the profiteers or the machine. We are men. We will make a Revolution.[9]

He repeats the idea more than once:

> I tell you the machine is in our midst already, there! And we have got to decide to go and work it rather than sulk....[10]

Ananta's message to his brotherhood to have a right approach to the machine is not pleasing to the reactionaries. If one machine can do the work of fifty ordinary men, rejecting it is a sign of madness. If Japan and Germany were to have only people of the mental disposition of Ralia and the *Arya Samajist* Mahasha Hans Raj, could they become economic super-powers? The martyrdom of Ananta, the machineman, for the cause of the machine and modernization comes as an eye-opener to his community to realise the immense utility of the machine in ending their poverty.

Industrialization played almost a revolutionary role in the life of Indian people. It made the Indian economy more unified, cohesive and organic. It raised the tone of the economic life in India. Further, it gave birth to modern cities which became the centres of modern

8. *Ibid.*, p. 19.
9. *Ibid.*, p. 85.
10. *Ibid.*, p. 89.

culture and increasing democratic social life and from which all progressive movements, social, political, and cultural, emanated. The establishment of modern industries, in addition, generated two important classes of the contemporary society, the bourgeoise and the proletariat. By the time Anand wrote *The Big Heart* there were more than 9,000 factories in India giving employment to about 17,00,000 workmen.[11] No one can deny their role in national formation and their voice in the formulation of policies for the emerging nation of the Indian Republic.

The social critic in Mulk Raj Anand is seen in his spokesman Poet Puran Singh Bhagat, with something positive which can make our social life a source of happiness. The poet wants people to practise the true religion which would re-assert "man's dignity, reverence for his name and a pure love for man in all his strength and weakness, a limitless compassion for man, an unbounded love especially for the poor and the down trodden so that those who have been left to rot on the dusty roads can be raised from their dreaded position and given the 'izzat' which is theirs by the miracle of their birth in this world".[12] He wants the Indian society to have confidence in the fact that by abandoning dead habits and evil customs and shams, "there can emerge a new kind of brotherhood, a new sense of devotion like the BHAKTI which our saint, Kabir preached and practised".[13] He insists on the need for drastic social change as he knows that "in this country only an overturning of the old social order will bring the healing balm of love among men, only a revolution will complete the reformation and the renaissance that is going on among us and produce the new community with a new morality in which, and through which, men can live creatively ...."[14]

By living in accordance with the above-quoted views of Poet Puran Singh Bhagat, every person can possess a big heart like the hero of the novel, Ananta, possessed. The greatness of poet Puran Singh Bhagat lies in the fact that his entire life is an unceasing plea for a big heart.

---

11. Desai, A.R.: *Social Background of Indian Nationalism*, Bombay, Popular Prakashan, 1984, p. 112.
12. Anand, Mulk Raj: *The Big Heart*, New Delhi: Arnold-Heinemann, New Revised Edition, 1980, p. 149.
13. *Ibid.*, p. 157.
14. *Ibid.*, p. 150.

Though the central theme of *The Big Heart* is the need for selective industrialization which will not prove disadvantageous to any section of society, the author also devotes some space in the novel to the evil of caste-system. The novelist efficiently knits together the theme of casteism with the main theme of the novel. The criticism of casteism in *The Big Heart* is mainly concerned with its evil effect on human relationship. While *Untouchable* and *The Road*, draw our attention on the relations between the untouchables and the high castes, *The Big Heart* points up the tensions within the high castes themselves whose sense of caste superiority spoils their interpersonal relations on the basis of equality. As the influence of mach. :- products has penetrated into Indian life (as stated in the beginning of this chapter), Lala Murli Dhar, the headman of the *thathiar* coppersmith brotherhood and *kasera* Gokul Chand, the *chandri* of utensil sellers' community of Amritsar undertake a joint venture, The relations between these managing partners, expected to be cordial on account of pecuniary considerations, is strained because of caste feeling. *Kaseras* and *thathiars* are sub-castes of the *Kshatriya* community – the second highest in the hierarchy of castes. The orthodox *Kaseras* ossified by megalomania look down upon the "lower orders" by the belief: "To Ram was given an arrow, to Sita a bow, and from them the truly noble order of *Kshatriya Kaseras* is descended!"[15], a belief which makes them think that their 'purity' would be defiled by coming into contact with the sub-castes. To assert their superiority they refer to the *thathiars* with the epithet 'low'. The spiritual philistinism and insularity of caste-consciousness is reflected in every contact the *Kaseras* have, under unavoidable circumstances, with the *thathiars*. Soon the headman of the *Kaseras*, Gokul Chand, realises the risk of losing his own caste in opening "a new account book in partnership with people whom he considered to belong to a lower caste"[16], which in this case happens to be that of the *thathiars*:

> He had been forced by the circumstances of the market, where there was little or no money in house-hold utensils, to open a factory and take on Government contracts. In order to assure the employment of skilled workers he had to choosc and select, first, the boys from Murli's family, who were highly skilled silversmiths, and then such other *thathiar*

15. *Ibid.*, p. 136.
16. *Ibid.*, p. 135

> boys as had been to a technical school or were young enough to go to one and learn to handle machinery. Old Murli was the headman of the *thathiar* brotherhood. For this reason, he had given him shares in the factory on the same footing as to some of his own *Kasera* brethren. But he had never intended the partnership to involve eating and drinking with the low *thathiars*, or to be on intimate social terms with any member of this community. For though both the *Kaseras* and *thathiars* were Hindus of the *Kshatriya*, the second highest caste, they had kept distinct because the craftmen, doing dirty, grimy, ill-paid work with their hands, had come to acquire a low professional status in Hindu society. Now he was on the horns of a dilemma, for his solidarity with his fellow partner in the factory, Murli, was in conflict with his affiliations with the *Kasera* brotherhood. And all these and other fears and doubts tangled up inside him to make his face a knot of worry.[17]

Thus, *The Big Heart* deals with one aspect of Casteism that has not received a significant consideration in either of the two novels, *Untouchable* and *The Road*, that is snobbishness. The caste snobbery among the upper-castes makes their social life filled with unnecessary hardships. The 'superior' sub-castes within a caste treat the 'lower' sub-castes as untouchables. To dispel this 'untouchability' from the public eye, the lower sub-castes do anything on earth to cultivate friendship with the superior sub-castes. Lala Murli Dhar's ridiculous insistence that Gokul Chand should attend the marriage of his grandson is only due to his desire to assimilate his family with the 'superior' caste of *Kaseras* through friendship and social intermingling. His proud feeling that his family has attained a 'superior caste status' makes him turn his back on his community of coppersmiths without actually establishing deep and intimate connections with the 'superior' *Kaseras'* community. He insists on the presence of Gokul Chand at any cost at Nikha's marriage with Kausalya; but he does not care to invite the members of his own brotherhood for the ceremony.

When the young men of the *thathiar* community come to know of this, they, under the leadership of Ananta, prevent the few rich *thathiars* that are invited for the marriage from attending it. The bride and her relatives now understand the attitude of Murli Dhar and his family to their community. The bride's father, Lala Ram Saran and

17. *Ibid.*, p. 134.

his brother Binde Saran protest. Their protests and in reaction to those protests the statements made by Lala Gokul Chand and the High Priest of the *Arya Samaj* are worth quoting:

> 'If we had known this, Lala Murli Dhar', said Lala Ram Saran, shocked, 'we wouldn't have stayed. After all, if our *thathiar* brothers are not coming, how can we celebrate the ceremony?'
>
> 'We will be turned out of the brotherhood if we don't honour our kith and kin with invitations on this sacred occasion', said Lala Binde Saran, echoing his brother's concern.
>
> 'I think', said Lala Gokul Chand, 'these folk from Jandiala are right. If you don't have the men of your own brotherhood, who will you have? The *Kaseras* are not coming. And if possible our visit here to-day must be regarded as secret.'
>
> 'We *Arya Samajis* have no such scruples, brother Gokul Chand', said the high priest in orange robes. 'We do not agree with the Orthodox *Sanantani* Hindus in keeping the old caste and sub-caste divisions. We have come here openly and I wish more of us had been informed. We must form a new community based not on caste prejudice but the revival of the true ancient vedic religion.'[18]

Lala Gokul Chand's fear of being expelled from his *Kaseras* community for attending the marriage of a *thathiar* and Lala Murli Dhar's ambition to attain the caste of *Kaseras* and the problems that accompany it are basically due to the perpetuation of the caste system and they could be avoided only if society were willing to abandon the old caste and sub-caste divisions. What the High Priest of the *Arya Samaj* tells Gokul Chand is what the social critic in Mulk Raj Anand has to say to the caste fanatics.

The central split in *The Big Heart* is between those who believe in Fate and those who show defiance to such a concept. The fatalists like Bhago and Ananta's step-mother Karmo (as in the case of Laxmi in *Coolie*), resuscitating their belief in *karma* would humbly say: "We belong to suffering, sister. We belong to suffering! This life is not worth living! All we can do is to do some good deeds and prepare for the next....'[19] For Ananta and his friends, the doctrine of Fate is non-sensical :

18. *Ibid.*, pp. 161-62.

19. *Ibid.*, p. 101.

> 'Fate! Fate! Fate doesn't dictate anything. I beg you to stop this kind of talk, ohe brothers, all of you, students, Maulvis and Pandits!' shrieked Ananta, desperate with anger and futility. 'Ohe, come to your senses and let us call all our brotherhood together and resolve upon some course for our betterment. Men make of their own deeds, they make of their own character, good or bad; and they shape of their own Destiny! So come and make your own fate.'[20]

Ananta considers fatalism as a self-destructive, fiendish belief, a serious obstacle to human progress.

The Big Heart has many similarities with *Untouchable*. Anand's touching treatment of the complex Indian problem in just over two hundred pages is magnificent and a further marvel is that the action is limited to the happenings of a single day as in *Untouchable*. Many writers who restrict the action to a short unit of time, deceive the readers by embracing the technique of flashbacks to surmount the limitations they have imposed on themselves. But Anand does not do so. As in *Untouchable*, so in this novel we have a poet whose long utterance is boring, but significant in the articulation of Anand's ambivalence towards the machine. *Untouchable* deals primarily with caste-problem. Though *The Big Heart* primarily does not deal with the caste problem, it devotes quite a few pages to the evils of the old caste and sub-caste divisions. The hero of *Untouchable*, Bakha and the hero of *The Big Heart*, Ananta are closely modelled after people Anand had known in his childhood. "I remembered the innocence of the original of Ananta", Anand wrote, "when he would borrow money to buy me sweets as he took me to bathe in the tank of the Golden Temple. I recalled the way he cooked meat on the monthly holiday of 'Akashti' and fed all his friends. I even admired the way he would buy liquor from his hard labour as a coppersmith and defy the elders by distributing drunkenness all around. He was among the few semi-literates who thought that God was dead, but himself seemed to have become a kind of God...." The Poet, Puran Singh Bhagat says of him: "I wish I had his courage, his love of action – even a little of his roguery".[22] Ananta's compassion for the poor and the helpless,

20. *Ibid.*, p. 205.

21. Anand, Mulk Raj: *Author to Critic: Letters of Mulk Raj Anand to Saros Cowasjee*, ed. Saros Cowasjee, Calcutta, Writers Workshop, 1973, p. 122 (letter dated Nov., 1971).

22. Anand, Mulk Raj: *The Big Heart*, New Delhi: Arnold-Heinemann, New Revised Edition, 1980, p. 92.

well illustrated in the novel, and his natural goodness easily observable in it, confirm the sincerity of his often repeated words: "There is no talk of money, brothers; one must have a big heart."[23] In fact, as Alastair Niven wrote, "*The Big Heart* is saved from being an economic tract only by the vitality of its central character Ananta, and the dramatic energy of its machine-wrecking climax."[24] Ananta is one of Anand's best realized characters. According to Elizabeth Bowen, "Ananta is an outstanding creation."[25] Anand portrays him thus:

> For the rogue and scoundrel that he was to the elders of the *thathiar* community, he was the idol of the youth of the craft. Partly it was the contagious warmth exuded by his well-knit body, the rounded proportions of a frame which seemed to combine a tiger's fury with the casual dignity of an animal who did not need to throw his weight about. Also, there was the air of the rebel about him, the man who worshipped no god and feared no mortal and had travelled farther by train than anyone else in the neighbourhood. And there was his large, expansive, generous manner, the open, frank, hearty speech which endeared him to those whose impulses were yet free from all restraint....[26]

The Big Heart is perhaps, the most argumentative of Anand's novels. Large portions of it have the tone of debate as different spokesmen among the coppersmith brotherhood suggest alternatives for modern India. It is also not free from exaggeration. Anand's 'moving' exposition of poor men's plight in this novel, to a great extent makes dismal reading. In a typical incident, Ananta is overcome with annoyance at the sight of a begging family and mutters to the elder child about its refusal to sit when it begs, only to realise that "starvation had bent their spines till they were doubled up like circus clowns, only without the gift that excites laughter".[27] He is horrified by an unsufferable sense of futility, the inadequacy of one

---

23. *Ibid.*, p. 19.
24. Niven, Alastair : *The Yoke of Pity : A Study of the Fictional Writings of Mulk Raj Anand*, New Delhi, Arnold-Heinemann, 1977, p. 81.
25. Quoted by K.N. Sinha, In: *Mulk Raj Anand*, New York: Twayne Publishers, 1972, p. 55.
26. Anand, Mulk Raj: *The Big Heart*, New Delhi: Arnold-Heinemann, New Revised Edition, 1980, p. 53.
27. *Ibid.*, p. 65.

man's sympathy to "spread the balm of pity over the rotting flesh of the whole of Hindustan".[28]

The novel is prefaced with a liberal speech made by Lord Byron in the House of Lords on 27th February, 1812, when the Luddites, the Nottinghamshire weavers, were agitating against the new industrial techniques that were a colossal threat to their employment. As Anand comments at the end of the Preface, "Although human conditions have changed much since Lord Byron spoke in the House of Lords, his words might still have some relevance to our time."[29]

What had happened to the Luddites, Anand obviously does not want to happen to the local artisans in India. So, through *The Big Heart*, he discourages the people who are over-enthusiastic to turn the emerging nation into an industrial super-power without giving due weightage to the multifarious problems rapid industrialization can bring. Though the novel has elements of propaganda and exaggeration, they are assimilated in the artistic whole. "In no other novel has Anand so attempted to organize a whole social, economic, and political picture"[30], writes Margaret Berry. There is no character in the novel who is totally deprived of soul. The complication of its plot, the dynamism of action, the excellence of characterisation, the authenticity of its moral vision and above all its human centrality are redeeming features powerful enough to withstand the charge of propaganda against it and make it a singular triumph.

Death of a Hero

Death of a Hero (1964) is the story of Maqbool Sherwani, the hero who was captured and executed during the first invasion of Kashmir by Pakistani raiders in 1947. It describes the real life story of Maqbool Sherwani and presents him as a patron-saint of secularism.

Maqbool, the hero of this novelitte is a young poet of the National Conference. In the late October of 1947, when the raiders from Pakistan have advanced to Baramula, he flees to Srinagar to consult the leaders of National Conference Volunteer Corps. They advise him to go back to Baramula in order to rally the people to fight against the invaders. As he gets near to Baramula, he becomes tired. So he spends the night in a field making a cave out of some hay. His

28. *Ibid.*, p. 67.
29. *Ibid.*, p. 6.
30. Berry, Margaret: *Mulk Raj Anand : The Man and the Novelist*, New Delhi: Arnold-Heinemann, 1971, p. 49.

sound sleep there, is suddenly disturbed by a lengthy exchange of distant rifle and machine gun fire. The distant rat-tat-tat of the machine gun increases. He feels that he must go and reconnoitre the position in Baramula. The cover, which the darkness affords, will help him. So he crawls out of the hay stack. A shiver goes down his spine as he realises that he may walk straight into the arms of Pakistani sentry. As he walks towards Baramula, he sees the Presentation Convent, a little away from the town, smoking. He wonders how the Pakistani Officers, who know of the help given to them by the White Generals, have allowed the burning of a missionary centre. Soon he comes to know that Baramula is completely in the grip of the Pakistanis and that they are filling their trucks with loot. He does not know where to go. After a pause he feels that entering the house of the businessman, Muratib Ali is the safest thing. From Muratib Ali's workers of carpet factory, Maqbool comes to know that the factory is looted by the Pakistanis and later it is set on fire. He meets Muratib Ali in his sitting room. Muratib Ali asks Maqbool to flee from the town if he values his life. In response Maqbool tells Muratib Ali:

> I am under orders... Besides, I feel that, on principle, we must struggle.... If we believe in freedom from these 'Muslim Brethren' as we believed in freedom from the British and their friends....[31]

From the conversation that follows Maqbool comes to know that his trusted friend and lawyer Ahmed Shah whom he made the president of the National Conference Branch of Baramula has joined the Pro-Pakistanis. Another friend of his, Ghulam Jilani who is a business partner of Muratib Ali, is gradually leaning towards the Pro-Pakistanis under the influence of his father and landlord of Baramula. So, after leaving the residence of the generous and good natured Muratib Ali, Maqbool goes towards the mansion of Ghulam Jilani in order to strengthen him from faltering and falling towards the Pro-Pakistanis. When Maqbool enters the big old Kashmir style reception room of Ghulam Jilani, he sees Ghulam sitting with the lawyer Ahmed Shah and Khurshid Anwar, an official of the invading army. Maqbool feels that he has walked straight into the lion's mouth. Soon there erupts a heated argument. At the peak of it, Khurshid Anwar wants to arrest Maqbool. Ghulam Jilani protests against it by saying that Maqbool is his guest. As Maqbool descends the stairs, one of

---

31. Anand, Mulk Raj : *Death of a Hero*, New Delhi: Arnold Heinemann, 1985, p. 47.

Ghulam's woman servants, Ibil, informs him that the Pakistanis are waiting outside to arrest him. The old woman takes him to Begum Sahib as she wants to meet him. Ibil then suggests a plan to save Maqbool from being arrested by the Pakistanis. Begum Sahib agrees with the plan. A *tonga* is arranged. Maqbool is asked to put on the *burqah* of Begum Sahib. It is an old strategem of the feudal households. On their way, though the Pakistani sentries challenge the *tonga*, Ibil's aggressive words prevent them from verifying the identity of the person in woman's veil. The carriage advances slowly. At a suitable place it halts. From there Ibil leads Maqbool to his house. There is real rejoicing in the family on his return. But it does not last long. There is a knock at the door. A whole group of Pathans is there to capture Maqbool. Aware of the impending danger, Maqbool rushes to the roof top. He then jumps from one roof top to another. Bullets ring through behind him. In the chase that follows, the pursuers manage to capture him. His captors, after treating him brutally, drag him and throw him into a lock-up. After some hours three warders drag him out of the cell and thrust him forward before Khurshid Anwar's improvised court. Ahmed Shah takes the role of a public prosecutor. After a summary trial, he is shot to death, in the middle of the night. Ahmed Shah then orders the sentries to tie the corpse to a pole and write the word 'Kafir' on his shirt with his own blood and place it for the people of Baramula to see.

The next day, when the conquering Indian troops enter Baramula, they find the body of Maqbool Sherwani tied to a wooden pole. They search the pocket and find a letter written by him from the prison cell for his sister, Noor. It is written with words that weep and tears that speak and they reveal the real source of his poetry: "....in our country, the most splendid deeds have been done by people, not because they were great in spirit, but because they could not suffer the tyrant's yoke, and learnt to obey their consciences. And conscience, howsoever dim, is a great force, and is the real source of poetry."[32]

As *Death of a Hero* was written in memory of Maqbool Sherwani who was a missionary of the religion of humanism who willingly accepted martyrdom for the propagation of that religion, Anand also gave another befitting name to the novel: "Epitaph for Maqbool Sherwani". The author's firm faith in the religion preached by Maqbool Sherwani probably encouraged him to write this historical novel.

32. *Ibid.*, p. 125.

Death of a Hero is a beacon light beckoning people to the harbour of liberty and secularism. Those who come to this light can make no mistake in recognizing the evil of religious fanaticism and the new nationalism based on it.

Though Anand has, as a passing criticism, in all his novels allotted some pages to his disapproval of institutionalized religion, only in *Death of a Hero* does he present religious chauvinism as a dominant theme. The novel points out how zealotry can destroy human right, freedom, peace and happiness and turn society into a hell. Religious fanaticism blurs a person's vision and provokes him to quarrel for the cause of unseen and non-existant forces. To a zealot anything other than his belief is blasphemy. The pro-Pakistani teacher Ishaq in the novel, who considers anyone of a faith other than his own as infidel, is a representative of all religious fanatics. It is his fanaticism that makes him think that murdering persons who do not belong to Islamic faith is permitted by the Koran. Fanaticism, in fact, prevents him from knowing the message of the Koran: "Let there be no compulsion in religion. Truth stands out clean from Error"[33] or "Let not the hatred of others make you swerve to wrong and depart from justice. Be just; that is next to Piety."[34] So he believes that the brutal Pakistani soldiers who are involved in random killing, looting and raping women are 'brothers engaged in a holy war'.

Maqbool Sherwani's belief in a good life as the only religion, makes him laugh at the way murderers engage in prayer. When he has entered Baramula guarded by invaders he sees :

> half a dozen men, raiders by the look of them, kneeling in the attitude of *Sajdah* prayer, their eyes closed, their faces turned towards the West.
>
> Would they break off from their prayers and challenge him?
>
> His heart beat fast. His face went pale. And his eyes were full of mist.
>
> All the six men got up with hands folded before them and did not look this side or that, but persevered in their prayer.
>
> He was safe.
>
> It was a miracle that none of them had been walking about or sitting down, preparing for prayer. And the irony of it

33. *The Koran* : Surah II: The Cow, Ayat: 256.
34. *The Koran* : Surah V: The Table Spread, Ayat: 8.

> struck him, as he reached past the tomb, to the cover of some fishermen's huts, that these brutal men could be devoutly praying, though only the previous night, perhaps they had been looting and murdering....[35]

The best religion is the most tolerant. It is nothing but love towards God and man. People, like the invaders referred to above, who simply perform certain religious rituals have in them only the cosmetics and not the substance of true religion.

Human history is full of religious persecution and religious wars. In the name of religion perhaps more blood has been shed than in any other name. Arousing religious fanaticism is sure to pay rich dividends to any invading nation. The Pakistanis act on the religious sentiments of Kashmiris for their territorial gain. The result is fantastic. The religious fanatics abandon their independent stand for Kashmir and in no time they turn to Pro-Pakistanis and welcome the invaders as liberators and call the barbarism let loose by them a holy war for the glory of Islamic democracy. Fanaticism darkens their mind. So they cannot see the true motive of the invaders. The Pakistanis have come not to consolidate Islam but to expand their territory and, in compensation for their trouble, to loot the people. This is evident from the words of one important Pakistani Officer, Khurshid Anwar:

> Let my boys secure the base in Baramula and compensate themselves for their trouble in coming all the way from Peshawar and Abbotabad – then we shall move forward. There are still riches hidden in the houses of Kashmiri Pundits, even if they have taken the *Panditanis* away![36]

Unfortunately many educated and intelligent people too do not care to understand the Pakistani motive. Under the influence of fanaticism they lose their dispassionate thinking. A typical example is Ahmed Shah, a lawyer and president of the National Conference Unit of Baramula. His view of the situation, as given below, shows how fanaticism has led him to wild and unreasonable position :

> I believe in a Central Muslim State, which will be a counter to Communism in the North, and to the *Bania* Hindu *Raj* in the South.... And we can connect up with our brethren in the

35. Anand, Mulk Raj: *Death of a Hero*, New Delhi: Arnold Heinemann, 1985, p. 47.
36. *Ibid.*, p. 37.

> Middle East and revive the glory of ancient Islamic democracy in a world ridden with unbelief![37]

To Ahmed Shah, the Pakistani invasion is a war of liberation. He considers it a historic event, thereby provoking protest from Maqbool:

> 'I will certainly not be bullied by you', interrupted Maqbool. 'I don't believe in this historic event — we were living peacefully enough and struggling against wrongs... And then these people came, with guns pointed at us, demanding accession by force.'[38]

Maqbool and Ahmed Shah are both patriots but of different perspectives. Ahmed Shah's nationalism is based on religious fanaticism. Any one who does not believe in Islam is not a member of the nation Ahmed Shah dreams to establish. In such a country laws are based not on reason but on the belief in a being whose existence no one is sure about. We all know that the Holy Roman Empire was not very holy. Nations built on religious fundamentalism justified the butchering of millions of political enemies in the name of God. For Maqbool, who has no belief in the existence of God, the concept of Islamic democracy is an idiocy. His patriotism urges him to fight for what is good for Kashmir. He wants the people of Kashmir, in whatever God they believe, to live in peace and harmony, without breaking up into fragments by building parochial domestic walls. Knowing the advantages of secular democracy over all other forms of government he struggles hard to establish in Kashmir a government of the people, by the people and for the people. He makes his position clear to the fanatic teacher Ishaq in this way:

> I am for Kashmir. Not for its usurpation by force, but for its freedom to choose where it wants to go.[39]

Maqbool does not succeed in his plan of rallying people to fight for the freedom of Kashmir, as a good many of his supporters are engulfed in the sea of fanaticism and the remaining few sympathetic to him are resigned to their fate. Fatalism makes a person inactive. It unmans man and destroys his heroism. Maqbool knows that fatalists would never openly come out for the cause of Kashmir. As

37. *Ibid.*, p. 72.
38. *Ibid.*, p. 75-76.
39. *Ibid.*, p. 22.

it is a serious impediment to the self-determination of Kashmir, whenever Maqbool comes across fatalistic remarks, he challenges it with the intention of removing its grip on the mind of the people. He becomes deeply annoyed with his own people who follow the path of fatalistic neutralism and inaction while the invaders are ruthlessly carrying on terrorist activities, disturbing and destroying the peace and tranquillity. When Maqbool visits the house of Ghulam Jilani, Begum Jilani tries to inspire him with the philosophy of humble acceptance in this way:

> Life is cruel. As a woman I have known this truth. We have to accept, because, in the eyes of Allah, we deserve the punishment. The only way, son, in which this cruelty can be offset is by obedience to destiny. What is written in one's fate will be.[40]

Maqbool, like Ananta in *The Big Heart* believes that man is the maker of his own destiny. Therefore he protests against Begum Jilani's fatalistic view of life by saying, "when death is opposed to life, then life must oppose death".[41] When he returns home, he finds that his father's reaction to what the Pakistanis have done to them is not different from the fatalistic belief expressed by Begum Jilani. The father tells the son pathetically:

> What can we do against such odds, I ask you! The salvation of our souls lies in the hand of Allah and his prophets. If we pray, perhaps Allah will hear our prayers.[42]

To the rationalistic and atheistic Maqbool, the belief in fate is an absurdity. He is pained to see how his fellowmen become particularly vulnerable to Pakistani invaders by their religious fanaticism and fatalistic belief. He wants people to resist the invaders with all their strength instead of accepting invasion and its ugly concomitants as a scourge of Allah. As the novelist remarks, "He (Maqbool) knew that this sudden descent of murder on his land was not an act of God, but a planned brutality to cow people down to submit, and resistance to it was the only virtue".[43] Therefore he laughs at the fatalists with these words of caustic and bitter humour: "Allah has sent his apostles, the Pakistanis, our 'Muslim brethren', to liberate us by

40. *Ibid.*, p. 80.
41. *Ibid.*, p. 80.
42. *Ibid.*, p. 88.
43. *Ibid.*, p. 52.

depriving us of our breath!"[44] After he is captured by his enemies, he becomes more blunt in his attack on the religion of fate which is a serious hindrance to the salvation of Kashmir. So he speaks out most passionately:

> Allah! Where was Allah? Why was He always against the innocents?.....There would be no salvation unless the religion of fate went by the board, and the soul became alive?[45]

From the discussion so far, it is evident that the main social criticisms in *Death of a Hero* are directed against religious fanaticism which invariably poisons the noble ideals of secularism and fatalism which freeze all our enthusiasm to struggle in life. Along with these main concerns, the author also introduces a subsidiary theme: brutality and ill-treatment of prisoners. It is the age-old story of man's inhumanity to man. The ill-treatment Maqbool receives from his enemies is tyrannical :

> The advance guard of the pursuers was on him. Hitting him with the rifle ends, shouting abuse and filth in their broken speech, slapping his face, and thrusting their fisticuffs into his sides, they pulled him from side to side, slapped him again and pushed him foward, till he fell.[46]

Not only the soldiers but also his old friend and lawyer Ahmed Shah is among the gang of tormentors kicking and abusing him. Dazed by the assault, Maqbool just watches his ex-friend, "still unable to believe that the thread of connection between the two Kashmiris should break so completely through the change in political allegiances. Somehow, he could not believe in the scene in which he was involved. He had the hallucination of being in hell".[47] Unable to suffer the torture any more Maqbool shouts: "You can kill me without all this....Why do you want to prolong the farce?"[48]

Anand, apart from protesting against the barbarism let loose on helpless prisoners like Maqbool, also condemns the unhygienic prison cells provided to them. The captors kick Maqbool from behind and push him to a prison cell. He sees in the cell "a cockroach steadily

---

44. *Ibid.*, p. 89.
45. *Ibid.*, p. 100.
46. *Ibid.*, p. 101.
47. *Ibid.*, p. 110.
48. *Ibid.*, p. 112.

advancing between the planks and he realised that there must be other insects about in the cell, possibly scorpions and rats, and even a snake. His eyes wandered across the dirty surface of the string bed and he was sure that there would be bugs in it."[49] Within a short time of stay in that cholera-causing prison cell without any proper place for excretion, he has to learn to do without self-respect.

In many of his novels Anand has protested against the cruel treatment of prisoners in India. He wants reform in Indian prisons so that the unfortunate inmates will not suffer from the feeling that they are reduced to a subhuman status. The way a nation treats its prisoners is a reliable measuring yard of its level of civilization. Though for the past many years Amnesty International and other International human rights organizations could not come out with any major shocking revelations about India's treatment of its prisoners, the frightening level of torture for confession practised in India and rightly reported by our newspapers is a fatal blow to our age-old traditions of compassion and kindness.

As asserted by the title of the novel, Maqbool Sherwani is a hero. But his heroism is quite different from the heroism of arms and ammunition brought out by Emperor Napolean or Alexander the Great. His heroism is founded on moral courage and love of humanity practised by Jesus Christ, Mahatma Gandhi, Mohammed or Joan of Arc. The heroism born out of moral courage and love of humanity is infinitely superior to the heroism carried out by arms and ammunition. The great Napolean admitted this when he wrote about Jesus Christ: "Alexander, Caesar, Charlemagne, and I myself have founded empires; but upon what do these creations of our genius depend? Upon force. Jesus alone founded His empire upon love; and to this day millions would die for Him."[50] Maqbool Sherwani, like Jesus Christ, valiantly faced his tormentors. He could escape persecution by "the recantation" his persecutors wanted him to make. But he never allowed the fear of death to grip his immortal soul. That makes him heroic. The heroism of Maqbool Sherwani is evident in the way he reacts to his tormentors' vulgar talks:

> 'Come to your senses! Raper of your sister', shouted Khurshid Anwar. 'Do you not value your life?'

49. *Ibid.*, p. 105.

50. From, *Best Quotations for all Occasions*, arranged and edited by Lewis C. Henry, London: Premier Publishers Pvt. Ltd., 1968, p. 36.

> 'I value my sister's honour more than my life!'
>
> Maqbool answered. 'So, please do not abuse me like that'.
>
> 'Insolent swine!' shouted Ahmed Shah. 'You are persisting in your treachery and don't realise that a word from Mr. Khurshid Anwar — and Zaman Khan will finish you off!.... Recant your treacherous stand or I shall have no option but to ask the court to pronounce judgement on you!.....!.
>
> 'Truth has no voice', he (Maqbool) began... I cannot move you....This land, which gave birth to me, this land which is like a poem to me — how shall I explain my love for it to you? From out of its valleys there has risen for centuries the anguish of torture... And we were trying to emerge from the oppression to liberate our mother, because we know her each aching cares..... you have come and fouled her! How could any of us stand by and not protest.....'[51]

It is easy to draw in Maqbool's life and death a parallel with the life and crucifixion of Jesus Christ. Maqbool was an admirer of Jesus Christ. He told Salaama: "*Jessuh Messih* was a real person and suffered for mankind — was crucified!"[52] Both Jesus Christ and Maqbool Sherwani protested against the evils which had been thrust upon their society. For this, they both were tortured by their enemies and paraded on wooden poles in order to discourage the public from following their path. When the Indian soldiers entered Baramula, they found the body of Maqbool Sherwani tied to a wooden pole. It reminded them of "*Yessuh Messih* on the cross".[53] On the lapel of Maqbool's shirt his tormentors wrote the word "Kafir" to show his crime. On the wooden pole (cross) on which Christ was crucified, according to the traditional belief, his enemies wrote the letter I.N.R.I., representing the words, "Iesus Nazarenus Rex Iudaeorum", meaning "Jesus of Nazareth King of the Jews", to mock at the plight of the man they had nailed to the cross. Both Maqbool Sherwani and Jesus Christ were aware that their life would end up in torture and death for protesting against their society. Yet both faced death

---

51. Anand, Mulk Raj : *Death of a Hero*, New Delhi: Arnold Heinemann, 1985, pp. 114 -15.
52. *Ibid.*, p. 39.
53. *Ibid.*, p. 124.

courageously. In Maqbool Sherwani's words, "But we still have to struggle; we will have to suffer, and.... But that is how we grow"[54], it is easy to discover at least a mild echo of the Biblical statement about Christ: "He learned obedience in the school of suffering".[55]

Death of a Hero is Anand's twelfth novel. It appeared one year after the publication of another short novel, *The Road*. In *Death of a Hero*, as M.K. Naik observes, "The entire action is rooted in a set of real historical incidents which constitute its framework, and by its very nature, this framework needs a great deal of elaboration, in terms of historical perspective, situation and character. Deprived of this elaboration the narrative was bound to appear sketchy and superficial, and covered in a miasma of vagueness."[56]

Death of a Hero, however, is an important question of Indian novel. It has not dated. Its voice still make reverberations !

54. *Ibid*., p. 95.
55. The Bible: Hebrews, 5:8.
56. Naik, M.K.: *Mulk Raj Anand*, New Delhi: Arnold Heinemann, 1973, p. 106.

VI

PRIVATE LIFE OF AN INDIAN PRINCE

The advent of Indian independence gave rise to a new literary awareness. The re-organization of the states, the plight of the Anglo-Indian community in India, the departure of the British after centuries of colonial rule, the sensations of the Independence movement, the repatriation of people either to Pakistan or Hindustan, the communists' effort to turn India into a Bolshevik state, the activities of the Congress, the response of 562 or more princely states to the call to join the Indian Union etc., were dexterously exploited by many creative writers.

In the years just before Independence, one of the most popular topics of discussion in India was the obstacles caused by some princely states to the formation of the Indian Republic. The common man, intoxicated with the newly acquired democratic rights, openly criticised the princes, without trying to understand their position or deep resentment at having been deceived by the Crown. The princes, whose principalities had solidly supported the Empire during the two World Wars and had fought the nationalists at home for the comfort of the British Raj, fervently hoped that when the rulers leave India they would stand up to the pledge given by Her Majesty Queen Victoria in 1858 "to respect the rights, dignity and honour of the native princes as our own", a pledge which was solemnly affirmed by her successors to the Crown. However, the British Government came up with a different interpretation of the pledge. They said that the pledge to the princes was solely based on Paramountcy, on their effective control of India as a part of British Crown and not merely on treaties and assurances. By their giving up of that effective control of India, the Paramountcy automatically lapsed and so they were no longer in a position to protect the princes and their principalities. However to the complaining princes the British Government gave a hint to seek their own means to remain Independent of the Indian Union. They were assured that Paramountcy would not be transferred to any successor Government. But this assurance meant nothing to the princes. The then Viceroy and Governor-General of India, Lord Mountbatten in fact advised the princes against seeking a path of Independence. Most of the princes accepted the advice but there were a few who by all means wanted to preserve their independence, like the Maharaja of Travancore, Indore and Kashmir, the Nawabs of Junagadh and Bhopal, the Nizam of Hyderabad and of course, the hero of Mulk Raj Anand's *Private Life of an Indian Prince*, the Maharaja Ashok Kumar of Sham Pur. The then Deputy Prime Minister, Home Minister and Minister in-charge of the States of Indian Union, Sardar Vallabhbhai Patel adopted various pressure tactics to force the recalcitrant princes to join the Indian Union: some were offered attractive Privy Purses and high ranking diplomatic assignments abroad, others were compelled to sign the Instrument of Accession on the grounds that they were no longer in a position to maintain law and order. The story of Sham Pur's accession to Indian Union as presented in the novel epitomizes what happened in several other princely states.

The hero of Anand's *Private Life of an Indian Prince*, the Maharaja of Sham Pur is an individual as well as a type. He is a type in the sense that he embodies all the weaknesses of his Maharaja class, namely pride, vanity, arrogance, political intrigue, flirtation and intemperance. He is also true to his type as he spends his days like most of the Indian princes by taking part in polo games, hunting expedition, orgies of drink and debauchery and by enjoying the company of his mistresses and English guests. At the same time he is an individual too, as his mind is obsessed with a unique problem which he can unravel only to his most intimate friends and which continually gnaws at his private life and ultimately drags him to madness:

Commenting on this novel, Mulk Raj Anand says:

> Actually my knowledge of Indian life at various levels had always convinced me that I should try to do a 'comedie humaine'. In this the poor, the lowly and the untouchables were only one kind of outcastes. The middle section, and the nawabs and rajas were also to be included as a species of untouchables. Unfortunately, there has not been time to show the poor-rich of our country, who deserve pity more than contempt.

> As usual, all the characters are taken from real life and transformed creatively from within in an almost Dostoevskian mood of pity, absolute pity, for those who love absolutely — in this case the prince. I taught 2 or 3 princes as a tutor in the early 20s, so I know the background.
> Malraux's novel 'Man's Fate' was very much in mind for ten years before I wrote 'Private Life'.[1]

Beyond that, there was also a personal reason which prompted Anand to write *Private Life of an Indian Prince*. As we noted in the introduction, it was written at the suggestion of Melpo, a Greek dancer who nursed him in Bombay, in order to save him from complete mental break-down. Hence, Anand's words that the novel "rushed out of me in one month", is understandable.

Anand's narrator in this novel is Dr Hari Shankar, a Post-Graduate in medicine, who has studied in London just like the author. In one of his letters to Saros Cowasjee, Anand says: "....In 1948, I had a breakdown. And the neutral narrator Dr Shankar was invented to become Shiva's third eye and to burn out the dross, confusion and the chaos of emotions in order to achieve a certain balance."[2] At the same time we cannot ignore what Anand has to say in the "Author's Note" to the novel: "The neutral 'I' of the first person singular has tended, in this book, to become a character in his own right.... the 'I' in this novel is not to be mistaken for the author."[3] We may be tempted to ask what necessitated this explanation. It may be to warn the reader who may be tempted to seek Anand in every utterance of the Doctor at the expense of the individuality of the narrator-character and at the same time ignore the presence of Anand in the other characters of the novel. If the strength of Anand is visible in the magnanimous doctor he created, one cannot ignore the weakness and agony of Anand equallly visible through the prince. As Saros Cowasjee comments in his book, *So Many Freedoms*, "There is as much of Anand in his prince as in his narrator, and this partly accounts for the penetrating analysis of the prince's character. Dr Shankar is the

---

1. Anand, Mulk Raj : *Author to Critic: The Letters of Mulk Raj Anand to Saros Cowasjee*, Ed: Saros Cowasjee, Calcutta: Writers Workshop, 1973, p. 12 (letter dated 18 Nov. 1967).
2. Anand, Mulk Raj : *Author to Critic: The Letters of Mulk Raj Anand to Saros Cowasjee*, Calcutta, Writers Workshop, 1973, p. 14 (letter dated 22 Nov. 1967).
3. Anand, Mulk Raj : "Author's Note" to *Private Life of an Indian Prince*, Delhi: Arnold-Heinemann, 1983, p. 23.

rational side of the author analysing the irrational side as seen in the prince."[4]

The Maharaja's full name is Victor Edward George Ashok Kumar: Victor after Queen Victoria, Edward after Edward VII; George after Emperor George V; Ashok after the ancient Indian Emperor, Ashoka. It appears that he wanted to please his British masters even by his "impressive" name in which East and West merge. His Highness's name also indicates his vasalage, his all-out attempt to please the Imperial Crown for the sake of safeguarding his little crown. Not only at ceremonial occasions but also when he finds occasions to seduce girls, as in the case of his seduction of the British shop girl Miss June Withers, he never fails to give his full regalia of titles and honours: "Maj. Gen. His Highness Farzand-i-Khas-i-Daulata-i-Inglishia Mansur-i-Zaman, Amir-ul-umra, Maharajadhiraj Sri 108, Sir Victor Edward George, Ashok Kumar Bahadur, K.C.S.I., K.C.I.E., D.L. (Benares), Maharaja of Sham Pur."[5]

The Maharaja has had his college education at the chief's college, Lahore. There he framed his motto of life, an inspiration from one of Shelley's passionate poems:

> I never was attached to that great sect
> Whose doctrine is, that each one should select
> Out of the crowd a mistress or a friend,
> And all the rest, though fair and wise, commend
> To cold oblivion, though it is in the code
> Of modern morals................
> ....Narrow
> The heart that loves, the brain that contemplates,
> The life that wears, the spirit that creates,
> One object, and one form.........[6]

With this motto ever in mind, he royally moves about, like the Absalom of Dryden, without being cursedly confined to a single woman, at a vibrant period of Indian history,

> When nature prompted and no law denied
> Promiscuous use of concubine and bride.[7]

The disastrous consequence of this attitude of the Maharaja is

4. Cowasjee, Saros: *So Many Freedoms: A Study of the Major Fiction of Mulk Raj Anand*, Delhi: OUP, 1977, p. 141.

5. Anand, Mulk Raj: *Private Life of an Indian Prince*, Delhi: Arnold-Heinemann, 1983, pp. 306-307.

6. *Ibid*., p. 46.

7. Quoted from John Dryden's *Absalom and Achitophel*, lines: 8-9.

given in the opening scene of the novel: "a first class scandal" involving Miss Bunti Russell, daughter of Captain Russell. Captain Russell, boiled with anger, rushes to the palace. He abuses the Maharaja and roars and the Maharaja and the Captain duel. The noice of the scuffle brings to the scene Captain Partap Singh, the A.D.C. and Munshi Mithan Lal, the Private Secretary to His Highness.

The Maharaja is furious that a commoner like Captain Russell, ignoring his divine right to rule Sham Pur dare to assault him. So he decides to personally meet his friend and Deputy Commissioner of Simla to put up a complaint against the Captain. He asks Munshi Mithan Lal and his personal physician Dr Shankar to accompany him. The entourage reaches Simla. But the Deputy Commissioner refuses to meet His Highness. Victor feels that things had gone very wrong and he tells his confidant, Dr Shankar, with greater pathos than ever before: "I am a rat in a hole."[8] When they get back to their hotel from the residence of the Deputy Commissioner, there is a wire for the Maharaja from the Prime Minister, Srijut Popatlal J. Shah, an ex-I.C.S. official from Central Provinces, appointed by the new Government of India, after His Highness had shown reluctance in acceding to the Indian Union. The wire asks the Maharaja to return to Sham Pur at the earliest for urgent consultation. Hard upon the telegram comes the Maharaja's political secretary who has been sent by the Prime Minister to fetch His Highness back.

Though they set out from Simla in response to the Prime Minister's telegram, after reaching Sham Pur the Maharaja is slow to respond to him. Therefore at their encounter, the *Diwan* in unequivocal terms states his position to the Maharaja:

> Maharaja Sahib, I am here in Sham Pur to fulfil the orders of the Sardar. I am an administrator and I have been sent here on duty. I am willing to send a memorandum, which you may give me, to the States Department. Only, if I may advise you in your best interest, I think you should consider acceding, because most of the princes in India have already done so. After all, these accessions are intended to promote the unity of the country. And, as a patriot, I am sure you will consider it your duty to come into the family.[9]

8. Anand, Mulk Raj: *Private Life of an Indian Prince*, Delhi: Arnold-Heinemann, 1983, p. 51.
9. *Ibid*., p. 90.

Victor calls this pious talk of the *Diwan* 'non-sense' and after the *Diwan* has left the palace, he discloses his future plan for Sham Pur to his nymphomaniac mistress Ganga Dasi and Dr Shankar: "I have some American friends....I shall call them here for Shakar......Actually, one of them sounded me about making a pact, for Sham Pur borders upon Tibet as well as Kashmir and India. I will show this *Diwan* a thing or two."[10] Joining in the discussion Gangi says that she can handle the *Diwan* and adds: "You leave him to me. He will be eating out of my hands soon."[11] Then Victor affirms: "I shall be strong enough to stand my ground against the States Department. I will offer the British and Americans the use of some strips of territory if need be. Later, I can turn them out."[12] While such discussion is going on inside the palace, the activists of *Praja Mandal* under the leadership of Pandit Gobind Das are preparing for a *hartal* to protest against the misrule of Victor and to gather support for the accession of the state of Sham Pur to Indian Union.

Unmindful of the *hartal*, Victor gets ready to welcome his foreign guests, Mr Peter Watkins of the American Embassy in Delhi who is 'nearly the Ambassador' and Mr Kurt Laudauer, a journalist and a few others. They are directed by Victor to proceed to the hunting lodge at Dharam Pur direct from the Station. At the lodge the guests and the hosts are introduced to one another. Mr Peter Watkins expresses his desire to begin the hunt for the panthers immediately and Victor orders the Chief *Shikari*, a middle-aged man, named Buta to urgently complete the arrangement. But that night or the next night could not be suitable to capture the panther. However on the third night they succeed in trapping the panther. Shooting starts. When the guests fail to shoot it down, Buta aware of the danger, takes a blind shot and the panther rolls over and falls without a struggle. The next day the mother panther comes to wail the death of her son and she is also shot dead.

Ganga Dasi who has managed to trap the Prime Minister Popatlal J. Shah just before the hunting expedition and who proudly declares, "I feel I could make him dance on my palm if I liked"[13], is caught in a passing fancy for Mr Kurt Laudauer, "a bright moon-

10. *Ibid*., p. 94.
11. *Ibid*., p. 95.
12. *Ibid*., p. 97.
13. *Ibid*., p. 170.

faced young man with auburn hair"[14]. Victor notices her turning her light of green eyes at him during the evening. And at night Victor and Dr Shankar see the shocking reality: Gangi lying in bed with Kurt in a passionate embrace. Victor wants to kill both of them but he calms down realising that he will ruin everything if the Americans come to know of his anger.

That is not the only incident that spoils the mood of Victor. Srijut Popatlal J. Shah and Mr Bool Chand leave the lodge without even saying good-bye to his Highness, leaving a wire the *Diwan* had received from the States Department at Delhi asking him to send His Highness to see Sardar Vallabhbhai Patel as soon as possible. Silence, the sister of gloom, spreads her dark cloud across the hunting lodge.

And then an awkward event takes place. Buta is not satisfied with the wage given to him. He protests and Victor gets annoyed and kicks him brutally. Buta falls back, bleeding in the mouth and nose. After this awful scene, the Americans lose all enthusiasm and without offering any help for the independence of Sham Pur, they leave for Delhi by the afternoon train.

Victor has no choice but to go to Delhi and meet Sardar Patel. So on that night itself, accompanied by Dr Shankar, Partap Singh and Mithan Lal, Victor sets out for Delhi by train.

At the prescribed time the interview starts. It is very brief and to the point. The Sardar firmly says: "I have called you to sign the papers for the accession of Sham Pur to the Indian Union."[15]

As they return to Sham Pur, Victor's face reveals his defeat, exhaustion and disillusionment. When he reaches his state, the most tragic news of his life has been awaiting him: Ganga Dasi has run away with Bool Chand. Victor beats his head with his fists, in a mad, incohate despair at being abandoned. He falls back on the settee, weeping and sobbing, his face covered with his hands. He begins to utter soliloquies: "Where have you gone? Oh, where have you gone?....Why have you left me like this?....I want you! I am dying for you....Why have you done this? Why?.... Why do you want to destroy me....?"[16] When Munshi Mithan Lal and others try to console him, he says with great abjectness: "But you don't understand!.....You can't see how my life was bound with her. She is coiled up in my

14. *Ibid.*, p. 178.
15. *Ibid.*, p. 241.
16. *Ibid.*, p. 249.

entrails...."[17] He is disconsolate. "Only in death shall I be able to get rid of her"[18], Victor says as he sighs.

After the accession of Sham Pur to Indian Union, the Administrator suggests to the Maharaja to take a holiday in Europe, a suggestion which emanates from an order to keep him out of the state.

So, Victor in the company of Dr Shankar and Captain Partap Singh, A.D.C., flies to London in the Air India International plane, "Malabar Princess". Even in this picnic-like situation, Victor is not happy because he has not been able to kidnap Gangi to London.

After reaching London, things do not change much for Victor. He is obsessed by the thoughts of Ganga Dasi. He is not able to sleep for more than an hour or two each night. And he is so split that he begins increasingly to talk to himself in his sleep, and also, when he is left alone. And sometimes he repeats like a child, "I want her. I want her."[19] One day, while shopping, Victor's libidinous hunger is aroused by a shop girl named Miss June Withers. So he arranges a party for her in the Mayfair Service Flat. It is a clever stage Victor sets for her seduction. He skilfully manages to win her over and in the week-end they are out for long drives in the country and soon without showing any restraint they are kissing and embracing each other even in the presence of Dr Hari Shankar and Captain Partap Singh.

> And yet, just when they were coming nearer to each other, Victor seemed to be thrown back into sudden moods of despair and to withdraw from the contest as it were. And it was only a small part of him, a kind of stop gap before the bigger reality of Ganga Dasi, whose memories were bearing him down, compelling him, encompassing him, murdering him, annihilating him.[20]

And one grey morning a C.I.D. man, an Inspector of Ward visits them and asks Captain Partap Singh to come with him to Scotland Yard for consultation. He also expresses his desire to meet the Maharaja. Then Victor confesses to the Doctor that Partap Singh's secret men may have succeeded in murdering Bool Chand as a

17. *Ibid.*, p. 261.
18. *Ibid.*, p. 262.
19. *Ibid.*, p. 295.
20. *Ibid.*, p. 322.

punishment for his taking away Ganga Dasi with him. Soon he receives an order from India House asking His Highness and his staff to return to India immediately to give evidence. Victor is numbed by the shock. "Oh, why did I have to get bound up with this murder?"[21], he wails. The suffering of his mind seems to become physical. He is disintegrating. Soon he is found trying to stand on his head. He has lost consciousness and he does not know the meanings of the words he is uttering:

> 'I can fly', he babbled suddenly. 'I can fly. I can fly away on my own....' And he got up and, stretching his arms out, began to flap them like a bird taking off. And he fell so that his head dangled on the side of his bed.[22]

Then he begins to weep and sing.

The next day they leave by Air India International "Moghul Princess" to India. "Throughout the flight he kept up a continuous monologue, interrupted by songs sung in a raucous voice, and by sporadic violence, until he became a complete nuisance to the other passengers and had to be strapped up and bound to his chair."[23]

During the flight, Dr Shankar realises that the best thing to do with the mad Maharaja is to admit him immediately in the lunatic asylum in Poona. A rich young English writer, Mr Ashley Gibson who travels with them in the plane, offers his car and he himself accompanies Dr Shankar sharing the burden of taking the Maharaja to Poona. The next day early morning they reach the asylum. Captain Bhagwat, the superintendent of the asylum is sympathetic to the Maharaja and he kindly allots to him a private room furnished with an iron bed, a table and a chair.

On hearing the news of the tragedy of Victor, Maharani Indira, the real wife of Maharaja Ashok Kumar who has been neglected by him under the irresistable influence of Ganga Dasi, contacts Captain Bhagwat and Dr Shankar and informs them of her coming to Poona to look after her husband, revealing "the irony and tenderness of a woman's love that would pursue a man even to hell to rescue him when the love was selfless and real".[24]

Feudalism is the chief social concern of *Private Life of an Indian*

21. *Ibid.*, p. 329.
22. *Ibid.*, p. 331.
23. *Ibid.*, p. 332.
24. *Ibid.*, p. 357.

Prince. Throughout the novel, Anand exposes and denounces all feudal values and their heavy handed proponents, the Rajas and Maharajas, represented in this novel by Victor, the Maharaja of Sham Pur. The social and economic system in Sham Pur is directed only to extort and exploit from the wretched people of the state innumerable varieties of taxes for the luxury, comfort and happiness of Victor, his nymphomaniac mistress Ganga Dasi and his intimate friends. The people of his state dramatically calls him "the 'tyrant of Sham Pur', the levier of illegal taxes and the egotistical head of a lawlessly lawful government, whose sanctions lay in his whims and fancies".[25] The oppressions, extortions and deprivations are chiefly conducted by Victor under the influence and for the benefit of his mistress Ganga Dasi. He knows that the Government of India would not allow him to bestow any legal status on her. So he begins to amass wealth for her by direct and indirect means. Various draconian taxes are levied upon the people in order to build up a fortune for her. Illegal dues, known as *nazaranas*, are taken from people, money is extorted from reversioners or heirs of those who died childless, from people who adopt children and even from people who arrange rightful succession. Any one who dare disobey those decrees is cruelly treated and his property is confiscated.

Victor's uxoriousness for Ganga does not prevent his hunting of other hearts. He "demanded any women who came within the orbit of his lustful vision".[26] Instead of procuring essential commodities for the miserable masses of his state he keeps many agents in different parts of his state for procuring young girls for him. As the author tells us, "not a virgin or a rupee was safe in his realms".[27] Those who protest against his exploitations are arrested and detained without any trial in prisons which are dark chambers of Death. The wretched condition of the living hell of the Udham Pur Jail narrated by one of the detenues shows Victor's tyranny and callous indifference to his subjects. The so called class I cell of the prison is nothing but a small black hole continually smelling of the smell of their own urine in open pots. The detenues in class III dormitory have no lavatory and have to relieve themselves at night "in one corner which has caused all of them to go down one by one with malaria, hook-worms, anaemia and

25. *Ibid.*, p. 315.
26. *Ibid.*, p. 175.
27. *Ibid.*, p. 60.

T.B."[28] The jail is worse than the concentration camps of the Nazis. Day in and day out the prisoners' necks, hands and feet are kept in fetters with heavy iron chains resulting in the formation of pus. In the evenings they are made to hold compulsory prayers, during which they are made to chant "Maharaja Sahib *ki jai*! Sham Pur Raj *ki jai*!"[29]

Even when people under the banner of *Praja Mandal* are observing *hartal* in protest against starvation, illegal extortion of taxes and other crimes of the ruler, Victor, unmindful of them, is entertaining his American friends at Sham Pur Lodge with French Champagne of 1905, delicious food, panther hunt, wild orgies and egg eating competition. As the narrator tells us:

> After drinks the guests wandered on to the lawns of the lodge in twos and threes, while the villagers, particularly the shrivelled-up old men, the large-stomached, naked little children and wiry *Shikaris*, gathered together on the fringes of the garden, admiring the exalted guests and nursing various hopes in their hearts for bounteous gifts of *bakshish*.[30]

The abject poverty suffered by the people of Sham Pur is well reflected in the *Shikari* Buta's desire even to dispense with his most cherished souvenir of hunt, the head and skin of a panther, in return for some money: "I will present the *Amrikan* sahib with the head and the skin, and he can take it home and say he shot it. I don't mind, *Huzoor*. To me a little cash is more valuable than a lot of prestige!"[31]

Victor's conducting of egg eating competition and generously offering champagne to the competitors to help them down the egg stands in marked contrast to his kicking of Buta which results in bleeding of mouth and nose for demanding a fair wage after spending many sleepless nights for the success of the panther hunt.

Victor's thoughts are nourished by the feudal, aristocratic idea that all excellence is inheritance. His ways as shown in the novel are the ways of feudalism. Anand's fear that India, "this very long-ago land" of ours, after its independence might not be able to completely shake off the feudal values which it embraced fervently for many centuries is based on his correct understanding of the Indian society with its attachment to the hangovers of history — the tolerance of

28. *Ibid.*, p. 162.
29. *Ibid.*, p. 163.
30. *Ibid.*, p. 179.
31. *Ibid.*, p. 183.

feudalism and a mystic veneration for the princes as the descendents of God. As Anand says in the novel, "The trouble with liberal democracy is that it takes a long time to mature."[32] Hence, during the quick accession of and change over in Sham Pur as in other parts of India, there is complete confusion. So instead of reforming the society, old values are pooh-poohed and the Inspector of Police comes to be more honoured than the Inspector of Schools and "intrigues, corruption, nepotism and black market spread in intricate coils around the houses and offices of Sham Pur, until, in the darkness that was day light, one could not recognize oneself or anything else".[33] Anand knows that independence from the colonial rulers or accession of kingdoms to Indian Union mean nothing to the majority of the people unless they are able to attain economic independence. So he wants the social and economic systems of the country to undergo a thorough transformation so as to give a fair deal to all sections of society and thereby ring the knell of feudalism once for all.

Another social criticism found in the novel is the unwillingness of the educated people in India to give up the age-old superstitious beliefs. Victor and his entourage on reaching the Sham Pur railway station wait there at the suggestion of Munshi Mithan Lal for the *Mahurat* to enter the state. As the narrator tells us "He was a prince who had been educated in the English Public School tradition and yet whose home background encouraged the darkest superstitions and the most obscurantist ideas. The most barbaric impulses of both civilizations dominated him."[34] The discovery of the *mahurat* by the state astrologer is an essential ritual for Victor. Not only for important trips of the Maharaja, "but sometimes even the shopping expeditions or visits to the club were preceded by the ostentatious reckoning by the state astrologer of the position of the stars *vis-a-vis* the day, the hour and the minute of His Highness's toings and froings."[35] The narrator-character, an Anand-like person, is irritated by the absurdity of waiting in the station for Pandit Dhanpat Rai to come and sort out the planets and the stars. So he asks the Maharaja: "Why are we waiting here when we know that Pandit Dhanpat Rai can persuade the stars to get into an auspicious array any time he

32. *Ibid.*, p. 268.

33. *Ibid.*, p. 266.

34. *Ibid.*, p. 69.

35. *Ibid.*, pp. 69-70.

likes?"[36] Meanwhile the astrologer arrives and says: "Maharaj, you are blessed.... The hour and the moment is ever auspicious for you. And your path is strewn with flowers all the way"[37], which provokes the critical Dr Shankar to whisper to the Maharaja: "Please look out for the few thorns that might have got mixed up with the roses."[38] The episode is an open criticism of educated men with rational outlook slavishly holding on to superstitious beliefs, the remnants of primitive thinking. The social criticism voiced by Dr Shankar in this episode perfectly expresses with Anand's own protest against superstition.

The disastrous consequence of infatuation is the pervading theme of *Private Life of an Indian Prince*. Victor's misrule, misery, crime and madness are solely due to his foolish attachment to his mistress, Ganga Dasi. The history of man is punctuated with such eccentrics. As Chamfort says, "A woman is like your shadow; follow her she flies; fly from her, she follows".[39] Hence, mad attachment to a woman is bound to keep a man in a fool's paradise. Anand's opaque criticism of infatuation observable throughout this novel may have resulted from his own involvement with the young girl, Anil de Silva.

Critics differ widely on the artistic quality of *Private Life of an Indian Prince*. While G.S. Balarama Gupta considers the novel 'a failure'[40], Saros Cowasjee finds it 'his best work'.[41] Commenting on this novel, Jack Lindsay says, "As a psychological novel on a grand scale, its scope is Dostoevskian".[42] K.N. Sinha in his book *Mulk Raj Anand* disagrees with this view as he feels that the Dostoevskian "etching of life in its depths" cannot be realised in *Private Life of an Indian Prince*.[43] On this dispute one may find a clearer stand in this commentary by K.R. Srinivasa Iyengar:

> Bad and mad though he may be, and pursued by fatality, the prince isn't devoid of a certain distinction. He quotes Manu

36. *Ibid*., p. 70.
37. *Ibid*., p. 71.
38. *Ibid*., p. 72.
39. Quoted from, *Best Quotations For All Occasions*, arranged and edited by Lewis C. Henry, London: Premier Publishers Pvt. Ltd., 1968, p. 252.
40. Gupta, G.S. Balarama: *Mulk Raj Anand : A Study of His Fiction in Humanist Perspective*, Bareilly, Prakash Book Depot, 1974, p. 87.
41. Cowasjee, Saros: "Introduction" to *Private Life of an Indian Prince*, Delhi: Arnold-Heinemann, 1983, p. 11.
42. Lindsay, Jack: *The Elephant and the Lotus: A Study of the Novels of Mulk Raj Anand*, Bombay, Kutub-Popular, 1965, p. 27.
43. Sinha, K.N., *Mulk Raj Anand*, New York: Twayne Publishers 1972, p. 63.

> and Plato and Shelley; he discusses philosophy and statecraft; he is cunning and cruel; he is vily and vain; he is self-righteous and self-pitying, and always he has a residual human charm of his own. Both Prince and "Queen Bee" are Dostoevskian characters in the sense that they exemplify the Russian novelist's dictum, "Human nature is broad". And Dostoevskian too is the Prince's capacity to indulge endlessly in the "hopeless wailing of the helpless."[44]

The above quoted views of critics show that *Private Life of an Indian Prince* is not unanimously admired by all critics. It remains, however, one of the best novels of Mulk Raj Anand. Anand is better placed in this novel in comparison to his other novels especially dealing with the lower dregs of society. In novels where the stage is dominated by illiterates like *Two Leaves and a Bud, Gauri, Untouchable* or *Coolie* one or two persons involving themselves in philosophical discussion appear odd and it amounts to intrusion. But in *Private Life of an Indian Prince* most of the characters are educated persons and in such an atmosphere, a college educated Maharaja and his personal physician, a Post-Graduate in medicine from London discussing Buddhism, Hinduism and Christianity or O' Casey's conception of 'state of chasis' or the status of woman in Europe, seem quite appropriate. Moreover most of such discussions are brief and so they do not destroy the focus of the novel.

Commenting on this novel G.S. Balarama Gupta says: "As a whole, the novel is a perplexing medlay of sex, intrigue and politics and is definitely not Anand at his best. It would probably have enriched the quality of the novel if Anand had enlarged the description of the gradual growth of the *Praja Mandal* rather than elaborating the nearly nauseating sexual ventures of Victor and Ganga Dasi."[45] It is hard to agree with this view as the novel's ultimate aim is not to present social problems or the opposition Victor faces but to expose his private life and personality trapped in a labyrinth of passion. If Anand were to enlarge the description of the gradual growth of the *Praja Mandal*, the novel would not have been a story of the private life of an Indian prince. The sexual adventures of Victor and Ganga

---

44. Iyengar, K.R. Srinivasa: "Foreword" to G.S. Balarama Gupta's *Mulk Raj Anand : A Study of his Fiction in Humanist Perspective*, Bareilly, Prakash Book Depot, 1974, p. (viii).

45. Gupta, G.S. Balarama, *Mulk Raj Anand : A Study of His Fiction in Humanist Perspective*, Bareilly, Prakash Book Depot, 1974, p. 87.

Dasi, as presented in the novel, are essential to our understanding of Victor's emotional disorder.

The plot of the novel moves in the right direction. The only minor irritant that can be noticed in the plot is the involvement of Mr Gibson and his subsequent discussion with Dr Shankar on many topics unsuitable at that grave situation permeated with the trepidation of Maharaja's madness. Mr Gibson's role in the novel is only to help Dr Shankar to take the Maharaja to the lunatic asylum at Poona. Instead of Mr Gibson, if a matter-of-fact figure, say, an official of the Union Government were introduced, the readers' concern for the Maharaja would not have been dissipated. As it is, Gibson arouses at first curiosity in the reader and later on boredom by his unwarranted talk and at his departure from the scene the reader realises that he had come only to spoil the intensity of feeling evoked by the pathetic condition of the Maharaja. Hence Gibson is a small parasite who could have been dispensed with.

The madness of the Maharaja is presented with complete psychological veracity. Anand seems to have been influenced by Shakespeare. After his mistress Gangi deserts him, Victor is deeply disturbed and he suffers pangs of jealousy. His state of mind is comparable to that of the jealous Othello. Later, when he comes to know that he has to return to India to give evidence on the death of Bool Chand, he is in the words of the author, 'like Caliban in the last throes of his revolt against his persecutors'.[46] Of all the Shakespearean plays, *King Lear* seems to have influenced *Private Life of an Indian Prince* the most. Mad Victor talks and acts like mad Lear. Dr Shankar is like the Fool in that Shakespearean tragedy, a philosopher and guide to the king. Ganga Dasi is an amalgam of Goneril and Regan; and Bool Chand who runs away with Ganga Dasi recalls Edmund, the bastard. Tikyali Maharani Indira resembles the virtuous Cordelia who came to help the king in his hour of helplessness. Apart from these similarities, the novel has many echoes of the Shakespearean voice. The words of one of the detenues in Udham Pur Jail, "And the whole hierarchy of officials and warders resembles the big flies who suck the blood of the little flies, with the little flies encroaching on the littler flies, until man begins to lose all faith in each other"[47], are comparable to Gloucester's pathetic utterance in *King Lear*: "As flies

46. Anand, Mulk Raj: *Private Life of an Indian Prince*, Delhi, Arnold-Heinemann, 1983, p. 329.

47. *Ibid.*, p. 163.

to the wanton boys are we to the gods/ They kill us for their sport."[48] Dr Shankar's reflective comment on the Indian princes, "The whirligig of time brings the strangest revenges",[49] is similar to Feste's comment on the 'mad' Malvolio, "... and thus the whirligig of time brings in his revenges"[50], in Shakespeare's *Twelfth Night*. Again, in the words of Victor, "I feel there are more disasters coming my way....I am afraid! I dread the future! I fear myself — my own thoughts! I feel a terrible sense of foreboding! It is all darkness...."[51], we can hear an echo of the words of Romeo in *Romeo and Juliet*:

> I fear, too early: for my mind misgives
> Some consequence yet hanging in the stars
> Shall bitterly begin his fearful date
> With this night's revels and expire the term
> Of a despised life closed in my breast
> By some vile forfeit of untimely death.[52]

There are a number of novels and semi-fictional accounts about the princes of India. The most popular among them are J.R Ackerley's *Hindoo Holiday* (1932), E.M. Forster's *The Hill of Devi* (1953), Mulk Raj Anand's *Private Life of an Indian Prince* (1953) and Manohar Malgonkar's *The Princes* (1963). Malgonkar's *The Princes* appeared only ten years after the publication of Anand's *Private Life of an Indian Prince*. The many similarities in episodes and structure that exist between these two novels indicate that Malgonkar was influenced by Anand's novel on the Indian Prince. *Private life of an Indian Prince* and *The Hill of Devi* appeared in the same year and so their authors might not have glanced each other's work before they were published. Mulk Raj Anand and E.M. Forster are the two most sensitive writers on the state of Indian princes. Forster in *The Hill of Devi* generously gives concession to the 'weakness of the flesh' of the Maharaja, His Highness Sir Tukoji Rao III of Dewas State Senior, whom he served for some time as private secretary. The novel gives a balanced, sympathetic account of the Maharaja. Though Anand does not strive for that kind of balance, he too treats his Maharaja with concession as 'a poor-rich of our country, who deserves pity

48. Shakespeare, William, *King Lear*, Act : IV : Sc. (i) : 36-37.
49. Anand, Mulk Raj, *Private Life of an Indian Prince*, Delhi, Arnold-Heinemann, 1983, p. 230.
50. Shakespeare, William, *Twelfth Night*, Act V : Sc. (i) : 380-81.
51. Anand, Mulk Raj: *Private Life of an Indian Prince*, Delhi, Arnold-Heinemann, 1983, p. 276.
52. Shakespeare, William, *Romeo and Juliot*, Act : I. Sc. (iv) : 103.

more than contempt".[53] Both writers handle the biography of their princes as more of an art than a branch of history. Their humane approach to the princes is greatly responsible for the success and glory of their works.

Referring to *Private Life of an Indian Prince*, Jack Lindsay says: "If Anand had written nothing else, his place in the history of the novel would be secure."[54] Some critics may find this too tall a claim, but Jack Lindsay is to a great extent correct in this assessment. It is a compassionate work on a passionate prince presented with irony, humour and understanding capable of giving great pleasure to the reader. This superb psychological novel is a milestone in Indo-Anglian fiction.

53. Anand, Mulk Raj : *Author to Critic : The Letters of Mulk Raj Anand to Saros Cowasjee*, ed. Saros Cowasjee, Calcutta, Writers Workshop, 1973, p. 12. (Letter dated 18 Nov. 1967).

54. Lindsay, Jack : *The Elephant and the Lotus : A Study of the Novels of Mulk Raj Anand*, Bombay : Kutub-Popular, 1965, pp. 27-28.

VII

GAURI

The Russian poet Nicholai Nekrasov's *The Peasant Woman*, the story of Sita in the *Ramayana* and the writings of Ali Sardar Jafri inspired Anand to write his tenth novel *Gauri*. It was first published in 1960 under the title *The Old Woman and the Cow* and later re-issued by Orient Paperbacks in its present name. It is unique among Anand's works as it is his only novel with a woman protagonist. The old title, *The Old Woman and the Cow* given by the publisher and a poet-friend of Anand[1] was not satisfactory to the author as the focus of the novel is not on the shameless old woman in the novel, Laxmi and her cow, Chandari, but on her virtuous, cow-like gentle and patient daughter, Gauri. So, the author rightly renamed the novel *Gauri*.

This novel, as indeed all Anand's fiction, expresses his indisputable concern for the suffering humanity of India. It forces one to ask a few questions about the Indian character. We call our woman 'Mata', 'Devi' and 'Laxmi' and claim that our society has always been giving due respect to women. At the same time, we also beat them, set them ablaze or turn them out of the house. Anand's novel *Gauri* eloquently exposes the hypocrisy of our society. It not only voices a strong protest against the ill-treatment of women but also explores through the example of Gauri what woman in India should do for her emancipation.

As Panchi struggles on the back of an unwilling pony to reach Piplan Kalan to possess the girl "whom he could fold in his arms at night and kick during the day, who would adorn his house and help him with the land"[2], curiosity and imagination take control of his

---

1. See: Premila Paul's *The Novels of Mulk Raj Anand : A Thematic Study*, New Delhi: Sterling Publishers Pvt. Ltd., 1983, p. 123 (Here the author quotes a personal letter Anand wrote to her on 21-12-1978 on the renaming of the novel).
2. Anand, Mulk Raj, *Gauri*, New Delhi : Arnold-Heinemann, 1984, p. 11.

mind: "Panchi tried to imagine what the girl, Gauri was like. Was she fair or was she dark? Beautiful or ugly or just plain? And in his fantasy, below the deafening roar of the *Angrezi* music, arose certain brief visions of how he would take her into his arms, as the hero always took the heroine in the films he had seen in the Hoshiarpur town."[3] He wishes that what his would-be-parents-in-law often repeated during the long months of negotiation is true: "Gauri is like a cow, very gentle and very good."[4]

As Panchi has taken the turn around the fire with Gauri tied to him from behind with her apron, he is anxious "to confirm the rumour that she was not ugly but was light skinned as her mother".[5] When the gyrations around the fire, and the whole embarrassing ritual of the marriage and the customary feast are over, the ceremony of 'showing' starts. While the females attending on the bride prolong Panchi's curiosity by not allowing Gauri to lift the *dupatta*, "overcome by a sudden and wild impulse to satisfy his curiosity he suddenly pulled aside the *jhund* of her *dupatta* and saw — a light wheat brown face with regular strong peasant features and the bloom of innocence on it".[6] He is very happy. Within a short time Gauri's mother, Laxmi comes in with ceremonial tears in her eyes and asks her daughter to get ready to go to her husband's house. She advises Gauri to be like Sita.

After the marriage, Panchi continues to stay with his guardians, uncle Mola Ram and aunt Kesaro. When Mola Ram was away, in the past, Kesaro used to dote upon Panchi. Kesaro's secret attachment to Panchi causes hatred in her against any woman coming in between her and Panchi. So she calls the famine, drought and poverty that have accompanied Panchi's marriage, as God's curse for his marrying the unlucky woman, Gauri. Under the influence of Kesaro, Panchi's admiration for the cow-like gentle and comely Gauri slowly vanishes.

Kesaro, taking the role of a ruthless mother-in-law continues her hate-campaign against Gauri. She abuses Gauri calling her "a whore from Piplan", "filthy woman", "sweeper woman shamelsss" etc. She blames her for going about at home without putting the *dupatta* on her head and maliciously accuses her of being free with

3. *Ibid*., p. 10.
4. *Ibid*., p. 11.
5. *Ibid*., p. 21.
6. *Ibid*., p. 29.

young men like the subedar's son Rajguru, while Panchi is away. Kesaro's insinuations arouses jealousy and fire in Panchi. One day it explodes and he slaps her many times.

Panchi and his uncle Mola Ram are not able to pull on smoothly for long. One day their hatred detonates. They exchange blows and Mola Ram asks Panchi to leave the barn he occupies. One of Panchi's Muslim friends, Rafique Chacha, the potter of the village then readily offers a part of his barn for Panchi and Gauri to stay.

Away from the joint family and undisturbed by Kesaro, Panchi and Gauri come closer. He slowly begins to understand her love and affection for him.

One day the wicked Kesaro visits them and poisons Panchi's mind against Gauri. She speaks to Panchi about his horoscope: "Our house would break up with the coming of an inauspicious girl...."[7] Hearing these destructive words, Gauri picks up unexpected courage and catches hold of Kesaro by the bun of her hair and pushes her out of the barn. After the departure of Kesaro, the idea of Gauri's bad stars injected in him by Kesaro continues to possess Panchi. Above all, Kesaro's accusation of Gauri's liaison with Rajguru in his absence arouses suspicion in him over her character. But Gauri's devotion to and ardent love for him makes his mind oscillate between loving and hating her. One morning she tells him shyly: "Now the rains will have to come, because I am with a child and we shall soon have another mouth to feed".[8] Instead of getting excited by the news, for days he is plunged into the biggest confusion, a veritable whirlpool of doubts and one day he kicks her shouting:

> 'Go, go, get out of my sight. Go to your mother, the whore....'
>
> She fell at his feet, begged with hands joined before her forehead:
>
> 'Do not send me away'.[9]

But he kicks her left and right. So she gets up and walks towards her home in order to protect her womb against any further violence from him.

When she reaches home her mother, Laxmi welcomes her with

7. *Ibid.*, p. 95.
8. *Ibid.*, p. 101.
9. *Ibid.*, p. 102.

crocodile tears. But her uncle Amru bluntly speaks against her return, and in the middle of the night, he awakens Gauri. He asks her to get ready to go to Hoshiarpur, as he has made a deal with a rich *Sahukar* there, named *Seth* Jwala Prasad to offer her to the *Seth's* elder brother, *Seth* Jai Ram Das, "in lieu of cash and the wiping out of the mortgage on their two houses as well as the cow, Chandari".[10] Laxmi seems to have accepted the evil design of Amru in order to save her cow, the only source of her livelihood, from being taken away by the rich *Sahukar*. The old man, *Seth* Jwala Prasad, who looks pious with holy marks on his forehead is already there with his horse to take Gauri away. Gauri protests and refuses to go as she still loves her husband, Panchi. But Amru falls upon her and, catching hold of her by the plait of her hair, drags her down from the bed. He assaults her, ignoring the wailing and protest of Laxmi and at last he is able to lift and place her on the back of the horse. Then, as *Seth* Jwala Prasad wishes, Amru accompanies them to Hoshiarpur.

After Gauri is bought and brought by force to Hoshiarpur, she suffers from an acute fever. So the *Seth* goes and fetches Dr Mahindra. The doctor, while examining her, comes to know from Gauri that she is sold to the *Sethji* by her parents. Ever since Gauri came to the house, the *Seth* has been trying to win her heart by putting up a garb of religiosity and also by offering her jewellery. He is ready to give her everything but she is willing to accept nothing from him. Her only desire is to go back to her husband. After the doctor leaves the place, the *Seth* approaches her with a betel leaf wrapped in silver paper to put in her mouth. As he comes close to her he sees her breasts bursting out of her tunic. He becomes desperate with desire. During the struggle that follows, Gauri pushes him off her by a violent wriggle and she warns him: "I am guarded by the Goddess! So do not come near me. Or you will burn!"[11] She wants to ran away but she cannot as her fever has become more acute. When the doctor comes again to examine her, he finds her condition grave and so he sends the ambulance to bring her to his nursing home. The nursing home is under the ownership of Dr Mahindra and Dr Batra. After two days Gauri becomes better "and on the third day she was walking about the house, voluntarily helping Miss Clara Young, the middle aged Christian matron, who was the main hub around whom the life of this

10. *Ibid.*, p. 125.
11. *Ibid.*, p. 145.

small hospital, with twenty beds revolved".[12] When the *Sethji* comes to take Gauri away, the doctors refuse him the permission as she is not willing to go with him and also as she wants to be restored to her husband. So Dr Mahindra advises the *Seth* to wash his hands off her. He then asks Gauri to help the matron, Miss Clara Young, till he will be able to contact her husband and will be restored to him.

At a critical moment Panchi realises his wrongheadedness towards Gauri and one day he arrives at Piplan Kalan to bring her back. He meets Laxmi at her house and asks for Gauri. Laxmi tells him to find her whereabouts from Amru. Panchi rushes with anger to the house where Amru is. In the ensuing fight between Panchi and Amru's supporters, Panchi gets wounded and collapses. The Sub-Inspector of the place, Ganda Singh arrives on the scene. Panchi's uncle Adam Singh, who tries to save Panchi during the fight, reports to the police what had happened. Ganda Singh instead of arresting the real culprits, takes Laxmi into custody. He kicks her and orders her to bring back her daughter immediately and restore her to Panchi so as to keep the matter out of court.

Adam Singh volunteers to go with Laxmi to Hoshiarpur to get back Gauri. From *Seth* Jai Ram Das they come to know that Gauri has refused to come home after her treatment in Dr Mahindra's hospital and that the doctor has employed her as a nurse. So they go to the hospital in search of Gauri. When Laxmi is shown into the doctor's presence, "she saw her daughter Gauri, dressed in a simple white *dhoti* escorting a young patient to the door. She stood transfixed for a moment with her eyes dilated wide...."[13]

The doctor after giving Gauri's wages, allows her to leave for good with her mother and uncle. When they reach Chota Piplan, Rafique Chacha and Hoor Banu are there to welcome them. Panchi has been recovering from the assault of Amru. Gauri quietly sits down at the foot of the bed, drawing the edge of her white sari over her forehead and eyes. After some time Panchi and Gauri are left alone in the barn. Panchi then suddenly pulls her on to himself, and hugs her saying: "I have known...darkness. Now you come and....set me on fire".[14]

The next morning Gauri sets about putting her house in order.

---

12. *Ibid.*, p. 149.
13. *Ibid.*, p. 222.
14. *Ibid.*, p. 237

When Panchi opens his eyes, she is ready with a hot tumbler of milk and tea leaves for him. Later on she gives him a towel bath.

In the afternoon Rakhi, the old Muslim midwife of the village and a friend of Kesaro visits them and shamelessly begins retailing the village gossip. Unable to bear her talk, Panchi flings her out of the house into the galley.

The next day Panchi hears the familiar sound of Kesaro's call from outside the barn. Panchi does not allow her to come in. So she spreads the news to the people in the lane about the arrival of the prostitute from Hoshiarpur. The gossip of the villagers about Gauri's life in Hoshiarpur begins to obsess and oppress him. And suddenly the devil in him starts to work: "Tell me the truth, bitch?.... What is the proof of your purity?"[15], Panchi bawls. He then jumps up from the bed and kicks her. Unable to bear his cruelty any more she makes up her mind to go away from him for good. Weeping and sobbing she tells Hoor Banu:

> He is a weak, spoilt creature! Spoilt by Kesaro. He pretended to be a lion among the men of the village. But really he is a coward! They are telling him that Ram turned out Sita because everyone doubted her chastity during her stay with Ravana!.... I am not Sita that the earth will open up and swallow me. I shall just go out and be forgotten of him...[16]

Sorrowfully she fixes her eyes for a moment on Panchi and then rushes out through the lane in the direction of Dr Mahindra's hospital as the "love for the unborn babe urged her on".[17]

The removal of the disabilities of the Indian women and their freedom from various forms of oppression has been an unending process. Though the law of the land does not admit of inequality on the basis of sex, old social and psychological habits and the reactionary resistance of the orthodox sections of society militate against the law and so even at the turn of this century majority of the Indian village women are still martyrs to the conventions of our society in which they are born. The conventions of our society are cruel to woman. They are intended to give advantages to the selfishness of man. They permit man to have many rights and freedoms from which woman is

15. *Ibid.*, p. 262.
16. *Ibid.*, p. 263.
17. *Ibid.*, p. 264.

excluded. They adopt different standards to judge the individual and social conduct of man and woman.

Mulk Raj Anand is saddened by the fact that the average Indian woman only has the status of a slave "bound and fecund for the service of the hearth..."[18] He has introduced in many of his novels the theme of woman's hardships : Rukmani in *The Road*, whose marriage was delayed for want of money to give dowry, does not understand why males behave with superiority and she comes out with a rhetorical question: "Oh why, oh, why were the men of tribe so privileged?"[19] In *The Big Heart* Janaki says: "No one knows what a woman suffers. How much she has to bear silently and without protest the abuse and the condemnation."[20] Though in 1856, widow remarriage was legally permitted, Orthodoxy does not actually encourage remarriage and considers widowhood as a punishment for a woman's earlier *karma* and condemns the widow as an ominous person. She is generally ostracised. In fact she is made to live a life in a kennel for the rest of her life. The widowed Maya in *The Village* Trilogy being the landlord's daughter faces more restraints. A couple of strong servants guard the gate like 'watch-dogs', and she is always under the control of her mother.

Anand knew that social taboos against women, as in the case of untouchability, cannot be changed by legislation alone. He found in the novel a medium for making people sensitive to the ill-treatment of woman. That urged him to write *Gauri*. It is, as an artist, Anand's greatest contribution towards the movement for the emancipation of woman. It projects the evils of male chauvinism and the society's ambivalent approach with regard to woman and inspires the Indian woman to face the challenge by courageously working for her emancipation which alone can redeem the Indian society from the failure of communication and communion between man and woman, the animating and sustaining principles of life and creation, whose union is essential for the well-being of both as well as for the survival of our race.

The opening scene of the novel, describing Gauri's marriage ceremony, exposes the absurd and ridiculous proceedings that have

18. Anand, Mulk Raj, "The Bride : An Essay on the Status of Woman in India", In: *Lines Written to an Indian Air,* Bombay, Nalanda Publications, 1949, p. 165.
19. Anand, Mulk Raj, *The Road*, Bombay : Kutub-Popular, 1961, p. 100.
20. Anand, Mulk Raj, *The Big Heart*, New Delhi, Arnold-Heinemann, 1980, p. 84.

become part of an Indian marriage: the loud music, the procession, the uncontrollable crowd of uninvited guests for the feast, children fighting for the showered copper coin, the quarrel over dowry, complaint over the quality of jewellery, the ceremony of the 'showing' conducted by the females with a chorus of lampoons and throwing of riddles at the bridegroom until he loses his patience and forcibly pulls aside the *jhund* of the bride's *dupatta* to see her face and so on. The marriage here is a most rigid type of arranged marriage prevalent in some parts of India in which the bridegroom is not even allowed to have a glance of the bride before the ceremony is complete. Since the bride's face remains hidden until the ceremony is over, the bridegroom has to depend on rumours regarding the appearance of his wife to be:

> He (Panchi) was anxious only for one thing: that when the four turns were finished and the whole embarrassing ritual of the marriage and the customary feast were over, he would be able to lift the red *dupatta* which enshrouded the girl's face, to confirm the rumour that she was not ugly but was as light-skinned as her mother. Sometimes rumour made an ugly bride into a beautiful one. And he was a trifle afraid that the praise of Gauri may be false. But many people had reported that she was fair. In this hope he had been willing to endure the heat, the sweat and the words of the priest.[21]

The marriage of the sort described in the novel is a mechanical action in which love, the force behind marriage, is drowned in the long negotiation for dowry. In such marriages, parents simply impose a wife or husband upon their children unmindful of his or her likes and dislikes. Whatever religious interpretation is given in support of such marriage, it is a mockery of love. The inhibitory nature of such marriages often leads to male barbarism on the first night. In one of his letters to Saros Cowasjee, Anand wrote: "You know that every Aryan rapes the helpless female in the arranged marriages of India on the first night. The cries are drowned in the music outside. And yet many of our modernists accept *vedic* rites at their weddings. This hypocrisy stinks."[22] Mulk Raj Anand, through the series of thoughts expressed by Panchi as he goes to Piplan Kalan on the back of a pony to 'own' Gauri and also through the comedy of the ceremony vividly

21. Anand, Mulk Raj : *Gauri*, New Delhi, Arnold-Heinemann, 1984, p. 21.
22. Anand, Mulk Raj : *Author to Critic : The Letters of Mulk Raj Anand to Saros Cowasjee*, ed. Saros Cowasjee, Calcutta : Writers Workshop, 1973, p. 28 (Letter dated 5 July, 1968).

presented in the opening chapter of the novel, laughs at arranged marriage and in unequivocal terms condemns a marriage which lacks the full approval and sufficient knowledge of the concerned partners.

Panchi after having gone through a conventional marriage wants his wife to lead a conventional life. He forces Gauri to submit to his impatience and pettiness without any protest. Her duties are to cook, to clean, to please her husband's libidinous desires and to submit herself humbly to his male chauvinism and physical violence. One day during their love-making, Gauri taking advantage of the situation pleads to Panchi not to beat her again at Kesaro's bidding. Even at that passionate moment he does not hesitate to remind her of his conventional right to beat her:

> 'But the husband has to chastise the wife if she goes wrong', he said airily. 'So says, our *Dharam*'.[23]

Ironic enough, Panchi himself does not appear to be an whole-hearted devotee of traditions. For instance, he calls the convention that forces women during their menstruation to the corner as untouchables, a 'stupid' thing. He defies convention by eating and drinking with the Muhammadans, but in the treatment of Gauri he strictly applies the conventions with the sole aim of asserting his right over her.

An understanding and sympathetic mother-in-law is an extremely rare phenomenon and for most Indian woman marriage means getting trapped in a horrible den where they get nothing but physical and mental torture. In a joint family, the misery of a woman begins from the moment she incurs the displeasure of the mother-in-law. Very often the mother-in-law's ill-treatment of the daughter-in-law is due to fear and jealousy. The mother-in-law's unquestionable position and influence in the house turns the daughter-in-law into an enemy. In such an atmosphere only a responsible and far-sighted husband can boldly come to the aid of his wife. As portrayed in *Gauri*, the vast majority of Indian homes are made up of Panchis and Kesaros who have no scruples about the tears of Gauris. Panchi's failure to defend Gauri against the evil tongue of Kesaro typifies the immoral and tragic nature of our domestic life.

Anand's usual protest against the belief in *karma* and superstition is voiced in this novel too. The villagers accept all misfortunes as part

---

23. Anand, Mulk Raj : *Gauri*, New Delhi, Arnold-Heinemann, 1984, p. 51.

of their *karma*. But Panchi, as in the case of all other Anand's protagonists, does not believe in *karma*. His explanation of *karma* as an euphemism for exploitation reflects the author's own mind:

> And he righteously felt the contradiction of life: the burning apperception of his own youth and strength, of his ability to do things, his capacity to eat and love and roll about in the shades of the mango groves and the degrading fact that this was all denied, for no fault of his or of any other peasant, but their *karma*, fate, which brought drought after drought. Bah — what lies the Brahmin dogs told — *Karma*! The white sahibs were aliens and had sucked the blood of the country, as Gandhi said. The Congress Sarkar could have damned up the rivers, or dug new wells and given the villagers the gift of water. But the white caps (sic) were in the big *chor bazar*. And then big schemes for giving water and power were affording bribes, so that by that time all the money was eaten away by the contractors, there were many more mouths to feed – that was *Karma*![24]

Gauri, like all village women believes in *karma*. But the education she has received by coming into contact with the enlightened Dr Mahindra makes her realise the foolishness of believing in it. She tells Rafique Chacha:

> When I first came to this house, I worried so much about what the village would say, I had no tongue in my mouth. I only did the house work and lay down to sulk and weep on that little cot. I certainly could not think. Now, how can you fly if you have no wings? The villagers accept the behests of Lalla Birbal and the other elders. And we are content to be pigs. *Daktar* Mahindra says: "Where there is poverty there is a money-lender, a priest and a landlord — and God is always on their side". But, he says, it need not be so......... 'Education', Gauri said quoting the big *Daktar*, 'education will make us master fate'.[25]

The villagers are blinded by superstition and they mistake superstition for religion. To such a people Kesaro telling that from the day Gauri set foot in their house, they have had bad luck, is bound

24. *Ibid*., p. 90.
25. *Ibid*., p. 240.

to sound sensible. Though Panchi has never believed in superstition and always laughed at his mother and Kesaro for the religious ceremonies they used to conduct, Kesaro's campaign of hate against Gauri based on her horoscope and bad stars gradually begins to work on him:

> The idea of Gauri's bad stars continued to possess him, because the circumstances which were said to have been created by her arrival continued to grow worse: the drought seemed to become permanent, the rains would not come; more birds were found dead with the heat in the fields; the wells were drying up completely; and the cattle was dwindling through the owners taking their cows (sic), buffaloes and bullocks away to villages further down the valley towards Hoshiarpur town to sell them to the slaughter house.[26]

Superstition victimises Gauri. Panchi who is in the beginning proud of Gauri's comely and innocent appearance and her cow-like meekness, forms a completely different picture of her under the influence of superstition planted in him by Kesaro:

> She has ruined me.... My aunt Kesaro is right when she says that this bride is the incarnation of Kali, the black goddess who destroys all before her, who brings famine in her breath and lays bare whole villagers. Like Kali Mai in the temple of Dharamsala, who wears a garland of skulls round her neck....[27]

Beaten by Panchi and insulted and abused by Kesaro, Gauri finds her life in Piplan Kalan a veritable hell. When she returns home with the hope of getting affection and happiness, again superstition drags her to greater misery. Her uncle, Amru, bluntly tells Laxmi about her: "Her husband has turned her out. This unlucky girl must have brought him troubles, as she brought difficulties to us...."[28] Amru, affected by superstition, thinks that misfortune will overtake them by her stay there and on the very day of her return he goes to Hoshiarpur and finds a market for her.

Blaming Nature's failure on Gauri, failures which affect not only her husband's family or village but vast territories of land and

---

26. *Ibid.*, pp. 97-98.
27. *Ibid.*, p. 33.
28. *Ibid.*, p. 107.

labelling her as the cause of all misfortunes is sheer scoundrelism. If Gauri were to stick to her husband Panchi in spite of his beating, and tolerate her aunt Kesaro in spite of her insults, there would have been every chance of her being put to death, under the pretext of appeasing god's anger which brought drought and famine and no one would have uttered a word against that horrible deed of human sacrifice on the altar of superstition. The accusation of Gauri as inauspicious simply shows how superstition has deprived people of their senses. It is deplorable that the villagers, instead of fighting against superstition, indirectly work for the strengthening of it by following many meaningless rituals involving a lot of their hard earned money to ward off supposedly evil influences.

The worship of Mammon or the greed for money is at the root of many social evils. The introduction of money into the rural economy is responsible for the moral decadence in village life. When Panchi promises a rent of Rs. 5 per month to Rafique Chacha for the barn he is allowed to occupy, the generous and compassionate Muslim potter is annoyed and speaks of the curse money brought in their otherwise peaceful life:

> Money ! money ! .....There is no talk nowadays except the talk of money — about the prices of things. Don't let me hear the word money again. The curse has blighted my house. My father and my grandfather used to exchange pots for grain with you farmers. It is only when I was forced to sell pots for cash to the shops that our troubles began....curse it...[29]

Whatever one may say about the curse brought about by money in our social dealings, it has become an indispensable force. As the Russian proverb says, "When money speaks, truth is silent." Terrifying are the brutalities committed for the sake of money. According to Union Home Ministry's report, in 1985 alone there were 6326 dowry cases and 837 cases of wife-burning in India. Money, when it becomes our master, is a great monster. It is money, the modern god that presides over all our social intercourse, that turns Amru and Laxmi heartless enough to carry out their evil design of selling Gauri away to a sixty year old greasy money-lender. Laxmi tells the city confectioner :

> In the part of the hills where I really come from...... women always taught men to love...But when you shopkeepers came

29. *Ibid.*, p. 59.

with your money you taught us hill people to buy and sell girls.... I am not ashamed of having gone to bed with men, but I am ashamed that I had to sell my daughter......[30]

Dr Mahindra sees through the situation more clearly and tells Laxmi how man's madness for money has brought falsity and wretchedness into the life of the village:

> .... we tie as many oxen and cows and buffaloes to the halter as we can, and when we have no money we sell our daughters – ..... I am not blaming you.... I am just saying those *Banias* who buy and sell, have brought falsity into the life of the village. In the old days, there was often scarcity. But, as no one owned the land, the five elders could give fertile land to whoever complained that his land was fallow. And all the grazing land was in common. And there was milk and butter and whey.... Now, every peasant owns his land (sic) can sell it.... 'And as he is often in debt to the *Seth*, he sells out and becomes a labourer in the town factory. And cash has become more valuable than the earth. So there is wretchedness everywhere.... your Amru turns crook and you sell your daughter, even as folks elsewhere are selling their daughters!'[31]

Man should certainly fight against poverty, but poverty should not make us brutes. Panchi's chasing out his wife to her home when he hears from her "we shall soon have another mouth to feed"[32], is a brutal act. Poverty should not make us inhuman. Rafique Chacha's attitude to life should be a model to the poor. He is rich in spite of his poverty. He maintains goodness in the face of all miseries. He tells Panchi: "Never give up faith, son! There is still life in us! This is not happening to one person, the drought! Thousands are suffering the pangs of hunger. Crops, fields, stocks have all gone. People are selling their daughters. So the damage to the land is nothing like the damage to men themselves....."[33] Rafique Chacha not only generously allows Gauri and Panchi to stay in his barn but also tries to make their life there a memorable one. The life of Rafique Chacha illustrates that a dignified approach to life and hard work are the solutions to poverty.

30. Anand, Mulk Raj: *Gauri*, New Delhi: Arnold-Heinemann, 1984, pp. 212-213.
31. *Ibid.*, pp. 224-225.
32. *Ibid.*, p. 101.

Anand, while condemning the wrong doings of male chauvinists in India, does not absolve woman of her sins against her own race. The ill-treatment of Gauri is mainly organised by women themselves. If Kesaro and the midwife Rakhi had not aroused suspicion in Panchi by questioning the purity of Gauri, she would not have been deserted by him. Anand, through the situation in the novel, tells us that the greatest enemy of woman is her own race. Hence, the first step towards the emancipation of women should be taken by women themselves. If the mother-in-laws of this Mother India become compassionate, our homes will be a place of happiness and we will hardly see in our Press the shocking reports on bride-burning and dowry deaths.

The technique of contrast adopted in the characterisation of Panchi and Gauri successfully brings out the nobility of Gauri as against the meanness of Panchi and makes the reader emotionally involved in the ill-treatment of Gauri. In the beginning of the novel we are told that on his way to Piplan Kalan in order to possess Gauri, "Panchi felt like a holy bull going off to marry the little cow Gauri".[34] The subsequent happenings in the novel turn upon the bull-cow paradigm. Panchi's annoyance at knowing that soon he would be a father is in sharp contrast to the joy Gauri felt in attaining motherhood. Gauri's parting with her ear-rings willingly, the only possession of jewellery she got as dowry, in order to buy seeds for cultivation; her defence of Panchi in the presence of her relatives and friends in spite of the fact that he inhumanly turned her out, and her earnest prayer to God to bless him with a good harvest even when as a consequence of his ill-treatment she was forcibly kept in the house of *Seth* Jai Ram Das are examples of her deep affection for Panchi. This deep affection shown by Gauri to her master and lord is a contrast to the superficial love of Panchi who tries to woo her with Hamam soap and stolen mangoes for his sexual satisfaction.

If Gauri is helpless at the beginning of the novel, at the end she emerges victorious. The transformation that has taken place in Gauri from an obedient, gentle and meek person to one 'with a will of her own' is indeed a triumph of womanhood. But the portraits of the suffering Gauri sulking on her string cot in a dark room, the Gauri kicked and insulted by her mean husband and the Gauri putting up

33. *Ibid.*, p. 99.
34. *Ibid.*, p. 13.

a defence for her husband in front of friends and relatives may be more attractive to the reader than the defiant Gauri telling her husband "if you strike me again, I will hit you back...."[35], or the eloquent Gauri lecturing to the old potter, Rafique Chacha. Her strength of character is best seen in her unwavering love for Panchi and her silent resolution "to get to the source of that antagonism and hatred which he showed to her".[36]

Panchi, despite his brutal treatment of his wife is not drawn unsympathetically. He is not altogether deprived of self-awareness and therefore he is able to acknowledge his faults in certain redemptive moments of his life: "And in the dim border land of his awareness, where reason rose above instinct.... he acknowledged to himself, that he had bullied her since she had come to his home, first at the instigation of Kesaro and then through habit."[37] Like Laxmi who is forced to choose between a cow that gives milk and a daughter who would soon bring forth another mouth to feed, Panchi too is a victim of circumstances. As the novelist tells us, Gauri "had not known much tenderness from her strong limbed husband ever since her marriage because the vigil and eyes of her mother-in-law Kesaro seemed to prevent him always from coming near her".[38] Panchi finds it impossible to rid himself of antiquated customs and social taboos against women active in his society and so he helplessly oscillates between his love for Gauri and the tyrannical influence of Kesaro. Yet the wavering Panchi is more impressive a character than the self-disciplined Colonel Mahindra — the most inartistically conceived voice of Anand in the novel. As Saros Cowasjee correctly observes, "Colonel Mahindra resembles John de la Havre in *Two Leaves and a Bud*, and the good he does to Gauri is largely negated by the damage he does to the novel."[39]

For some years before the publication of *Gauri*, Anand had been annoyed by certain literary critics with revivalist tendency who complained that his novel did not approximate to the mythical pattern and are therefore merely documentary. Anand's sharp

35. *Ibid.*, p. 263.
36. *Ibid.*, p. 40.
37. *Ibid.*, p. 77.
38. *Ibid.*, p. 51.
39. Cowasjee, Saros, *So Many Freedoms: A Study of Mulk Raj Anand's Major Fiction*, Delhi : OUP, 1977, p. 158.

reaction to such critics is contained in one of his letters to Saros Cowasjee:

> spontaneously, I feel, that the revivalists want to take us back to the filth of Hinduism, to the worship of Sabala the cow, and Hanuman the monkey, to the god-king Rama, who was a casteist and allowed his wife to be consigned to the fire, because the dhobis said she had been abducted by Ravana and had stayed in his ashram. They want to bring back the philosophy which smothered the rationalism of the Buddha and divided India into hierarchies, weakening it, so that it fell before every conqueror who could bring 500 horsemen through the Khyber Pass and descend upon the fertile plains.[40]

In this context Gauri has a special significance among all Anand's novels. It is Anand's only novel using Hindu myth as part of technique. But he does it not as a concession to the revivalists but "to prove that a new contemporary myth (of growth to awareness) of the potential man is possible, as against the myths of the *Ramayana* and the *Mahabharata*".[41] He says, "The old myths of the *Mahabharata* and the *Ramayana* and the *Puranas* can be safely left to those who want to bring back the civilization of the pre-Christian eras to the machine age. I have myself deliberately tried to create and live up to a new contemporary myth-man, in his dignity of weakness, struggling to be an individual, a god, and, of course, failing in the attempt."[42]

Anand does not try to hide the fact that the framework of *Gauri* comes from the *Ramayana*. In the first chapter of the novel itself there is a reference to Sita. Before Gauri's departure at the end of the marriage ceremony to her husband's home, Laxmi advises her daughter: "Be like Sita...."[43] Towards the close of the novel, Rakhi with sustained viciousness compares the case of Gauri to that of Sita and asks: "When Sita was abducted by Ravan, and her husband went and fetched her back, what did people say?"[44] Panchi is embarrassed

40. Anand, Mulk Raj, *Author to Critic : The Letters of Mulk Raj Anand to Saros Cowasjee*, ed. Saros Cowasjee, Calcutta : Writers Workshop, 1973, p. 32 (Letter dated 5 Aug. 1968).
41. *Ibid.*, p. 27 (letter dated 31 July 1968).
42. *Ibid.*, p. 31 (letter dated 2 August 1968).
43. Anand, Mulk Raj, *Gauri*, New Delhi : Arnold-Heinemann, 1984, p. 30.
44. *Ibid.*, p. 246.

by almost the same malicious talk from his old friend Damodar: "Ohe ja and, look after her! She has come back, after her exile like Sita who had stayed with Ravana!"[45] Gauri's enemies as well as mere gossip-mongers compare her forced stay with the banker in Hoshiarpur to Ravana's abduction of Sita and her forced exile in Lanka. Crushed under this village gossip, following the path taken by Ram under similar situation, Panchi challenges Gauri to give proof of her purity. At this painful climax in the novel, the parallelism between the story of *Gauri* and the *Ramayana* crumbles. Gauri asserts that she is a Sita of the twentieth century quite different from the Sita of the *Ramayana*. In the *Ramayana*, the earth opens up and swallows Sita to save her from further humiliation. Though Gauri wishes the earth to "open up to rescue her as it had opened up to receive Sita, the ground was hard and solid under her feet and showed no sign of opening up to prove her innocence"[46], and she realises that the only answer lay in forgetting Sita and taking "the road to the town". Anand seems to be saying here that in this modern era of existential struggle, man instead of blindly depending on the strength of the old myth, must find strength in his own physical and mental powers through hard work and devotion to duty. As Gauri takes the road to the town, the novel says that she "waved her head to forget Sita".[47] She seems to have made a correct assessment of her era in which the gods are no longer helpful to the helpless and so she courageously goes towards the town to seek her emancipation. The road she takes is a road to progress, free from the stumbling-blocks of old myths. Gauri could hold her own only through the education and qualification in nursing she has obtained, and which ensures for her an employment. The solution Gauri finds against her predicament is the solution Anand offers to the predicament of Indian woman: Education can free her from the clutches of superstition and employment can give her economic independence and together these can ensure for her a life of dignity and freedom.

Anand's message in *Gauri* is explicit in the speeches of Dr Mahindra and implicit in Gauri's assertions for social amelioration. Interestingly, Saros Cowasjee who has defended most of Anand's works against hostile criticism, in his commentary on *Gauri* or *The*

45. *Ibid.*, p. 259.
46. *Ibid.*, p. 264.
47. *Ibid.*, p. 264.

Old Woman and the Cow says: "I can think of no novel of the sixties by a reputable writer which has more overt propaganda than one encounters in the last fifty pages of *The Old Woman and the Cow.*"[48] Towards the end of the novel, Anand seems to appear under the mask of Dr Mahindra for the sake of airing his views. Who can deny the red-hot voice of the author in the following words of Dr Mahindra :

> Our Dharma is feeding the Brahmins and paying interest to the *Banias*. And ill-treating the untouchables. And Vinoba can convert a good man here and a good man there. And some tigers may learn to eat vegetables. But can you tell me of how many sons of ministers have given away their land to the poor at the bidding of Vinoba?.....[49]

Some of the speeches of Dr Mahindra, like the one quoted above, are directed more towards the readers than to his peasant audience, Laxmi and Adam Singh. Mahindra's eloquence cannot be disputed but his words to the rustics, parading his scientific knowledge about making food out of sunshine or on controlling the energy of the universe are out of place as his audience are incapable of understanding them and also as their minds are obsessed only with the thought of how to take back Gauri to her husband. As Alastair Niven says, Mahindra's "role is to impinge upon Gauri's consciousness, to be the agent of her awakening. From the moment he enters the book his abstract function is clear".[50]

Undoubtedly, the obtrusive role played by Dr Mahindra does some damage to the novel. However, the novel is saved from lapsing into propaganda by virtue of its artistic design, descriptive power and the sensitive portrayal of its heroine, Gauri. Gauri symbolises the strength and purity of Sita and she is one of the most memorable female characters in the whole range of Indian fiction. She represents some of the most applauded qualities of Indian womanhood. The novel, as the author rightly tells us, is his "offering to the beauty, dignity and devotion of Indian women".[51] It is also remarkably different from other Anand's novels in its tightness of structure. The

---

48. Cowasjee, Saros : *So Many Freedoms: A Study of Mulk Raj Anand's Major Fiction*, Delhi : OUP, 1977, p. 159.
49. Anand, Mulk Raj : *Gauri*, New Delhi : Arnold-Heinemann, 1984, pp. 225-26.
50. Niven, Alastair : *The Yoke of Pity : A Study in the Fictional Writings of Mulk Raj Anand*, New Delhi : Arnold-Heinemann, 1978, p. 111.
51. See: Blurb, In : Anand, Mulk Raj, *Gauri*, New Delhi : Arnold-Heinemann, 1984.

cow-like gentle Gauri presented in the first chapter, undergoes epic transformation mainly through suffering and at the end of the novel, she succeeds in vindicating her right to an independent life free from the violations and abrasions of male supremacy.

VIII

LAMENT ON THE DEATH OF A MASTER OF ARTS

Mulk Raj Anand's shortest novel, *Lament on the Death of a Master of Arts*, published by Hind Pocket Books (P.) Ltd., is only of 66 pages in length. The author rightly calls it "a long short story".[1] Anand wrote this during a sea voyage from Tilbury to Bombay harbour. In a letter to Saros Cowasjee the author gives the background to this novel:

> It is well known that before death, or the final null and void, sometimes a man of vision can see the important parts of his life come before him. During his prolonged illness as a T.B. patient, my college friend had written to me of the things he remembered about our life together. When the news of his death came to me, I had jotted down a poem about his painful experiences. Bored with the talk of the tea planters on the P & O boat, I had extended this poem into a long Whitman ballad. I was under the influence of Lorca's *Lament on the Death of a Bull Fighter* which I had just then read.....And it was one of the first publications of the Progressive Writers' Association. It was printed in Allahabad, on hand-made paper, by the Law Journal Press. Jawaharlal Nehru read it at a sitting and heard the recital in the company of a few of his secretaries and made the flattering remark that it was the best book produced by the Progressive Writers. I added, "the intensest if not the best".[2]

Anand's *Untouchable*, *The Big Heart* and *Lament on the Death of a Master of Arts* are novels of single day span. In the case of

1. Anand, Mulk Raj : *Author to Critic* : *The Letters of Mulk Raj Anand to Saros Cowasjee*, ed: Saros Cowasjee, Calcutta : Writers Workshop, 1973, p. 107 (Letter dated 20 April, 1971).
2. *Ibid.*, pp. 107-108.

Untouchable, the hero's single day described is not his last day, but a day on which he can look forward to the flush-system and future happiness. This is not true of *The Big Heart* and *Lament on the Death of a Master of Arts*. The day described in *The Big Heart* at the beginning appears normal like the village craftsmen's all other days of despondency but it ends with the unexpected death of the hero. The situation in *Lament on the Death of a Master of Arts* has no unexpectedness: The hero's condition is such that he has nothing much to look forward to and so, instead of looking at the featureless future, he makes a philosophical search into his past and in the afternoon of that day his death-wish triumphs over his wish to struggle ahead. The protagonist of this novel is a T.B. patient of name, Nur, who has been an object of frequent ridicule among his near and dear ones. They sneered at him saying: "....there goes Nur, the son of a confectioner, who is M.A. Pass, but who sits idle, with one hand on the other, and kills flies because he can't get a job..... he fancied himself a Babu, but now he has come down to his real state, became a coolie."[3]

The locale in the novel undergoes no shift: Mourners come and go but Nur is always on the bed from the beginning to the end. Death lies on him, like an untimely frost. The first person to visit him in the stillness of that early hour of his day of doom is his father, a gigantic, padded faced, wry-mouthed Chaudhari, who always terrified Nur like Nero. He asks him to wake up and mention the name of Allah-Mian. The conflict of his desire to die and the determination to hold on to life begins to toss him in the early hours of the day. "One side of him urged him in to death, while the other held him back to survival".[4] For the past five months he has been bed-ridden. "From the first cry at birth his life had been pain-marred....."[5]. His mother died when he was only five years old. Memories of the past eddies his mind and he suddenly recollects the day when his grandmother took him to the pir (burial ground of his mother):

> He remembered the horror of a moment when his grand mother had taken him there and he had seen a skull beside a crumbling mound in the empty sockets of which millions

3. Anand, Mulk Raj: *Lament on the Death of a Master of Arts*, Delhi: Hind Pocket Books, 1963, pp. 52-53.
4. *Ibid.*, p. 9.
5. *Ibid.*, p. 13.

> of ants were crawling. He had wondered whether his mother had become an ugly demon with a malevolent steady stare in the pits of her head and a terrible changeless grin on the thrusted teeth exposed from hard indrawn lips, under the burqah as she appeared in his dreams.....
> But surely she wasn't eaten by the worms..,. No, no, not his mother......though why not?[6]

In the remote past, he had seen many fearful days. The punishment given by the teachers frightens him. His father's insistence that he should say his prayers irritates him as the prayers make no sense to him. Suddenly he hears the voice of the Mullah calling on the faithful to pray:

> "Dur, dur, dog", Nur murmured, rising out of his resignation, angered by the groans of a dry-as-dust formalist..... "Call the faithful to prayer, call them to prayer, dog! I hate you all! to incur your wrath I spit on your face and I spit on the face of your God!"[7]

His thought is just then disturbed by the arrival of his grandma, aged seventy. She offers him tea and enquires about his condition. His grand-mother loves him but he dislikes her as she allowed his father to marry again after his mother's death. When the grandma leaves the place his mind again gets involved into the recollections of the past. As he dreams of the horrible school days, his old school mate, Gama, now a *tonga-driver* visits him. They discuss the uselessness of the modern system of education and comment on the malice of their masters.

Nur tells Gama the first line of a poem he has framed in his mind: "Why did you drag me into the dust by making me an M.A."[8] Nur then lectures to Gama on happiness, death, and their class-mate and poet Maulana Muhammad Hussain Azad's feelings on India and his vast knowledge of the works of Goethe, Shakespeare, Dickens etc. It is the poet Azad who has initiated Nur into the mysteries of poetry and philosophy. In the opinion of Nur, Azad's vast knowledge is due to his hard work. "He spent most of his time in odd corners of the college, while all of us just wasted our time ragging each other and

6. *Ibid.*, p. 14.
7. *Ibid.*, p. 17.
8. *Ibid.*, p. 38.

gossiping as we sat in the fields outside the college buildings during the free hours."[9]

Nur is happy to reveal his painful personal life to Gama. He tells Gama in a cynical voice that his father wants him to apply for admission to all Government services one after another as he places too much reliance on his Master degree.

Now Nur's mother-in-law, his wife and her aunt visit him. Thereupon Gama leaves the scene. They weep and wail. They have come as if to spoil Nur's discussion with Gama on his grouse against the world. The women's wails grow louder and shriller as his grandmother, his step-mother and other women of the lane join the chorus. His wife Iqbal, a woman of great character, tries to prevent them from beating their breasts in vain. His father also joins the crowd, angrily quoting the names of young men who could become big officers after getting degree and questioning his son's failure:

> The son of Sheik Pir Baksh has become a deputy collector, why can't you? The son of Sardar Kalyan Singh has become a sub-judge, why can't you?[10]

The Chaudhri's words spoken with blood-streaked eyes churn Nur's blood with fear. He has felt that every breath he breathes is in jeopardy and that every morsel of food he eats in the home is being watched.

Just then Nur's physician, Captain Pockkanwala, an ex-I.M.S. Officer, arrives on the scene. After the check-up he advises Nur not to excite himself.

Soon Nur is alone in the room. Within a short time, his whole form is numbed, as if he had been struck by lightning. His throat suddenly brings up a profusion of saliva rich with blood, and he lurches over to throw it into the spitoon. When his grandma comes with essence for him to drink, he has taken the last voyage, the great leap into the dark.

Nur lives only a short time and it is full of misery. He comes up and is cut down like a flower. In most of Anand's novels one or the other character speaks of his or her "belonging to suffering". Nur begins to die as soon as he is born. Anand's view of the philosophical implication of suffering is obvious in *Lament on the Death of a Master of Arts*. The author's own comment in this respect is worth quoting:

9. *Ibid.*, p. 38.
10. *Ibid.*, p. 52.

> Unlike the Buddha, who says pain is the essence of the Universe, I believe pain can help the growth to awareness. Perhaps the ascetic Indian in me makes me feel this way. And, I believe, the cruelty and barbarism implicit in the senseless, tough people when they are dealing with the poet in India, is more terrible because it condemns the sensitive man to needless suffering. Nur was a saint who was sacrificed through the ignorance of his father and his moralist tutor, Master Ishaq. The innocence of his young wife, to whom he was married by arrangement, alone redeems his days of agony, as also the devotion of his grandmother.[11]

Anand considers suffering as an instrument for the growth to awareness. Man is inclined to learn more from suffering than from entertainment. Nur is able to probe into his soul and society only during his bed-ridden days of five long months.

According to K.N. Sinha, "*Lament on the Death of a Master of Arts* bears a close resemblance to what is designated as existentialist art. It points up the limitations of human life without choice of action and touches on the philosophical implications of human misery and pain. The novel clearly demonstrates that the human condition itself is perilous and that erosion of contours (the fissures of being) is inherent in existence."[12] As against this statement made by K.N. Sinha, it may be interesting to quote Anand's own comment about this novel given in one of his letters to Saros Cowasjee: "I admit the novel is morbid, but then so is all truth, and my crime is that, though the hero goes into the night, I still try to give hope of the poetry of innocence of Nur's wife, of the mad Azad and even grandma's sentiments become a redeeming feature. You see, I am not an existentialist. I still believe in human beings."[13] Anand's denial of his being an existentialist is ambiguous. Existentialism has various "schools" and they differ markedly in doctrine and attitude. Anand is certainly not an existentialist of the Kierkegaard school which stressed the idea, "That in God man may find freedom from tension

11. Anand, Mulk Raj : *Author to Critic : The Letters of Mulk Raj Anand to Saros Cowasjee*, ed : Saros Cowasjee, Calcutta . Writers Workshop, 1973, p. 108 (Letter dated 20 April 1971).
12. Sinha, K.N. : *Mulk Raj Anand*, New York : Twayne Publishers, 1972, p. 45.
13. Anand, Mulk Raj : *Author to Critic : The Letters of Mulk Raj Anand to Saros Cowasjee*, ed. Saros Cowasjee, Calcutta, Writers Workshop, 1973, p. 109 (Letter dated 20 April 1971).

— for in him the finite and the infinite are one".[14] This is obvious from the attitude of most of Anand's heroes, who come out strongly in defiance of God. But Anand is certainly an existentialist of the school of Jean Paul Sartre and Martin Heidegger which says that "man is alone in a godless universe".[15] Anand's appreciation of this school's protest against conformism which teaches that man, "as a screw in the gigantic bureaucratic machine, is unable to change anything in the chain of events"[16], is evident in all his novels. Anand's heroes protest against many foolish social conventions and thereby they are unconsciously disciples of Jean Paul Sartre's school of existentialism which preaches that "man has no reality if he thinkingly follows social law or convention".[17] Anand's concern for man's being easily observable in all his novels is the soul of existentialism too, which one can easily discover in the fictions of the greatest existentialist writers like Dostoevsky and Kaska.

The prime concern of Anand as a social critic in this novel is to give a clarion call to the nation to reform its educational system. Not only Nur but also his creator, Anand was a victim of an ill-framed system of education. As Anand wrote in *Apology for Heroism*, the education imparted to him was "imitative giving very little idea of Indian tradition, but mainly bastardized version of English curricula in English, with particular emphasis on English history, ideas, forms and institutions, deliberately calculated to show everything relating to Indian history and tradition as inferior."[18] This pernicious education never answered his obstinate questionings. It kept the realities of life at bay. The whole system was exam-oriented and attending classes was only for getting good marks. Anand's father was like Charles Dicken's Gradgrind, whose only worry was how to turn his children into "Mathematical Thomas" and "Metallurgical Louisa". He bothered only for the examination result ignoring the proper development of Anand's personality. During the first two years of Anand's college life, he felt cheated, because none of the questions about the world

14. See : *A Dictionary of Literary Terms* by A.N. Gupta and Satish Gupta, Bareilly : Prakash Book Depot, 1983, p. 125.
15. *Ibid.*
16. See: *Dictionary of Philosophy*, edited by I. Frolov, Moscow: Progress Publishers, 1984, p. 137.
17. See : *A Dictionary of Literary Terms* by A.N. Gupta and Satish Gupta, Bareilly : Prakash Book Depot, 1983, p. 125.
18. Anand, Mulk Raj : *Apology for Heroism*, Delhi : Arnold-Heinemann, 1975, pp. 32-33.

which he wanted to ask were answered. In *Apology for Heroism* Anand recollects, "our appointed task, according to the syllabus, was to mug up Professor Sharma's two elementary text books on Logic and to cram Professor J.S. Mackenzie's *Outline of Ethics* for the First of Arts examination. The method of teaching adopted by our lecturer was to read these books aloud to us, Chapter by Chapter, asking us to underline various passages for cramming with a view to vomiting them out in the examination hall. He did not explain what logic was good for and why ethics was necessary; he merely paraphrased the difficult English of the texts into his idea of simple English!"[19]

Anand had realised after graduation that the educational system in which he had been nurtured was false, stupid and barely adequate even to fulfil the standards set for subordinate services for which it was a kind of recruiting ground. The system of education which turns millions of youths in this country into educated illiterates angers Anand and he transfers this anger on to his character Nur, who through his interior monologue, stream-of-consciousness and recollective dialogue with his old classmate Gama exposes the vanity, hollowness and futility of the modern education system. On the ideals of education, Tagore once made the following substantial comment:

> In education, the most important factor must be the inspiring atmosphere of creative activity. And therefore the primary function of our University should be the constructive work of knowledge. Men should be brought together and full scope given to them for their work of intellectual exploration and creation: and the teaching should be like the overflow water of this spring of culture, spontaneous and inevitable. Education can only become natural and wholesome when it is the direct fruit of a living and growing knowledge. Our education should be in full touch with our complete life, economical, intellectual, aesthetic, social and spiritual; and our educational institutions should be in the very heart of our society, connected with it by the living bonds of varied co-operations. For true education is to realise at every step how our training and knowledge have organic connection with our surroundings.[20]

19. *Ibid.*, pp. 37-38.
20. Quoted by Balachander, K.K., "Higher Education in India: The Shifting Perspectives — I", In: *University News* (Published by Association of Indian Universities, New Delhi), Vol. XXVI, No. 12, March 21, 1988, p. 3.

The objectives of education presented by Tagore were totally absent in the education Anand and his contemporaries received. In a letter to Saros Cowasjee, Anand wrote: "The destiny of Nur became to me symbolic of the youth of India, who are condemned to earn the degree of Master of Arts for respectability. The poetic talent is denied. And the poets accept, in our country, this condemnation and are content to weep away."[21]

Nur wants to be only a confectioner like his father. But taking no note of his son's desire, the Chaudhri sends his son for college education and thus Nur obtains a Post-Graduate degree. It brings great hope to his father that soon his son would be a big officer. But the M.A. degree does not help Nur in any way to climb the rungs of the social ladder. Instead, it makes him an object of laughter. With the M.A. degree he finds himself in an awkward position. The possibility of getting a respectable job and his inability to obtain it torments him. The degree stands as an obstacle even to his going back to his father's profession. Disappointment drags him to the fringe of despair and he becomes bed-ridden with consumption. The degree, instead of giving him comfort and happiness forces him to intense feeling of agony and he versifies: "Why did you drag me into the dust by making me an M.A."[22] Nur realises that a degree without the power to influence high officials will not help a man to get a 'respectable' job. So, in response to Gama's mocking question — "What is there in education, brother!" — Nur, affecting a learned voice says:

> "Education, education, brother....education means wisdom; wisdom means the correlation of the growth of body and mind; the correlation of the growth of body and mind is achieved through knowledge : and knowledge is power, if you have enough recommendations, that is."[23]

The books prescribed for Nur's Matric and College courses include *High Roads of History*, Southey's *Life of Nelson* and Rawlinson's *Selection of Essays*. The novelist's reference to these books is not

21. Anand, Mulk Raj : *Author to Critic : The Letters of Mulk Raj Anand to Saros Cowasjee*, ed. Saros Cowasjee, Calcutta : Writers Workshop, 1973, p. 109 (Letter dated 20 April, 1971).

22. Anand, Mulk Raj : *Lament on the Death of a Master of Arts*, Delhi : Hind Pocket Books, 1963, p. 38.

23. *Ibid.*, p. 28.

unintentional. The British curricula in India made no sense to an Indian student as it was divorced from the actualities of Indian life. It simply gave a distorted account of India's past history, glorified the British conquerors and the British as civilizers of India. It tended to weaken national pride and self respect. Further, as this education was given in English, it created a chasm between the educated Indian and the common people of India.

Gama's laconically expressed comment on education — "What is there in education, brother! Waste of time!"[24] — is a reaction to his deep, unpleasant feelings on his schooling under masters who have belittled that highly esteemed profession by their cheap behaviour with the children. One such teacher is Kaushi Ram. Gama asks Nur whether he could remember Master Kaushi Ram who taught them in Class V. Nur simply smiles. Kaushi disliked Nur, as Nur refused to take private tuition from him along with the sons of the opulant merchants of the cloth market. Kaushi charged ten rupees a month from each of the boys and Nur didn't know how he could ask his father for the money, specially as it was well known that the master made immoral suggestions to the boys who went to his house to be coached. One day when he had been left alone in the class-room, filling his satchel at the end of the school session, Kaushi had even tried to kiss him, and because he had refused to be kissed, the Master had beaten him on the knuckles with a ruler the next morning by making the flimsiest excuse about his pronunciation as he read aloud. When Gama came to know this, he caught hold of Kaushi by the scruff of the neck and threatened to kill him if he did not behave well. Only Gama's hooliganism could help the master to come to his sense.

Nur's teachers were worse than "The Village School Master" of England described by Oliver Goldsmith. Instead of spreading knowledge they spread terror in the mind of the children. One day Nur arrived late at School. The master, whose meanness and cruelty made the children nick-name him as "the greedy dog" and "the demon", found it a suitable situation to take revenge on Nur: "The master had asked him to bring a basket of sweets from his father's shop and when he (Nur) had begged his father to give him the gift to offer to the Master, the Chaudhri had refused..."[25] So the master found Nur's late coming a pretext to take revenge. When the demon

24. *Ibid.*, p. 27.

25. *Ibid.*, p. 22.

lifted the cane, Nur stricken by terror started to shriek, whereupon the Master shouted to him: "Be quiet or I will give you one stripe more for every one after which you howl!"[26] Nur, as he lay on his death bed, recollected that not only his school master but also the religious teachers had been mean in their approach to him. When he stopped reading *Suras* for a moment in the mosque,

> suddenly, from the darkness behind him, there was a kick in his ribs and Maulvi Shahab-Din stood, caressing his beard and shouting: "Beware, swine, and recite the *Suras* or else your mean, dirty father will tell me that I don't deserve any new clothes this year because I haven't taught you to remember the *Suras*."[27]

The failure of the teachers as portrayed in Anand's novels is mainly due to their lack of familiarity with the modern scientific method of teaching, in which the outdated maxim, "spare the rod and spoil the child" has absolutely no place. So, instead of correcting the mistakes of students by remedial methods, they terrorise them with horrible punishment. When Nur had made a spelling mistake, "the master was putting pencils between his fingers and pressing them hard, hard, harder and Nur could see himself writhing and shrieking and crying as he rolled on the floor to release his cracking bones from the Master's grasp..."[28] A master like the one referred to above is still part of this nation's labour force, who forgets his mission as a teacher and behaves like a policeman, equating the mental weakness of the children to crime and torturing them for it and thereby obstructing their healthy mental growth.

Frequent are the reports of brutalities on school going children. They are mainly heard from primary or middle schools for the obvious reason that the Guliver-like masters have no fear of retaliation against their brutalities from the helpless Lilliputian-like little children. Instead of bringing inspiration to the class room if they only bring canes and use them indiscriminately, "the twinkle twinkle little stars" in the noisy little mansions of our country will fail to twinkle and in the course of time they will declare like Gama, "What is there in education, brother! Waste of time! "Nur too felt the uselessness of the type of education imparted by "the greedy dogs" and he used to

26. *Ibid.*, p. 22.
27. *Ibid.*, pp. 23-24.
28. *Ibid.*, p. 23.

pray in secret for illness in order that he might escape the master's beatings with the perpendicular rod.

Anand vehemently opposes this barbaric method of teaching. In his book, *On Education*, he writes: "suppression, repression and cane driven sense are not education at all".[29] He does not want children to go to school in fear as he knows that education will be fruitful only when children could feel joy and happiness in going to school and could get inspiration and illumination by attending classes. To achieve these goals, Anand is for liberal education which would ensure "learning by playing", "learning by doing", "learning by seeing", "learning by experimenting" and so on.

Like all Anand's heroes, Nur is also a severe critic of the traditional religion reduced to mere rituals. Nur finds his father's ill-treatment of him and his insistence on his saying prayers contradictory. He finds the saying of prayers a useless exercise. But out of fear for his father, he everyday unwillingly wakes up to the *Muezzin's* call: "He had to run to the mosque to do the *wuzu*, wash himself, join the congregation and follow it in the various postures: sit, stand, kneel, rub his forehead on the ground and murmur the verses in Arabic which the Mullah had taught him by rote...."[30] The Mullah, Shahab-Din, teaches him *Suras* not out of any desire to fill the mind of the young Nur with the Islamic spirituality but for merely getting new clothes from the Chaudhri. To Nur, the traditional religion is non-sensical:

> He had never been able to learn Arabic well enough to understand the Koran, though he had repeated the *Suras* from the first page to the last, hundreds of times.... And though he had never told anyone, while he was saying prayers on a constipated belly he had involuntarily discharged a stinking wind which had fairly resounded back from the walls of the mosque to his own ears, so that it had made him burst out with an embarrassed laugh.... The body seemed to bring the soul back to the earth. He had been afraid that God must have heard it, but then he had reassured himself that since he discharged wind, because of the exercise involved in kneeling, bending, standing, sitting and kneeling

29. Anand, Mulk Raj : *On Education*, Bombay: Hind Kitabs, 1947, p. 35.
30. Anand, Mulk Raj : *Lament on the Death of a Master of Arts*, Delhi : Hind Pocket Books, 1963, p. 15.

> again, which was the prescribed method of saying prayers, surely God would forgive him for his sin.[31]

Nur's failure to get a dignified job in spite of his possessing a first class M.A. degree, the death of his mother when he is only five years of age, the unnatural cruelty of his father and the death that lingers on him day by day due to consumption, make him question the very existence of a Benevolent, Merciful and Compassionate Being described in *The Holy Koran*. So, Nur like the handicapped Ahab in *Moby Dick*, shows defiance to God. The very voice of the Mullah calling "Allah-ho-Akbar", arouses his anger and condemnation of God. Nur might have had his own reason for challenging God. The society in which he is placed is totally deprived of any godliness and the writings of Huxley and Darwin which he read might have encouraged him to disbelieve in the existence of God.

Nur's marriage with Iqbal is also imposed on him by his father. The decision-making is solely done by the Chaudhri. He does not consult Nur's liking. He does not care to probe into his son's lack of enthusiasm or unpreparedness for marriage. The Chaudhari considers his son's M.A. degree a free ticket for admission into the paradise of officialdom. And in anticipation of Nur's future position as a dignified member of the Government of India, the Chaudhri marries him off to a rich veterinary surgeon's daughter, Iqbal, obviously after collecting a huge dowry. She is a devoted wife. On the last day of his earthly sojourn Nur recollects Iqbal's virtuous nature and his own wickedness towards her. The author voices Nur's redemptive recognition of his sin of male chauvinism this way:

> And when she had proudly presented him with the gift of a little red-faced girl child, who frowned and cried with closed eyes, he had felt like murdering her and the child, and had gone out reading among the tall valerians of the city garden, its towers and its lawns.... Poverty had come between him and her, how cruel it had made him to her, how stubbornly aloof and hard and neutral, so that now when he wanted to smile at her, to touch her, he had turned his eyes away frozen and rigid, too proud and too ashamed to look at her......[32]

If Iqbal is like the other Anand heroine, Gauri, Nur could be

31. *Ibid.*, p. 16.
32. *Ibid.*, pp. 50-51.

likened in some aspects to Gauri's husband, Panchi. Both Panchi and Nur are frightened as well as angered by the news of their wives bringing forth their offsprings which would bring to them the responsibility of feeding one more mouth. Both of them ill-treat their virtuous wives to the degree of being ashamed to look at them later. Both of them under the pangs of poverty fail to maintain equanimity and transfer their anger with the exploiting world and annoyance with hunger on to their better halves in the form of ill-treatment and torture, notwithstanding the fact that the women are paragons of devotion. Anand's condemnation of male chauvinism eloquently presented in *The Big Heart* and *Gauri* is also echoed in this novel. The social critic in Anand finds it hard to be silent about the foolishness of men involved in wife-beating merely to divert attention from their inability to solve the problems of hunger and poverty.

In *Lament on the Death of a Master of Arts*, Anand successfully introduces the device of a confidant to reveal the thoughts and feelings of the hero. Gama is Nur's confidant, a trusted friend, to whom the protagonist confides his secret thoughts or feelings. The author efficiently handles the device to unravel the hero's heart and thereby avoids many lengthy and inartistic use of monologues. The tête-à-tête between Gama and Nur focuses the main theme of the novel, the futility of modern education which offers degrees, but not always jobs. Nur with a first class M.A. degree has to remain content with the job of a postal clerk, for which the qualification required is only Matriculation. Aware of the fate of a highly educated person like Nur who has no ability "to pull wires" is to end up unemployed or under employed, Gama, the confidant of the protagonist, who has long since bade farewell to modern education by accepting the vocation of a *tonga* driver, points out, during the discussion, the uselessness of modern education. The poetic-hero's response to it is a pathetic poem with the opening line: "Why did you drag me into hell by making me an M.A."[33] Anand's presentation of the futility of modern education is artistically admirable and it stands as the greatest merit of *Lament on the Death of a Master of Arts*.

The theme of lament in the novel is frequently concretized through the outer curve of the action. As Nur struggles for breath due to the suffocation caused by cough and hamorrhage, the women among his kith and kin and neighbours chant a dirge of lament:

33. *Ibid*.

> "Hai, hai" his mother-in-law and her sister cried the more loudly, and beating their heads till the old grandma came slowly down the stairs and the women of the neighbouring houses rushed to the windows of their houses and began to shout, "Is he dead? Is he dead?"
> The women's wail grew louder and shriller as his grandmother, his step-mother and the other women of the lane joined the chorus to their shrieks a violent show of beating their breasts, and smiting their foreheads in a rhythmic sequence attuned to the dirge of "Hai, hai! Hai, hai! Hai, hai!"[34]

A sharper kind of lacerating lament from these compassionate women is heard, as Nur's life sinks towards death beyond any point of return:

> The women on the top storey came screaming down, beating their breasts, their thighs, their foreheads, their cheeks and their bare breasts again and again and cried, "Hai, hai! Hai, hai! Hai, hai!" The women of the neighbourhood rushed and entering the room, began to beat their heads deliberately crying and wailing, "Hai, hai!"[35]

The lament of these wailing women produces what would be a rehearsal scene of Nur's actual death. This death rehearsal enacted by the women, with gestures, tears and words "borders on the ridiculous, but serves to heighten the tragic effect as well. It also provides comic relief by illustrating the absurd nature of death itself. But, more important, the anxious women act in the way of the Greek chorus."[36]

The undoubtedly loveliest part of the novel, "the Nur-Gama scene", is slightly mildewed by the author's unconscious intrusion into the scene by the introduction of his ideas on liberty and socialism. Anand's plea for socialistic democracy which according to him would reduce the gap between the haves and have-nots in contrast to the liberal democracy of the west, is introduced in the novel by Nur. The words are not Nur's own. He simply quotes what, his most admired college mate and poet, Azad said:

> The whole world is in search of happiness, all mankind seeks

34. *Ibid.*, pp. 47-48.
35. *Ibid.*, pp. 64-65.
36. Sinha, K.N. : *Mulk Raj Anand*, New York : Twayne Publishers, 1972, p. 44.

> the privileges of glory and power and wealth. But it is vulgar, I tell you, it is vulgar and stupid, the way in which society distributes her favours. The bitch has no morals, she yields herself to the embraces of any robber, brigand or cheating idiot who has secured for himself the traditional right to a vested interest.[37]

The above passage, a quotation from the fiery speech of Azad, is reproduced by Nur with an element of unconvincing fire. Azad has no role in the novel. And so the sincerity of his words and actions cannot be independently judged by the readers or critics. Azad's words in the novel, being reported speech and that too reported by a man on his death bed, lack immediacy and authenticity. In response to this political view quoted by Nur, Gama, the *tongawallah*, voices his view on how the nation should be set free from British Imperialism:

> "Child, you are easily led astray", said Gama, out of a clash of kindness for Nur, a contempt for Azad and a sense of inferiority. "All those speeches of his are no use. We want a workers' raj just as it is prevailing in Russia, because the condition here will be as it is in Russia. There was a time when the Czar ruled Russia as the *Badshah* of *Vilayat* rules us. But one day he was shot down. And the peasants and the labourers are ruling there .... The labourers of Hindustan are realising that the Sarkar can't go on...."[38]

The above words of Gama as well as the part of the fiery speech of Azad cited by Nur, sound hollow and completely out of place. They are instances of the artist's failure to assimilate propaganda to his art. They manifest Anand's obsession with political ideas that were sometimes unwarranted by the fictional situation. Moreover, the workers' raj the author has introduced here, is now a non-entity. The recent happenings in the erstwhile Soviet Union, such as, its rapid dismantling of socialism and moving towards a market economy and privatisation, shows how the people have been disillusioned of workers' raj or "the dictatorship of the proletariat". For today's reader, understandably, Gama's cock and bull story of a cloud-cuckoo-land ruled by the workers, offers no delight.

Lamet on the Death of a Master of Arts is an impressionistic

37. Anand, Mulk Raj : *Lament on the Death of a Master of Arts*, Delhi: Hind Pocket Books, 1963, p. 38.

38. *Ibid*., p. 41.

work of art in the sense that its technique centralizes the mental life of the chief character rather than the reality around him. But the mental life of the hero around which the plot of the novel revolves is pregnant with sentimentality and the hero appears more as a pathetic character than a truly tragic one. The situation around which the plot of the novel develops is also highly magnified. "Its significance", in the words of G.S. Balarama Gupta, "has been inflated out of all proportion. The evidence for this is that the story chosen by Anand is material good enough for a touching little short story but it has been spun out into a long drawn out novel."[39]

Another defect in the novel is absence of variety. Nur from the first to the last page of the novel is fixed to a bed on the stage. Only the other "actors and actresses" have their "exits and entrances". So the novel lacks dynamism and action.

In spite of these defects, the novel successfully portrays the hero's great drama of self-consciousness through his memories.

39. Gupta, G.S. Balarama : *Mulk Raj Anand – A Study of his Fiction in Humanist Perspective*, Bareilly : Prakash Book Depot, 1974, p. 103.

IX
CONCLUSION

The foregoing study of Mulk Raj Anand's non-autobiographical novels with special attention to his social concerns and their implication for his art has brought us to certain conclusions. This Chapter contains a brief summary of the major findings and conclusions of the study.

Anand's social criticism is sustained by his faith that an artist can contribute immensely towards social change. Of all Indian creative writers writing in English, Anand is perhaps the most concerned with the question, what is literature? His views on the subject are spread over many essays and articles. Some of the more important ones are: "Preface" to *The Hindu View of Art* (1933), "Introduction" to *The Golden Breath* (1933), *Apology for Heroism* (1946), "English Novels of the 20th Century on India" (1943), "New bearings in Indian Literature" (1961), "The Writers' Role in National Integration" (1962), "Creative Writing in the Present Crisis" (1963), "A Note on Modern Indian Fiction" (1965), "Is Universal Criticism Possible?" (1966), "The Role of Creative Writers and Artists in the Developing Countries of Afro-Asia" (1966), "The Story of My Experiment With a White Lie" (1967), "Old Myths and New Myths: Recital *versus* Novel" (1969), "I believe" (1969), "Pigeon-Indian: Some Notes on Indian English Writing" (1971) and "The Changeling — an Indo-Anglian Novelist's Credo" (1972). By far his clearest and most acceptable views on the functions of a novelist are to be found in his long confessional essay, *Apology for Heroism*. In it he says:

> Because of his addiction to truth, the writer can help to educate humanity.... far more enduringly than can the scientist or educationalist. For, as I have insisted before, the creative writer or the poet is in a position to expose the perverters of words, aspire to truth, to take a whole view of the world, a view which is both extensive and intensive. And he is possessed of the necessary apparatus to help to exault

> men to the full heights of their dignity, to equip them with the necessary spirit to tackle the tasks before them. By giving vent to their inmost desires, by revealing to them the true nature of men and by informing their will, the writer thus helps men to take part in the drama of revolt from which emerges the new society. And he trains the higher type of human being who may not always have to seek sanction for his behaviour in the external and arbitrary rules of conduct enforced on him by others, but is an individual with the inward monitor of his own conscience, who will bend before no tyrants but only follow his own enlightened will.[1]

In the same book, the author speaks of "the revolutionary aspect of art"[2], by which he means "the way in which it can change life". He agrees with Shelley that creative writers or poets are "unacknowledged legislators of mankind" and says that "the writer alone, if he is honest and brave, is in a position to understand the world qualitatively, to perceive the most delicate processes of the human sensibility, on the aesthetic as well as the cognitive and conative planes. And, if he is possessed of true creative ability, he can transform his knowledge into a vision such as can claim the loyalty of men in his own locality, and across national frontiers, and lead them to a universal awareness of life, thereby possessing them with the will to renew it and change it. The writer is like a God who realises his own many freedoms and confers them on others."[3]

George Orwell, celebrated for his committed writing, is one English writer who analysed his own attitude to writing and to commitment in depth. He, in his essay "Why I Write?", points out four reasons that urged him to write which, he thought, were to be found in every author, though mixed in different proportions. They are: (1) sheer egoism, the desire to be remembered after one's death and to be talked about during one's life; (2) aesthetic enthusiasm, an understanding of beauty, a pleasure taken in the impact produced by the contiguity of sounds, a sense of rhythm, a desire to share important aesthetic experiences; (3) historical impulse which, he explains as a "desire to see things as they are, to find out true facts and to store them up for the use of posterity"; (4) political purpose,

1. Anand, Mulk Raj : *Apology for Heroism*, Delhi: Arnold-Heinemann, 1975, p. 135.
2. *Ibid.*, p. 131.
3. *Ibid.*, pp. 130-131.

the enthusiasm to guide the world in a certain direction, to "alter other people's ideas of the kind of society that they should strive after". Orwell in the same essay ("Why I Write?") goes on to tell us that these impulses may be at war with each other, each contesting for supremacy. He himself felt that had it not been for his involvement in the Spanish Civil War, the strength of the first three would have outweighed the fourth.[4]

Like Orwell, Anand too participated in the Spanish Civil War and like him Anand too found a new direction for his art after experiencing the terrible days of malaise and darkness during the war. Like Orwell, Anand too analysed his own attitude to writing and to commitment in depth and presented it in an essay of the same title as Orwell wrote, namely, "Why I write?". The essays of Anand and Orwell of the same title and revealing almost the same attitude of commitment show that they both are apostles of the same aesthetic philosophy. In a characteristic passage in "Why I Write?", Anand speaks of what became a mission of his life:

> But the compulsion to pursue the truth of human relations has, I confess become the mission of my life. I could not have written all the twenty or so novels, and hundreds of short stories, if I had not been possessed with the sources of love which Gandhi touched off in me, and if I had not had the deep inner desire to reveal the beauty, the terror and the tenderness in the lives of the characters. I wanted, against the injunctions of the critics, to write in the time-bound contemporary world, about the here and the now, seeing everyone with a naked vision, in all the starkness of the human predicament, relieved by people's smiles, by the smiles of women for their children and by love. I wanted to see people as they were, growing in this world.....
>
> My searches have led me to roam round the world. And I have written in the rough ballad rhythms of an Indian-English, in which there are inevitable echoes of the mother-tongue, about the agony of aloneness of people, in the depths of degradation, in the wretchedness beyond wretchedness forced upon human beings by other human

4. Orwell, George, "Why I Write?", In: *Collected Essays, Journalism and Letters of George Orwell*", Vol. I, edited by Sonia Orwell and Ian Angnus, London : Penguin Books, 1970, pp. 25-28.

> beings through causalties often unknown to them. I had to soak myself in the lives of men and women from within their tormented senses. I immersed myself in the sub-world of the poor, the insulted and the injured, through continuous pilgrimages to the villages, the small town and the big town *bastis* of our country. I had to journey away from the Bloomsbury literary consciousness to the non-literary worlds, whose denizens have always been considered "vulgar" and unfit for respectable worlds. I had to become uncertain as my anti-hero heroes. I had to go through their sufferings and little joys as my own. I had to become weak with their weakness. I had to become strong with the strength of their resilience.[5]

Such passionate pronouncements in several of Anand's critical essays clearly spell out his "predilection d' artiste". They are also helpful to the critics to determine the nature of his commitment. "Commitment, strictly, is conscious alignment or conscious change of alignment".[6] Sartre, Orwell and Anand are great exemplars of committed writing. Sartre's arguments for commitment, in the specific conditions of Post-War Europe, rested upon his belief in its inevitablility:

> If Literature is not everything, it is worth nothing. This is what I mean by 'commitment'. It wilts if it is reduced to innocence, or to songs. If a written sentence does not reverberate at every level of man and society, then it makes no sense. What is the literature of an epoch but the epoch appropriated by its literature?[7]

The statement reveals Sartre's total disapproval of pure art and his whole-hearted support for commitment in creative writing. Anand and Orwell have a different level of commitment. Their commitment does not make them zealots. However, their mild and tactful revelation of commitments is detectable from what they have to say.

The story of Anand's emergent commitment is told in many of

5. Anand, Mulk Raj, "Why I Write?", In : *Indo-English Literature*, ed. K.K. Sharma, Ghaziabad, Vimal Prakashan, 1978, p. 14.
6. Williams, Raymond, *Marxism and Literature*, Delhi : OUP, 1977, p. 14.
7. Sartre, Jean Paul, Quoted by Raymond Williams, In : *Marxism and Literature*, Delhi : OUP, 1977, p. 90.

his critical essays. His observations and experiences made him lean towards Marxism and the Marxian postulate that, "It is not the consciousness of men that determines their social existence, but, on the contrary, it is their social existence that determines their consciousness."[8] However, he criticised communism for denying "to people the very liberties and human rights for which the revolutions were fought"[9], and he refused to join the communist party because he honestly believed that he would never, as an intellectual, be able to accept the almost religious discipline demanded by a group of people who evolved changing tactics around a minimum manifesto with maximum sanctions. He refused to be a votary of the dogmas propounded in the name of Marx by many of the verbal jugglers among his orthodox adherents. Besides, the influence of Tolstoy, Ruskin, Morris and Gandhi counteracted upon his views on socialism. The ethics of socialism and its humanism were more convincing to him than its dialectical aspect. Thus, instead of committing himself to a programme of political action, Anand dedicated himself to the grievous cause of suffering humanity. His commitment to the philosophy of humanism is at the very centre of his creative enterprise. He believes firmly in "a new conception of the role of man, an emphasis on the importance of the human being as such, a profound respect for man, love for him and faith in his capacity to straighten his back and look at the stars."[10] The following extract from his letter to Srinivasa Iyenger, written in July 1961, clearly shows where his commitment lies:

> I am .... doing some village social welfare work in order to integrate my love for the poor with actual work for them....I never realised, as intensely as I do now, the reasons why both Tolstoy and Gandhi chose the peasantry for their devotion. After writing for many years about pains of these people, I now feel that, for their sake, it may not all have been in vain. *The Old Woman and the Cow* and *The Road* will confirm the poetic truth that the alleviation of pain and its expiation are the only values given to our intelligentsia in the present time".[11]

8. Anand, Mulk Raj : *Apology for Heroism*, New Delhi, Arnold-Heinemann, 1975, p. 184.
9. *Ibid.*, p. 202.
10. *Ibid.*, p. 95.
11. Quoted by K.R. Srinivasa Iyengar, In : *Indian Writing in English*, Bombay : Asia Publishing House, 1962, pp. 356-57.

Anand was at the height of his powers in the thirties, when he wrote his first four novels, *Untouchable, Coolie, Two Leaves and a Bud* and *The Village* — all pregnant with his artist's understanding of the sociological situations he was writing about. Anand's presentation of the socialism of the thirties in these novels as solvents of the social problem of India was similar to the effort made by James Farrel and Richard Wright through their fictional works to call attention to the social problems of their communities in America. Anand was frank enough to admit that his literary efforts were directed towards a goal and that this goal was the alleviation of the suffering of fellow human beings. While Anand's commitment demanded that literary works have the power to move the world to compassion and kindness, his artistic purity can suffer no subjugation. He is thus able to bring to Indo-Anglian fiction new matter, new technique, new style and new attitudes. In the "Preface" to the Second Indian edition of *Two Leaves and a Bud* (1951), Anand says that until he began to write about the outcastes, the pariahs, the under-dogs and to resurrect them from the obscure lanes and alleys of India, nothing very much had been heard or written about them in polite literature in the languages of our sub-continent. In spite of their nationalistic concern, Bankim Chandra's novels were but romances distantly imitative of Scott with a historical or mystical slant; Tagore was chiefly interested in the upper-landed gentry of Bengal and the 'bhadra-lok', the middle-class section of Calcutta city; and Sarat Chandra in the lower middle classes; and Munshi Premchand chose his themes from the defeated peasantry and humble folk of Uttar Pradesh. Their forms and techniques hardly kept abreast of modern developments in the novel. None of them could produce realistic or naturalistic novels after a Balzac or a Zola. Anand's love for novelity and originality enabled him to carry the tradition of Tagore and Premchand, Bankim and Sarat Chandra to new heights. He modernised the Indian novel. By his creation of protagonists from the pariahs and the under-dogs who had not been allowed to enter the sacred precints of the novel he broke new ground and made a departure from the tradition of Indian fiction. What Anand actually succeeded in doing was interpreting the soul of India, the real India of the villages to the West in the form they could easily understand and appreciate. His interpretation of India is based on realism as his protagonists are based on real characters with whom he freely mixed for play and friendship, paying no attention to their caste, class or creed. As Anand himself acknowledges in the "Preface" referred to already:

> All these heroes, as the other men and women who had emerged in my novels and short stories, were dear to me, because they were the reflections of the real people I had known during my childhood and youth. And I was only repaying the debt of gratitude I owed them for much of the inspiration they had given me to mature into manhood, when I began to interpret their lives in my writing. They were not mere phantoms.... They were flesh of my flesh and blood of my blood, and obsessed me in the way in which certain human beings obsess an artist's soul. And I was doing no more than what a writer does when he seeks to interpret the truth from the realities of his life.[12]

The truth Anand the artist interpreted "from the realities of his life" focuses on man's inhumanity to man. It tells:

(1) Casteism is a crime against humanity and everyone who believes in human dignity should actively strive to eliminate it.

(2) Inequality in society and the ill-treatment by "haves" and "have-mores" of "have nots" is a national tragedy. The nation can be saved from this tragedy only by following the path of democratic socialism, "a way of life in which the moral and material urges of the people can have the fullest play".[13]

(3) Superstition, belief in Fate or *Karma*, religious fundamentalism and fanaticism are enemies of healthy social life, progressive thinking and individual and national prosperity. They should be totally removed from the mind of the people by inculcating rational thinking.

(4) Social, economic and political freedom is the birth-right of all men. To ensure this to common man, society should be set free from the influence of its arch-enemies, capitalism and imperialism.

(5) War is the greatest plague that can afflict humanity. It destroys not only states and families but also international harmony and world peace. As war is due to the failure of human wisdom, disputes should be settled by applying human wisdom across the negotiating table and not in the battle-field.

(6) Machine is important for the rapid growth and modernization of nation. It should be introduced keeping in mind the welfare of the

12. Anand, Mulk Raj, *Two Leaves and a Bud*, Delhi : Arnold-Heinemann, 1951, p. 2.
13. Anand, Mulk Raj, *Apology for Heroism*, New Delhi : Arnold-Heinemann, 1975, pp. 163-64.

society as a whole and not for turning the poor, poorer and the rich, richer.

(7) Feudalism is a terrible evil crushing the peasant folk. If land, the principal means of production in the village economy, is under monopoly ownership of the few people who are called landlords, then the landless peasants and tenants will remain in a state of perpetual beggary and slavery. Only the abolition of landlordism by land ceiling legislation and giving the right to ownership of land to all can the diabolical exploitation of the peasants and tenants be stopped.

(8) Ill-treatment of woman, the mother of mankind, is a barbaric act. Woman should be given equal right with man both in theory and in practice.

(9) Modern education is futile and produces only frustration as it gives merely degrees and not jobs. Education system should be reformed to suit the need of the times.

The first malpractice Anand has attacked as a social critic is the caste system, which in the words of Raja Ram Mohan Roy is, "the supreme root of all our social evils"[14], and it is presented through the painful experiences within a single day in the life of an untouchable boy, Bakha. This internationally renowned novel, *Untouchable*, is a *tour de force*. In point of technique the novel is superb. It reminds us of Joyce's *Ulysses*. The novel deals with the problem of casteism in general and untouchability in particular in vivid artistic terms and its artistic power is evident in every page. Anand has rarely achieved that concrete effect in any other novel. Art and idea are dexterously fused in this novel. As Professor C.D. Narasimhaiah rightly remarks, "In the novel (*Untouchable*) doctrines and dogmas are assimilated into a total sensibility which shapes his (Anand's) imagination and gives life to an epoch and its hopes and aspirations and its curses."[15]

Anand's depiction of untouchability in the novel has an ingenuous quality indicating the author's staunch sincerity and freedom from sentimentalism. The evil of untouchability is presented with moderation and equanimity and "the whole story is touching and tender". The natural progress of the novel and the author's determination to give the art an upper hand over the idea makes the novel really superb.

---

14. Raja Ram Mohan Roy : Quoted by A.R. Desai, In : *Social Background to Indian Nationalism*, Bombay : Popular Prakashan, 1984, p. 254.

15. Narasimhaiah, C.D. : *The Writer's Gandhi*, Patiala : Punjabi University, 1967, p. 70.

The immense popularity of the novel is evident from the fact that a play based on it, staged in London and the Provinces of the United Kingdom, could draw full houses for a period of four months.

Anand is not as triumphant in his novel *The Road*, which has the same theme as *Untouchable* and was published 25 years later. Though art and idea do not intermingle altogether well in this novel, they are somehow made to co-exist without any observable degree of artificiality. But the main defect with the novel is its weak characterisation of the protagonist. Bikhu, the central character in the novel fails to emerge as the hero. All his enthusiasm and energy is derived from another character, Dhooli Singh, who actually appears to usurp the cynosure in the novel. Further, the stage is cramped with too many characters and scenes and this distracts the attention of the reader from the central character. The author's gratuitous introduction of the love motiff too destroys the authenticity of the novel. In spite of these minor defects, *The Road* has a powerful focus and it points out that the untouchables tortured "and condemned for centuries deserve a better deal and this is possible only if men give up the age-old belief in caste and *karma* and spread the message of love and tenderness – and, of course, practise these values conscientiously."[16] According to Arnold Bennett, the "essential characteristic of the really great novelist is a Christ-like, all embracing compassion".[17] As *Untouchable* and *The Road* artistically reveal Anand's all embracing compassion for the oppressed and doomed people of India, they are fictional works of the highest order.

Anand's second and third novels *Coolie* and *Two Leaves and a Bud* are directed mainly, towards the evils of class system. These novels show class system to be a greater evil than caste system. A 'low caste' man can enjoy a lot of freedom in these modern days as long as he has money with him. But a "high caste man" who belongs to the wealthless class is in perpetual slavery. The tragedy of Munoo in *Coolie* and the horrible exploitation of Gangu and the ill-treatment of his beautiful daughter, Leila, in *Two Leaves and a Bud* amplifies this truth.

Coolie is a novel of the poor and the down-trodden. It offers a chance to the reader to really experience the unending pain, suffering

16. Gupta, G.S. Balarama: *Mulk Raj Anand : A Study of His Fiction in Humanist Perspective*, Bareilly : Prakash Book Depot, 1974, p. 36.
17. See: *Novelists on the Novel*, ed : Miriam Allott, London : Routledge Paperback, 1973, p. 133.

and prolonged struggle of the poor and as the misery of poverty is presented through an orphan boy, it particularly evokes a deep sorrow in the reader. The novel amplifies the view of Bernard Shaw that poverty is the worst crime of all and its eradication is the prime task of any socialistic society.

The novel contains some of Anand's best nature descriptions. The whole book is an impressive painting in black and white. As the action of the novel moves from the village of Bilaspur in the hills of Kangra, Punjab, to Sham Nagar, from there to Daulatpur, and then to Bombay, and finally to Simla in the North, the reader is made to experience a video vision of the varied scenes and sights of India that would rivet his attention.

The plot of the novel is episodic in character. It is a chain of incidents joined together keeping Munoo as its unifying figure. The portrayal of English characters, especially in the Bombay Chapter is not realistic. The author's zeal in over-emphasizing the picture of exploitation too does some damage to his art. The final part of the novel, Simla scene, is introduced in the novel by the hackneyed device of accident. This part of the novel gives the impression of being sketchy, hasty and it is slightly unconvincing. But the overall impression that one gets of this novel is that it is a sensitive and impressive work credibly portraying the tragic tale of a poor boy's hard and agonising struggle for survival and his ultimate defeat and death in a world where the poor man's blood is cheap and the bread he gets, very dear. It remarkably succeeds in rousing our humane feeling for the poor and the oppressed and it possesses enogh energy and fire to enkindle our soul to work for an egalitarian society where compassion and kindness will be an unwritten law. The novel may remind the reader of both Dickens' *Hard Times* and Thackeray's *Vanity Fair*. In its epic sweep and comprehensive coverage of society in which the hero struggles to survive, it is also reminiscent of Steinbeck's *Grapes of Wrath*. K.R. Srinivasa Iyengar rightly praises it for its unparalleled amplitude and power of narration, and calls it "a prose epic of modern India".[18]

Two Leaves and a Bud gives expression to the unending anguish of tea plantation labourers under extremely selfish British masters who treat the male folk among the labourers as bonded slaves and

18. Iyengar, K.R. Srinivasa : *Indian Writing in English*, Bombay : Asia Publishing House, 1962, p. 267.

their women and daughters as objects of sexual gratification. The novel is a powerful crusade against imperialism and capitalistic exploitation. As a social critic Anand is extremely sensitive to the evils of capitalism and imperialism and that sensitiveness sometimes tells upon his fictional narration. The author's portrayal and open criticism of the British here is harsh and unconvincing. Of the English characters in the novel, the most inartistically created is the author's own mouthpiece, Dr De la Havre. His frequent homilies condemning imperialism and capitalism and his very role in the novel lacks credibility. There is too much of Anand in the character of the doctor. Much of what the doctor says in *Two Leaves and a Bud* is available in Anand's own critical essays like *Apology for Heroism*. Andre Gide's advice to novelists is never to "present ideas except in terms of temperaments and characters".[19] Anand has failed to pay any heed to this good advice while writing *Two Leaves and a Bud* and therefore the artistic and the social strands do not merge well in this novel. His hatred against the evils of Imperialism and Capitalism accounts for the many gusts of barren tirades in the novel.

The evil of superstition, orthodoxy and war are Anand's social concerns in "The Village trilogy", comprising *The Village*, *Across the Black Waters* and *The Sword and the Sickle*. These novels present the struggle of a sensitive Punjabi peasant boy, Lal Singh, first against his own people, then as a soldier in British Indian army and at last as a freedom fighter. The first novel in the trilogy, *The Village* gives a realistic portrayal of an Indian village caught in the cross-road of transition — the poverty and ignorance of the villagers, their fear of accepting modernity, their exploitation by money-lenders, land-owners and priests, their zealotry, hypocrisy and arrogance, and the non-conformist hero's bitter stuggle against these soical predicaments and his eventual escape from his close-to-heart village. The novel is imaginatively vivid, refreshing and original. Readers are made to experience the simplicity of the village life not only through actions but also through the style and naturalness of speech in it. Though the plot is weak, the novel has many dramatically significant episodes, such as Lalu's visit to the 'King George Vth Hair Cutting Saloon' at the Fair and the events that preceded his enlistment in the army.

The description of nature in *The Village* is a remarkable

---

19. See : *Novelists on the Novel*, ed. Miriam Allott, London : Routledge Paperback, 1973, p. 104.

achievement. Saros Cowasjee while commenting on this aspect of the novel says:

> No Indian writer has pictured landscape as vividly as Anand, nor possessed the breath of his canvas which ranges from mountains to valleys, from the rich golden field to the parched, dried earth. And I am familiar with no writer, Indian or English, who has used the smells and colours to better effect. Even a psychological novel like *Private Life of an Indian Prince*, concerned largely with palace intrigues, is full of beautiful descriptions.
>
> Many Indian writers attempt to show some sort of inter-relation between man and nature. Anand as a realist makes no conscious effort to harmonize nature's moods with man's; he gives to nature an independent existence and reveals her both in her beauty and in her cruel aspects. Central to his theme is man's struggle in society: the poor are too occupied making a living to communicate with nature, the rich too engrossed in becoming richer.[20]

Against this evocation of nature in *The Village* stands the social critic's concern for the suffering of the peasants caused by the social leeches — the landlord, the money-lender and the lawyer. "Nowhere has money-lending been brought to a finer and more diabolical art than in India"[21], wrote Sir Malcom Darling. The money is lent at an unimaginably high rate of interest and from the very start there is little hope of it being repaid. Then the landlord comes in and he increases his territory by buying the mortgaged land. If the poor peasant ventures to approach a lawyer, he too jumps upon the penniless peasant to suck his remaining blood. *The Village* holds a mirror to these realities of Indian society and the novel admirably succeeds in blending together the author's art and social criticism.

Across the Black Waters is the continuation of *The Village*. It describes the hardships, agony, privations and frustrations of the first division of Indian troop who had been brought to fight in Europe during the first World War. The book is full of excellent characters:

---

20. Cowasjee, Saros, *So Many Freedoms : A Study of the Major Fiction of Mulk Raj Anand*, Delhi, OUP : 1977, pp. 103-104.
21. Darling, Malcom, *The Punjab Peasant in Prosperity and Debt*, Bombay : OUP, 1947, p. xxi.

Lal Singh, a non-conformist and the protagonist of the novel who under inevitable circumstance unwillingly said farewell to his village and got recruited in the army, together with his intimate soldier friends, Uncle Kirpu, Daddy Dhanoo and Havildar Lachman Singh, make up the conscience of the novel. Their silent suffering, terrifying actions tastelessly performed, and their quips, puns and comments at moments of relaxation expose the barbarism and immorality of war. The conversation between the soldiers is picturesque and is spiced with abuses. The story is told with vivacity and vigour. Though the novel is without much of a unified plot, the story remains interesting. The descriptions of the fight are very realistic and we see the trench warfare going on under our very own eyes. Anand's overriding concern in this novel, namely the devastating effect of war upon the individual is excellently exposed and the novel has a sentimental appeal for both the Indian and the English reader. The author's condemnation of war presented in a humorous manner makes the novel undoubtedly sovereign.

The Sword and the Sickle, the last volume of the trilogy, describes how the global imperialism of Britain which initiated it to be a participant in the World War I caused extreme misery even in the remote villages in India. The war took place at a time when Nature was particularly cruel to the Punjabi villagers. The monsoon failed to arrive in time and drought gave mortal blows to man, cattle and plants. When the war finally ended, the hero's heroic deeds during the war gave him nothing but a dismissal order and that made him a rebel and as a natural consequence, he joined the peasant struggle but that too ended in futility.

The stage of the novel is unmanageably cramped with just too many characters and episodes. Some of the episodes, like the funeral procession of Chandra's corpse, which has a melodramatic flavour, are not well integrated into the novel. The hero is not given a central position in the novel. It is the Count who dominates the scene. But the characterisation of the Count has no consistency. His regal, serious and lovable nature displayed here and there in the novel appears in sharp contrast to his ridiculous, silly and fantastic role in many other scenes. Anand who maintains distance from his characters in the first two volumes of the trilogy, fails to maintain the artistic requirement of distancing the author from his characters in this novel and the novel has many long speeches and orations on the evil of landlordism, British imperialism, on communism, Gandhism etc., almost directly presenting the author's point of view. Hence, *The Sword and the Sickle* is artistically inferior to the first two volumes of the trilogy.

In the pre-independent years, the progressive social and political groups in India recognized the benefits, direct and indirect, of industrialization. Though they differed in their views on industrialization – whether to follow the capitalistic or the socialist path – they all stood for rapid, all-sided expansion of industries. While sharply divided on many vital issues, they put up a united demand for it. They jointly worked for the removal of various obstacles to industrial development. The demand for industrialization thus became a national demand.

Anand's *The Big Heart* supports the demand for industrialization made by the progressive social and political group in India. But the author's support for it in the novel is not without reservation. He could foresee the disastrous consequences of industrialization if it ignored the welfare of the traditional village artisans. To avoid complications in society, Anand pleads in *The Big Heart*, for industrialisation with caution. Apart from this main concern, the novel has many other things to say, such as reproval of the caste system, capitalism, male-chauvinism and the need for practising the humanistic religion. As the hero of the novel, Ananta, is modelled after a person of the same name with whom Anand had intimate relation, the portrayal of him appears natural. It is the author's "real-life-application" that helps him to bring out the hero's perfections and imperfections. The supreme merit of *The Big Heart* is its powerful and realistic characterisation of the hero Ananta and his beloved Janaki. This vital experience of the novel helps the reader to extenuate its only weakness, that is, the polemical presentation of social problems. The theme of tradition *versus* modernity which forms the central conflict in the novel is convincingly portrayed. The death of Ananta in the defence of the machine as well as the society's cruel character assassination of Janaki for not living the conventional life of a widow are the sins of tradition. They are committed by a society which is extremely selfish and parochial as well as opposed to modernity and progressive thinking. Anand's social concern is evident in his downright castigation of the hide-bound society.

Most of Anand's heroes share the love for machines. Bakha, in *Untouchable*, at the close of the day could feel happy by the thought that one day machine, to be precise, the flush-system, will eliminate the dirty work he is forced to do. Munoo, in *Coolie*, is extremely excited at Sham Nagar when he sees things he has not seen before, like telephone, gramophone, shaving machine, "a box which talks", etc. The Indian soldiers after reaching France, as described in *Across the Black Waters*, become wonder-struck at seeing big vehicles, machine to milk etc. The conflict between tradition and modernity is well illuminated in the very opening scene of *The Village*. Nihal Singh who has spent a great part of his life travelling on bullock-cart faces a lot of difficulty in adjusting himself to travel by train. When he equates the arrival of the train to the arrival of "the age of darkness", his progressive minded son could not keep quiet. To Lal Singh, the train connecting towns and villages is a boon for the progress and prosperity of the nation. In *The Road*, the hero Bikhu considers the building of the road as the first step against social exploitation. The hero's mentor, Lambardar Dhooli Singh, proclaims, "it is only roads and roads and more roads, and electricity – that will bring prosperity!"[22]

Closely related to *The Big Heart* is Anand's novel, *Death of a Hero*. The heroes of both the novels are courageous men valiant enough to even face death for the cause for which they struggle. The protagonist of *Death of a Hero* is a Christ-like figure. He prefers to sacrifice his life rather than his cause. But as a work of art, *Death of a Hero* is not a great success. The vast framework of the novel he chose needed elaboration but he tried to present it in about 100 pages only and therefore the narration and the action in it appear sketchy and superficial. However, the principal social concerns of the novel, the author's condemnation of religious fanaticism and of the ill-treatment of prisoners are presented with accuracy and historical fidelity to the events that took place in the state of Kashmir in 1948.

One of the best works of Anand after his return to India is *Private Life of an Indian Prince*. The novel gives a crystalline picture of the dramatic changes that were taking place in the whole fabric of life in India – especially the life of Indian princes, torn between ambition to establish independent states with the aid of alien powers and the desire to avert any clash with the Indian Union. The story is authentic. It presents the predicament of an Indian prince, named Victor, at a most significant moment in the history of India. What happened to Victor happened to almost all the princes of India when they had to give up their Crown. They had to pass through the same

22. Anand, Mulk Raj, *The Road*, Bombay : Kutub-Popular, 1961, p. 22.

psychological stress and strain. The foul atmosphere of the Palace of Shampur as given in the novel is emblematic of what was going on in all other palaces in other states. Vicky, who quotes from Shelley and other poets typifies the superfluous polish of education common to all princes. But he is placed in a queer situation in which no man could escape being corrupt. His nymphomaniac mistress and eternal charmer, Ganga Dasi, is well developed, and so are other characters. In fact, *Private Life of an Indian Prince* is undoubtedly Anand's profoundest character study. The novel clearly shows Anand's characteristic merit as a novelist with a sociological imagination. It is indeed Anand's most powerful work and undoubtedly a great literary creation, deserving accolades of the literary critics.

The theme of tradition *versus* modernity artistically illustrated by Anand in *The Big Heart* is repeated in a more pointed form in *Gauri* or *The Old Woman and the Cow*. The author has chosen here, for the first time in his fictional undertaking the framework of a Hindu Scripture, the *Ramayana*, as part of his technique. The aim is not to endorse or justify the myth, but to use it as a fictional framework for a modern tragedy. Gauri is the modern version of Sita, not the self-effacing goddess of the *Ramayana*. In Sita's hour of trial, the goddess comes to her help and "the earth swallows her up, vindicating her honour, But this does not happen in the case of Gauri, however much she might will it! Hers is the glory of making a choice between alternatives. She prefers to break the labyrinth of an eccentric design rather than live in perpetual shame in her husband's house who wantonly mistrusts her. She battles her way out of the confines of her narrow, encircling world to a position of unbelievable strength. It is truely a pilgrimage of hope and faith that she undertakes. She sets an example for others to follow."[23]

Anand's presentation of the ill-treatment of Gauri by the disinterested aunt Kesaro, the selfish husband Panchi under the grip of male-chauvinism, the erotic employer Dr Batra and by her own mother Laxmi, and uncle Amru is a plausible and moving portraiture. The story of Gauri is in fact the painful story of most Indian women. Crimes against women, are rampant even until the present day. Most of us turn a blind eye in our day-to-day life to the macabre incidents such as dowry death, bride harassment, rapes and kidnapping. Though we are in the computer age and at the threshold of the 21st

---

23. Sinha, K.N., *Mulk Raj Anand*, New York : Twayne Publishers, 1972, pp. 69-70.

century, we even condone senseless practices like *Sati*. As women are an intrinsic part of the human race and an integral part of the nation, Anand makes a touching appeal through *Gauri*, for the women's cause.

Lament on the Death of a Master of Arts which presents the last day of Nur, an unemployed M.A. who has been suffering from consumption is, as the author rightly calls, a long short story. The protagonist's childhood, his hard times in school, his confidant Gama, his college life, his inability to get a suitable job, his married life with Iqbal are all presented as passing scenes before the eyes of the dying young man and the novel closes with his death. The novel reveals Anand's keen observation of the modern day Indian Muslim society. However the "novelette suffers from a flimsy situation which is more pathetic than tragic in its unrestrained sentimentality and its loose plot."[24]

Though *Lament on the Death of a Master of Arts* is not one of Anand's masterpieces, like the season of autumn, it has its music too, and the novel's greatness lies in its deep and authentic search for illumination, in its lyricism and in its powerful and appealing theme, which brings out vividly the dangers of having an obsolete educational system. Anand's protest is principally directed against the drawbacks and limitations of our system of education which harvest only frustration and disappointment. The novel exposes those aspects of our education system which stand as a major road-block to our national goal and prosperity. Nur symbolises the misery and misfortunes of millions of Indian youth who get university education and remain thereafter unemployed or under-employed.

After going through this book, some readers may feel that it wrongly takes for granted a uniformity and homogeneity in Anand's vision throughout his long career. But the fact is that Anand's vision throughout his long career has not undergone any major transformation. For example, in 1933 he wrote *Untouchable* to present the evils of untouchability. After a long gap of 30 years, in 1963, he took up the same theme in *The Road* and the second novel repeats some of the incidents given in the first and the concern expressed in both the novels is the same. To consolidate my point further, I quote here a passage from the great Indo-Anglian critic, Meenakshi Mukherji's article, "Beyond *The Village* – An Aspect of Mulk Raj Anand":

---

24. Mehta, P.P., *Indo-Anglian Fiction*, Bareilly : Prakash Book Depot, 1979, p. 185.

> He (Anand) published his first novel in 1933 and is still writing to-day, but there is very little to distinguish his earliest work from the latest. To take the example of the recent work, *The Old Woman and the Cow*, the characterisation here is done in the same black and white terms as before. There is the same number of good men (Rafiq Chacha, Adam Singh, Dr Mahindra) and bad men (Amru, Birbal, Panchi's uncle). There is the same saga of an individual persecuted by society as in *The Village*, the only difference being that the sufferer now is a woman; there is the same tyranny of the money-lender and the landlord. Like Lalu in *The Village* more than twenty years back, the new protagonist Gauri believes in progress, in the necessity of cleaning up the village, in the use of modern scientific methods.... No development from his earlier work is perceptible either in treatment of the theme or in style. But for a few references to Partition and Independence and Vinoba Bhave, one could mistake this novel to have been written in the "thirties" [25]

Anand's novels are marred here and there by an overdose of sentimentality, pathos, or excessive reformatory zeal. But a novel has to be evaluated not bit by bit, like the study of an organism under an electron microscope, but by taking into account the overall impact it has on the reader. In the microscopic analysis of Anand's novels, one is sure to see certain defects at least in some of his novels like *Two Leaves and a Bud, The Road, The Sword and the Sickle* and *Gauri*. However, when all is said and done, he emerges as a great artist possessing at once a sensuous and a moral understanding of life. The charge of propaganda levelled against him by some critics is largely false, but his presentation of ideas in some of his novels gives the impression that his art almost thrives on what may seem propaganda. This is mainly due to the author's unwillingness to distil out the social concerns from his art. But Anand is never an aggressive propagandist: he is what George Orwell was, an expositor, who makes artistic exposition of the exploitations he sees, a political novelist, who portrays his characters and their deeds in relation to the great and sudden social, economic and political changes of his time. Like R.D.

---

25. Mukherjee, Meenakshi, "Beyond *The Village* – An aspect of Mulk Raj Anand", In : *Critical Essays on Indian Writing in English*, edited by M.K. Naik, S.K. Desai and G.S. Amur, The Macmillan Co. of India Ltd., 1977, p. 243.

Charques, Anand believes that political passions are often nourished by literature and literary taste is much affected by politics. So, he considers those who appear to be politically inidfferent or who 'make a show' of detachment as tacit supporters of the prevailing system. According to him literature and life are parallel development. Obviously, it is impossible for him to say ditto to the Aubrey Menen's stand, "I am no reformer, only a writer"[26], as Anand cannot imagine how a modern writer with a conscience, can simply soar up in the wings of poesy, losing touch with the social predicaments and the hard and painful realities of life.

Anand's attempt to influence opinions and actions in his novels as a whole is inbuilt in a natural way within the dramatic or fictional situations he introduce in them and so, he is, in the strict sense, not a propagandist. If Anand was bent on propaganda, or was a hard-boiled leftist, he would not have presented the workers as both good and bad, thereby compelling the Marxist Progressive Writers' Association to declare him a decadent in 1949. He should, also, then have made his proletarian heroes ultimately victorious, a marked feature of proletarian literature of the thirties in Europe. But being a realist and not a propagandist, nor a doctrinaire writer, he cannot but see his heroes as finally defeated. It is the defeat of his heroes which has provoked even some of his friendly Russian literati to criticise him. To illustrate the point, one may quote Y. Tupikova, who, while admitting the ideological and artistic merits of Anand's early novels, regrets that in *Coolie*, Anand "underrates the conscious factor in the workers' movement in 1928-1929, often does not see where the struggle must lead, and presents his revolutionary characters in rather a sketchy manner...."[27]

Anand is particularly annoyed by the fact that the charge of propaganda against his novels is mainly an accusation of Indian critics and in a letter to Saros Cowasjee he complains:

> But nobody in the many languages into which *Coolie* has gone has suggested that it is propaganda, except some Indian critics who are unconsciously Sanskritists and regard contemporary themes, especially from the lower depths, as extra-literary material. They are still in the days of the

26. Menen, Aubrey, In : *The Week*, Nov. 6-12, 1988, p. 40.
27. Tupikova, Y., "Mulk Raj Anand", In : *Soviet Literature*, No. 9, 1953, p. 161.

> *Mahabharata* and the *Ramayana*. ...... And oddly enough, they take refuge behind the categories of Western academic criticism and dismiss anything about raw life as 'naturalism' or 'realism' or 'social realism'. They will accept Tolstoy and Dickens and Hardy, but should an Indian try to portray the peasants of India, or slum children, or the maid servants, you are then written off as a 'communist propagandist'.[28]

Whatever Anand says in defence of his works, there can be no denying the fact that some of his novels like, *Two Leaves and a Bud*, *The Road, The Sword and the Sickle* and *Gauri* are weak, primarily because they do not embody a harmonious fusion of art and idea, thereby giving them a look of propaganda much more than they actually are. The artistic weaknesses which are mainly responsible for this magnified appearance of propaganda in them are:

(1) The characters who voice the author's opinion are too good to be real; they are portrayed as if without any shades or weakness and therefore they and their words appear unnatural.

(2) Anand has created characters who could convincingly express his views, but has failed to create characters who could express views opposite to those he held. Hence his views are presented without any voice of dissent.

(3) The style and content of speech of the characters are not sufficiently individualised. There are instances of his illiterate characters speaking like scholars. Anand has not succeeded in exhibiting a diversity of styles, individualised in different ways in order to help the readers to identify the characters from the way they speak.

(4) The utterance of the characters who give Anand's point of view is noticeably too long. It contradicts the normal human dialogue in which no character would utter much above a dozen words at a breath.

If Anand were to rectify these weaknesses, the novels referred above could have had greater artistic credibility.

However, the central argument in this book has been that Anand could not have written even a single novel if he had not been deeply involved in social questions. His social concerns are catalysts

---

28. Anand, Mulk Raj, *Author to Critic : The Letters of Mulk Raj Anand to Saros Cowasjee*, ed. Saros Cowasjee, Calcutta : Writers Workshop, 1973, p. 22 (Letter dated 3 Feb. 1968).

that have enabled him to envision the lives and deeds of a heroic but ill-placed generation of Indians. In his best works like *Untouchable, The Village, Across the Black Waters* and *Private Life of an Indian Prince*, his social concerns strengthen his art immensely and in them art and social criticism make for the finest quality of fusion, giving a conclusive proof that the driving force behind his writing, namely, the undeviating concern for the welfare of the wronged and exploited sections of the human race, has acted as a great help to his creative achievement. "Like Aldous Huxley, Anand is more interested in life than in art, and in art only in so far as it serves life. He is a committed artist and we should be grateful to him for ably demonstrating in his best works that art need not be any the poorer for being the handmaid to life. Art has not suffered under dogma; it has suffered from second rate writers who failed to synthesize life with literature."[29]

Once William Golding, the Nobel laureate and the celebrated author of *Lord of the Flies* said: "If you sit a child upon your knee and begin, 'Once upon a time....', you know that you have got him."[30] Like Golding, Anand has always been "fascinated with the perennial power exerted by the story on human psyche".[31] That was the reason why he refused to write a tract on untouchability as suggested by Gandhiji and instead wrote a novel on that theme. Inaugurating the Diamond Jubilee celebrations of the *Samastha Kerala Sahitya Parishad* at Tripunithura, near Cochin, on January 9, 1988, which I attended, Mulk Raj Anand called upon creative writers to shift their emphasis from "evasions for easy sales, fake fame and cheap popularity to genuine passion".[32] Anand's novels reveal his passionate concern for the poor and the oppressed and his deep and abiding commitment to human values. He is a story-teller of the highest order – thinking through his stories about the agonising sociological questions of his society, as most great novelists have done in the English, Indian and perhaps many other traditions as well.

---

29. Cowasjee, Saros, In : "Preface" to *Author to Critic: The Letters of Mulk Raj Anand to Saros Cowasjee*, ed. Saros Cowasjee, Calcutta : Writers Workshop, 1973, p. xii.
30. See : "Keep Going, Write on and on..." (Excerpts from speeches made in India by William Golding), In : *Manorama Year Book*, Kottayam : Malayala Manorama Company, 1988, p. 305.
31. *Ibid.*, p. 305.
32. See the Newspaper item: "Sahitya Parishad Jubilee Celebrations Begin", In : *Indian Express* (Cochin Edition), January 10, 1988, p. 8.

SELECT BIBLIOGRAPHY

PRIMARY SOURCES

Works by Mulk Raj Anand

(a) Novels

Across the Black Waters (New Delhi : Orient Paperbacks, 1980)

Confessions of a Lover (New Delhi : Arnold Heinemann, 1976).

Coolie (New Delhi : Arnold Heinemann, 1985).

Death of a Hero (New Delhi : Arnold-Heinemann, 1985).

Gauri (New Delhi : Arnold-Heinemann, 1984).

Lament on the Death of a Master of Arts (New Delhi : Hind Pocket Books, 1963).

Morning Face (Bombay : Kutub-Popular, 1968).

Private Life of an Indian Prince (New Delhi : Arnold Heinemann, 1983).

Seven Summers (Bombay: Kutub-Popular, 1951).

The Big Heart (New Delhi: Arnold-Heinemann, New Revised Edition, 1980).

The Bubble (New Delhi, Arnold-Heinemann, 1984).

The Road (Bombay : Kutub-Popular, 1961).

The Sword and the Sickle (New Delhi : Arnold-Heinemann, 1984).

The Village (New Delhi : Arnold-Heinemann, 1984).

Two Leaves and a Bud (New Delhi : Arnold Heinemann, 1983).

Untouchable (New Delhi : Arnold-Heinemann, 1984).

(b) Other Books

Apology for Heroism (New Delhi : Arnold Heinemann, 1975).

Author to Critic : The Letters of Mulk Raj Anand to Saros Cowasjee, Calcutta: Writers Workshop, 1973.

Dancing Foot (Delhi : Ministry of Education, 1957).

Homage to Tagore (Lahore : Sangam Publishers, 1946).

Is there a Contemporary Civilization? (Bombay : Asia Publishing House, 1963).

Letters on India (London : Labour Book Service, 1942).

Lines Written to an Indian Air (Bombay : Nalanda Publications, 1949).

Marx and Engels on India (Allahabad : Socialist Book Club, 1939).

On Education (Bombay : Hind Kitabs, 1947).

Persian Painting (London : Faber and Faber, 1931).

The Hindu View of Art (London : Allen and Unwin, 1933).

The Indian Theatre (London : Dennis Dobson, 1958).

The Story of Man (Amritsar : Sikh Publishing House, 1952).

The Third Eye – A Lecture on the Appreciation of Art (Chandigarh, Punjab University, 1963).

(c) Articles

"*A Letter", A Souvenir Volume of Appreciations* (The Radhakrishnan Number), Madras-Hyderabad, 1962.

"Jawaharlal Nehru", *Cultural Forum* (Special Number on Jawaharlal Nehru), Vol. VI, No. 4 (November, 1964).

"How I Became a Writer", *Contemporary Indian Literature*, Vol. V, Nos. 11-12 (November-December, 1965).

"The Bride: An Essay on the Status of Women in India", *Lines Written to an Indian Air*, Bombay : Nalanda Publications, 1949.

"The One and the Many : Some Changing Social Patterns of New India", *United Asia*, Vol. 18, No. 1 (Jan-Feb., 1966).

"The Story of My Experiment with a White Lie", *Critical Essays on Indian Writing in English*, ed. Naik, M.K. et. al., Madras : The Macmillan Co. of India Ltd., 1977.

"The Writers Role in National Integration : A Discussion", *Indian Literature*, Vol. V, No. 1 (1962).

"Trends in the Novel" *Cultural Forum* (Tagore Number), 1961.

"Why I Write?", *Indo-English Literature*, ed. : K.K. Sharma, Ghaziabad, Vimal Prakashan, 1978.

SECONDARY SOURCES

(a) Studies of Anand

Cowasjee, Saros, *So Many Freedoms : A Study of the Major Fiction of Mulk Raj Anand*, Delhi : OUP, 1977.

Fisher, Marlene, *The Wisdom of the Heart : A Study of the Works of Mulk Raj Anand*, New Delhi : Sterling Publishers, 1985.

Gupta, G.S. Balarama, *Mulk Raj Anand : A Study of His Fiction in Humanist Perspective*, Bareilly : Prakash Book Depot, 1974.

Lindsay, Jack, *The Elephant and the Lotus : A Study of the Novels of Mulk Raj Anand*, Bombay : Kutub-Popular, 1965.

Mehta, P.P., *Indo-Anglian Fiction*, Bareilly : Prakash Book Depot, 1979.

Naik, M.K., *Mulk Raj Anand*, New Delhi : Arnold-Heinemann, 1973.

Niven, Alastair, *The Yoke of Pity : A Study in the Fictional Writings of Mulk Raj Anand*, New Delhi : Arnold-Heinemann, 1978.

Paul, Premila, *The Novels of Mulk Raj Anand : A Thematic Study*, New Delhi : Sterling Publishers, 1983.

Riemenschneider, D., *An Ideal of Man in Mulk Raj Anand's Novels*, Bombay : Kutub-Popular, n.d.

Sinha, K.N., *Mulk Raj Anand*, New York : Twayne Publishers, 1972.

Tilak, Raghukul, *Untouchable : A Critical Study*, Delhi : Rama Brothers, 1983.

—, *Coolie : A Critical Study*, Delhi: Rama Brothers, 1983.

(b) Articles and Reviews

Christesen, C.B., "Messages and Souvenirs", *Contemporary Indian Literature*, November-December, 1965.

Collins, Maurice, "Review of *Across the Black Waters*", *Time and Tide*, Vol. 21 (30 Nov. 1940).

Cowasjee, Saros, "Mulk Raj Anand: A Profile", *The Illustrated Weekly of India*, May 4, 1969.

Forster, E.M., "Preface", In : *Untouchable*, New Delhi : Arnold-Heinemann, 1984.

Gowda, H.H. Anaiah, "Mulk Raj Anand", *The Literary Half Yearly VI,* January, 1965.

Iyengar, K.R. Srinivasa, "Foreword", In : G.S. Balarama Gupta's *Mulk Raj Anand : A Study of His Fiction in Humanist Perspective*, Bareilly : Prakash Book Depot, 1974.

Kaushik, R.K., "Red, Brown and Grey – Ideological Commitment in Mulk Raj Anand's Novels", *Indo-English Literature*, ed. K.K. Sharma, Ghaziabad : Vimal Prakashan, 1978.

Marath, S. Menon, "Three Indian Novelists", *Life and Letters*, Vol. 59 (Dec. 1948).

Morris, Ira, "Messages and Souvenirs", *Contemporary Indian Literature*, Nov-Dec. 1965.

Mukherjee, Meenakshi, "Beyond *The Village*: An Aspect of Mulk Raj Anand", *Critical Essays on Indian Writings in English*, ed. Naik, M.K. et al., Madras : The Macmillan Co. of India Ltd., 1977.

Orwell, George, "Review: *The Sword and the Sickle* by Mulk Raj Anand", In : *The Collected Essays, Journalism and Letters*, Vol. 2, Harmondsworth : Penguin Books, 1970.

Ree, Goronwy, "Book Review: *Two Leaves and a Bud*", *The Spectator*, No. 5679 (30 April, 1937).

Spender, Stephen, "Mulk Raj Anand's *Two Leaves and a Bud*", *Life and Letters Today*, Vol. 16, No. 8 (Summer 1937).

Tupikova, Y., "Mulk Raj Anand", *Soviet Literature*, No. 9, 1953.

(c) Other Books

Allott, Miriam, *Novelists on the Novel*, London : Routledge Paperback, 1973.

Charques, R.D., *Contemporary Literature and Social Revolutions*, London : Martin Seeker, n.d.

Chandra, Bipan, *Nationalism and Colonialism in Modern India*, New Delhi : Orient Longman Ltd., 1979.

Chakravorty, B.C., *Rabindranath Tagore : His Mind and Art*, New Delhi : Young India Publications, 1971.

Darling, Malcom, *The Punjab Peasant in Prosperity and Debt*, Delhi, OUP, 1947.

Desai, A.R., *Social Background to Indian Nationalism*, Bombay : Popular Prakashan, 1984.

Frolov, I., *Dictionary of Philosophy*, Moscow : Progress Publications, 1984.

Gupta, A.N. and Satish Gupta, *A Dictionary of Literary Terms*, Bareilly : Prakash Book Depot, 1983.

Henry, Lewis C., *Best Quotations for all Occasions,* London : Premier Publishers, 1968.

Ingle, Stephen, J., *Socialist Thought in Imaginative Literature*, London : The Macmillan Press, 1968.

Iyengar, K.R. Srinivasa, *Indian Writing in English*, Bombay : Asia Publishing House, 1962.

—, *Two Cheers for the Commonwealth*, Bombay : Asia Publishing House, 1970.

Mukherjee, Meenakshi, *The Twice Born Fiction*, Delhi : Heinemann Educational Books, 1971.

Naik, M.K., *A History of Indian English Literature*, Delhi : Sahitya Academi, 1982.

Narasimhaiah, C.D., *The Swan and the Eagle*, Simla : Indian Institute of Advanced Study, 1969.

—, *The Writer's Gandhi*, Patiala : Punjabi University, 1967.

Nehru, Jawaharlal, *Bunch of Old Letters*, Bombay : 1958.

—., *Recent Essays and Writings*, Allahabad, 1934.

Plekhanov, Georgi V., *Art and Society*, New York, 1936.

Raymond, Williams, *Marxism and Literature*, Delhi : OUP, 1977.

Rubin, David, *The World of Premchand*, London : George Allen and Unwin Ltd., 1969.

Sartre, Jean-Paul, *What is Literature?* (translated by Bernard Frechtman), Northampton : John Dickens & Co. Ltd., 1970.

Shaw, George Bernard, *The Complete Prefaces of Bernard Shaw*, London : Paul Hamlyn, 1965.

Singh, Bhupal, *A Survey of Anglo-Indian Fiction*, London : OUP, 1975.

Singh, R.K., *Indian English Writing 1981–85 : Experiments with Expression*, Dhanbad : Bahri Publications, 1987.

Swamy Vivekananda, *Caste, Culture and Socialism* (Published by Swami Ananyananda), Calcutta, Ashutosh Lithographic Co., 1983).

Varghese, Paul, C., *Problems of the Indian Creative Writer in English*, Bombay : Somaiya Publications, 1968.

(d) Other Articles

Balachander, K.K., "Higher Education in India : The Shifting Perspectives-I", *University News* (Published by Association of Indian Universities, New Delhi), Vol. XXVI, No. 12, March 21, 1988.

Mathew, Mammen, "Keep Going, Write on and on....", Manorama Year Book, Kottayam : Malayala Manorama, 1988.

Orwell, George, "Why I Write?", *Collected Essays, Journalism and Letters of George Orwell*, Vol. II., ed. Sonia Orwell and Ian Angnus, London : Penguin Books, 1970.

(e) Newspaper Items

Indian Express, "Sahitya Parishad Jubilee Celebrations Begin", *Indian Express* (Cochin Edition), January 10, 1988.

Newstime, "Untouchability Still Prevalent in Bihar", *Newstime*, Hyderabad : Vol. 3, No. 4, Tuesday, January 28, 1986.

INDEX

F

G

H

I

J

K

L

M

N

O

P